# Educa
# Management for the 1990s

Brent Davies
Linda Ellison
Allan Osborne
John West-Burnham

Longman

Published by Longman Group UK Limited
6th Floor, Westgate House, The High, Harlow, Essex CM20 1YR
Telephone (0279) 442601
Telex 81491 Padlog
Fax (0279) 444501



First published 1990
Reprinted 1991

**British Library Cataloguing in Publication Data**
Education management for the 1990s.
1. Great Britain. Educational institutions. Management
I. Davies, Brent
371.200941
ISBN 0-582-06039-7

ISBN 0-582-06039-7

Printed in Malaysia
by The Commercial Press Sdn. Bhd.,
Serdang Jaya, Selangor Darul Ehsan

# Dedication

This book is dedicated to:

Clive Kendrick

and

Iain Smith

# Acknowledgements

The authors would like to thank Beryl Condliffe and Hazel Davies for help in the production of the book.

The publishers are grateful to the following for permission to reproduce copyright material:

Carfax Publishing Company for Fig. 4.3 and Fig. 4.4 from the article 'The purpose and function of budgets — some theoretical perspectives for education managers' by K. B. Davies from *School Organization* Vol. 4, No. 3 (1984); Gower Publishing Company Ltd for Fig. 6.3, Fig. 6.4 and Fig. 6.6 from *Handbook of Management Development* by A. Mumford (1985); Harper & Row, Publishers, Inc for Fig. 5.7, an adaptation of the Fig. 'Hierarchy of Needs' from *Motivation & Personality* by Abraham H. Maslow, copyright 1954 by Harper & Row, Publishers, Inc. Copyright © 1970 by Abraham H. Maslow; the author, T. Simkins for Fig. 4.2 from *Budgeting & Resource Allocation in Educational Institutions* by T. Simkins & D. Lancaster (2nd ed. 1987), *Sheffield Papers in Education Management* No. 35; University Associates, Inc for Fig. 6.7 (top) from 'Introduction to the Structured Experience Section' from *The 1975 Annual Handbook for Group Facilitators* edited by J. William Pfeiffer & John E. Jones (1975).

We have been unable to trace the copyright holders in the following and would appreciate any information that would enable us to do so:

Fig. 3.6 from *Build Your Own Rainbow* by B. Hopson & M. Scally (Lifeskills Associates, 1984); Fig. 6.7 (bottom) from *Experiential Learning: Experience as a Source of Learning & Development* by D. A. Kolb (Prentice Hall, 1984); Fig. 2.3 from 'A framework for management information systems' by G. A. Gorry & M. S. Scott Morton from *Information for Decision-Making* edited by A. Rappaport (Prentice Hall, 1975).

# Contents

# Contributors

**Brent Davies** is Head of Education Management at Crewe and Alsager College of Higher Education. Prior to this he spent ten years teaching in the ILEA. He runs a Master of Science Degree in Education Management. As an LMS consultant for a large number of LEAs he is extensively involved in middle and senior management training. Recently as an English Speaking Union Scholar he toured the USA evaluating Education Management programmes in universities and colleges. He has published a number of articles and books on educational finance and training and development approaches.

**Linda Ellison** is a Senior Lecturer at Leeds Polytechnic and, prior to this, worked in a large comprehensive school. She is the Course Leader for the M.Sc Education Management and is extensively involved with programmes of management training, particularly for heads and deputies. She has also been involved in the provision of staff development on LMS in a variety of LEAs and publishes in this area.

**Allan Osborne** is the Acting Head of Education at Leeds Polytechnic where he has been particularly involved in the development of modular In-Service provision. Previously he was Programme Leader for a Masters degree in Education Management and worked in schools in York and Humberside. He is currently involved in a wide range of consultancy activities and has published a number of articles concerning education management.

**John West-Burnham** is a principal lecturer in Education Management at Crewe and Alsager College of Higher Education. Prior to this appointment he spent 15 years teaching in secondary modern, grammar and comprehensive schools and in further and adult education. His teaching and research interests include management learning in education, the effectiveness of senior management teams and skills for teacher appraisal.

# Introduction

The 1988 Education Reform Act has brought about a revolution in the education system. National Curriculum, local management of schools, open enrolment and appraisal are but a few of the changes which are impinging on schools. The era of senior and middle management having primarily a curriculum leadership role is under challenge. What is being thrust on the system is a demand for a much more explicit approach to the management of schools.

This book aims to give the reader a clear understanding of some of the key issues in education management in the 1990s. The central task of schools in this decade is to provide effective education through curriculum provision to all our children. Management, however, does not just concern itself with organising an effective curriculum and its delivery. There are a large number of management activities which must take place to ensure that this learning process is successful.

This book is organised in chapters which reflect these management activities and in an order that may appeal to the reader in assessing a suitable sequence of events.

The first chapter reflects on the nature of education management and the perspectives which can be employed in managing educational institutions. With a view of the overall context of education management, the following two chapters consider the need for management information and management planning which underpin each of the succeeding chapters.

When information and planning needs have been assessed the book moves on to look at managing the resources that deliver effective education. Chapter 4 focuses on the budgetary processes in the resource management cycle while chapter 5 looks at managing human resources.

The manager, having gathered information and planned and organised human and non-human resources, should consider two factors which relate to the process of management. These are the management of change and of stress. Any management activity, and curriculum is the prime example since the 1988 Education Reform Act, involves change. Knowing how to manage this change can be as important as the substance of the change for determining the success of the activity. Chapter 6 aims to give the reader an understanding of this change process. Undoubtedly, the pressures of current and planned educational initiatives on managers and their staff in schools can be dysfunctional if they result in unmanageable and dangerous levels of stress in individuals. Chapter 7 takes a very practical approach to aid the reader in his/her professional role of minimising stress within this changing environment. This is followed by a more detailed consideration of one of the key factors in stress reduction, that of effective management of time, in chapter 8.

While schools may organise their management processes to deliver efficient and effective education, this, in itself, may not be enough to ensure the success of the institution. Virtue does not always bring its own reward, although virtue with a good marketing strategy may! In an era of open enrolments and formula funding, attracting pupils and students is a key management task. Chapter 9 looks at marketing to review the techniques and approaches which schools can use to promote themselves. Chapter 10 examines how education institutions can set about evaluating themselves in order to ensure the quality of their performance. It establishes a conceptual model to set the framework of school-based evaluation within which practitioners can operate.

If there is an area in the management of schools which makes it distinct from the management of other types of institutions, then that area is centred on the management of the curriculum. The final chapter therefore gives a strategic management overview of this important area and lays down a structure for the reader to undertake a more detailed review of the extensive literature in the field of curriculum management.

This sequence of management activities can be represented as:

The nature of education management
Management information
Planning in education management
Resource management in schools
Human resource management in schools
The management of change
Managing stress in schools
Effective time management
Marketing schools
Managing the evaluation of schools
Perspectives on managing the curriculum in schools

While there are other areas of education management to consider, which may be included in a future volume, this book provides an assessment of the key areas on which middle and senior management in schools can focus when dealing with the current management challenges facing them. It should provide the reader with the opportunity to stand back from his or her current practice and assess the underlying principles which will enable that experience to be evaluated and seen in context.

# 1 The nature of education management

## Allan Osborne

The following chapters in this book will offer the reader a great deal in the way of possible solutions to very specific issues in the management of schools — this one will not — or at least not in the same focused way. Whether the reader is willing or able, or even desires, to adopt to some degree the approaches put forward will be decided in large part by his or her wider set of beliefs and understanding concerning the nature of schools, schooling and education. We are all deeply immersed in our own understanding of these things — we live the reality of them every day. This is not therefore the place to discuss alternatives in these areas yet again, but simply to acknowledge that they do and will affect our response as managers within the education service. However, an explicit consideration of the broader themes of education management as such is a luxury which fewer people will have had the time, or perhaps the inclination, to undertake. It may though be useful to do just that, since our perception and understanding of them will also condition the way we approach the more focused sections following.

The basic view to be explored is that the nature of education management is undergoing major change as a result of the Education Reform Acts of 1986 and 1988 — and particularly by the local management of schools and open enrolment elements of the latter.

At the general level there is indeed already a wide consensus that managing schools in the future will be different — but once we move from the most general to more specific views, there is considerable and very important diversity as to the nature of those changes. At the most simplistic level there is a view which suggests the emergence of a 'chief executive' approach to management in schools. This is a notion often based in part upon perceptions of what is happening or is felt to have already happened in other countries, and the most widely used comparison is drawn with the USA in mind. This view is rooted in the separation of management and education within schools and suggests a greatly increased emphasis upon the former by senior staff. The premise of much of what follows is contrary to that view and is based on the view that to separate the 'educational' from the 'management' processes of schools is a fundamental misconception — at odds with the British educational tradition, with what is actually happening in other countries and even with its own origins in industrial and commercial practice. It is in fact a very good example of attempting to ape industrial and commercial practice which is either not appropriate or indeed is out of date even in its own context. We should be looking not at such practice in the past but rather in the future — more of that later.

This is not, however, to imply that nothing is different — far from it. The 'chief executive' view, often put forward as a radical set of ideas, is in fact profoundly conservative — based as it is upon a traditional, hierarchical mode of thought. A properly radical perspective would look instead at fundamentals — at the shape of schools as organisations, at the relationships between managerial and professional aspects of work in schools and at the whole question of the location of management as a set of tasks and processes; at who does what, where and when in the management process. In short the simplistic 'business model' is no substitute for a much more radical and exciting blend of management of and for professionality which may be within our grasp.

This chapter is therefore an invitation of sorts — an invitation to pause before plunging into the specific issues that follow and to consider some of the broader questions about the nature of education management. To those who are still reading, firstly my thanks, secondly a warning (this section is filled with questions rather than answers) and thirdly some encouragement to read on, in that doing so may help to maximise the utility of the book as a whole.

For ease of presentation the chapter is structured around the following themes:

- The nature of educational change
- A managerial perspective
- A professional perspective
- The location of education management.

## The nature of educational change

Managers in schools have long been involved in the management of change of various kinds and at various levels — particularly in relation to the curriculum or elements of it. West-Burnham in chapter 6 outlines an analysis which can be applied to a wide range of situations from the individual project to a whole school programme. At this stage, however, it is necessary to examine the relationship between our underlying approaches to managing change *per se* and the whole question of whether those approaches are applicable to, or congruent with, the task of *changing the nature of the management function itself.* Change, whether it be in the curriculum, in assessment, in the relationship between school and community, in resource management or in any other area of school, cannot be managed effectively (in anything other than the short term) without also making appropriate changes to the management structures and processes which are actually attempting to bring about the substantive developments. For this reason it is appropriate to take a base-line review of the nature of educational change as a whole before proceeding further.

All who work within the education service are acutely aware of the pressure for change at all levels. From the individual classroom, to the school as a whole, through the local authority and to the national level as represented by the DES, the pressure is enormous. Not only is there a great depth to the pressure for change, but it also exists on an enormously wide number of fronts — from the National Curriculum through assessment and on to open enrolment and the local management of schools and (for some) beyond that to grant maintained status or other 'exotics'. It is important however to dispel the 'big push' theory of change — that all we need is one last great effort to climb the next hill or round the next corner and we shall then arrive in the promised land of milk, honey and stability! Those who search for something and never find it become dispirited or cynical and eventually it becomes very hard to motivate them to climb the next hill. Those who pin their hopes on highly specified, short range solutions may or may not get it right. If they do not (and the track record is not good), they will be responsible for leading us up the wrong path (again) and they will create yet greater levels of exhaustion and disaffection. A more viable approach accepts the on-going nature of educational change — the journey is more important than the destination in the sense that one is real and the other never more than a shifting image. This is as true for attempts to change the nature of the management process itself as it is for the more obvious areas of change management.

It is also necessary to reflect upon at least one other dimension to the situation. The dynamic force for educational change this time around (in contrast to the sixties and seventies?) lies not within the profession but is social and political and, in the latter sense, is enshrined in the Education Reform Acts of 1986 and 1988 in particular. For some, this appears as a rapid move away from the consensus approach to change which characterised education up to the 1970s, and as a move towards imposed solutions at all levels of the service. We should make no mistake about the political nature of these developments, but a horrified throwing in of the towel is no response on the part of those who would manage the service in the interests of pupils. Major management questions start to emerge — questions which can only be answered from an *education management* perspective. At root, the educational changes with which we are engaged are fuelled by rapidly changing socio-economic patterns, and the particular political drive given to these at the moment is of much less importance (in anything other than the short term) than we may often feel to be the case. The present political initiative rests upon a consumer- or market-based perspective as the driving force for change, and upon the belief that managers within the service will respond to that direction. However, this begs many questions about the *ways* in which they will respond and some of these issues will be identified later.

It is not possible to establish, even in the broadest terms, educational needs for the present, or the immediate future, without taking into account the fundamental economic and social changes which are summed up in the phrase, 'a post-industrial society'. While some regard these changes with optimism and others with foreboding, there is a growing consensus that they are changes of a very different magnitude and nature to anything since the Industrial Revolution — and even that comparison may underestimate the process as far as time-scale is concerned. While crystal ball gazing is an absorbing occupation, for us the question raised is how do education and education managers relate to this scenario?

The enthusiasm of the sixties (it was not just naivety) would have held that education should lead the whole process, while the cynicism of the seventies and eighties would have us believe that education, that is schools at any rate, can do no more than mirror the society of which they are part. In reality, of course, the relationship between education and society is much more complex than either view would suggest. Education does reflect social, economic and political needs or pressures, but in doing so it also subtly refracts the image and modifies the pressures — the balance within the relationship is not constant. Moreover, on some occasions (and the present scenario could well be one) the economic and social pressures may be pushing in the same direction as educational forces. That is to say, what educators are promoting primarily as 'a good thing anyway' is, on this occasion, likely to receive considerable reinforcement because it coincides with what the economic-technical revolution requires. We should not regard this situation lightly or allow ourselves to fall into a purely reactive management position. A proactive approach to education management in the service is required as never before (see Benn 1984). What then, should this stance be?

Just as it is dangerous to predict the macro-scenario in anything other than the broadest terms, so it is dangerous to attempt to construct educational blueprints for the future — especially in curriculum terms. Yet this is exactly what is happening and it is also happening with the schools in a reactive stance. Having 'failed' to find the curriculum or examination version of the Holy Grail for themselves during the sixties and seventies (and having exhausted themselves in the process) the schools are, at the moment, resigned to accepting a string of panaceas from without — the YTS/TVEI initiatives are now being superseded or subsumed by the National Curriculum cure-all. It is not that these initiatives do not contain good educational practice which is being criticised here (for they do), but rather the way in which they are seen by some as panaceas which can succeed without full professional involvement. It is in the quality of the management of these initiatives that success or failure lies — not in the ideas themselves. There is an awesome truth here that managers at all levels must act upon rather than pay lip service to — that is, there will be no educational progress without the full commitment and motivation of the teaching force. Imposed managerial solutions will simply not work.

These programmes may fulfil the hidden agendas of some of their originators but they will not in their present forms fulfil the real educational needs of the future. Educators, both from a professional and management position, must become much more involved in developing (rather than simply operating) these programmes which could form the basis of a real way forward. It is suggested here that the major curricular change of the future lies in what Fullan (1982) has described as the balance between cognitive and social development goals. While Fullan writes in a wide educational context, his work can be applied directly to the initiatives now underway in the UK:

> Currently, the main attention and content of reform is largely imbalanced in favour of the more basic of the cognitive goals, to the relative neglect of higher-order cognitive goals, and to a very strong passivity when it comes to personal/social development goals.
>
> Fullan (1982) p. 289

This imbalance can be strongly related to a very restrictive view of teacher professionality and to an equally restrictive view of the nature of education management.

It is however not in curriculum thinking that Fullan's major contribution is to be found, but rather in the issues he raises about the nature of change as a process in educational terms, and the implications these have for managers in the service.

An important question in relation to change is what Fullan describes as 'fidelity and variation'. Should change be homogeneous and centrally directed in both design and implementation or should it be heterogeneous and decentralised? As he states:

> If the direction of the change is seen as desirable and if the means of

> implementation are proven and clear, there is nothing wrong with consistent homogeneous implementation.

However, he goes on to say that:

> . . . these conditions are not always or even usually the case . . .
>
> Fullan (1982) p. 290

Who would doubt this in the context of the post-industrial society? If variation rather than fidelity is required in the management of change, then the restrictive views of professionality and management currently underpinning much thinking would not seem to be the most appropriate model for the future. Indeed, Fullan identified several other important ideas; time and change, leadership and change, meaning and change, and the tension between grandeur and incrementalism as strategies for development. On all of these levels a similar analysis can be drawn — i.e. that restrictive views of teacher professionality and associated management perspectives provide an unlikely vehicle for progress. This is not the place to labour the points one by one, but the overall position is made clear by looking at what Fullan characterises as the difference between 'specific and generic capacity for change'. The implementation of a specific change is not the prime goal. Indeed, a single success if it is too costly in terms of time, commitment, motivation or any other resource, may be at the expense of future changes – and we may be seeing some evidence of this at the moment in terms of the reactive stance of large parts of the service. Rather as Fullan (1982 p. 292) says, 'the goal is to get good at change'.

It would appear therefore that changes in the nature (location?) of the management function must go along with all the other changes with which we are involved. Put in the language of this chapter, we should not be seeking the Holy Grail in the curriculum or anywhere else, but attempting to create relationships between management and professionality within structures which are good at bringing about change without exhausting or demeaning teachers in the process. It is to an examination of these managerial and professional perspectives that this chapter must now turn. Throughout it is held that professionals and managers are people and it is people who should be brought to mind whenever such terms as professionalism and professionality or management and managerialism are encountered. These characteristics and/or processes start with people and they affect other people — each other certainly, but also pupils.

## A managerial perspective

Classical management theory emphasises the conscious creation of procedures in opposition to the interplay of unco-ordinated activities. Consequently the basic concepts have been division of labour, organisational structure, job descriptions, but above all — hierarchy. Perhaps because they were the first in the field, or more probably for deeply rooted socio-political reasons, the classicists have never been seriously challenged — theories have come and theories have gone but the belief in the *control* function of management has remained — even more so at the level of practice than of theory, although at that level, some insights can be gained.

The most fully developed rationale for this view of management is Max Weber's bureaucracy with its positive emphasis upon rationality, predictability and impartiality. For this purpose the salient features are the role of 'office', the stress on procedural devices, the division of labour and the emphasis on hierarchy. The whole is tied together by the notion of control although later a distinction was to be made between the authority of office and the authority of expertise.

Certainly, bureaucratic organisational forms and processes can be very effective in the right conditions of a known product or service, 'mass production' and stability. Although, in its pure form, the bureaucracy concept cannot be applied fully to schools, it has been suggested that bureaucratisation is one of the most significant educational developments of the times. Spence (1981) argues that the theory is powerfully related to school life, seeing classroom behaviour as narrowly prescribed and highly institutionalised as a result of both direct and indirect control, the latter being perhaps more significant:

> . . . a person can be in a cage without being constantly under observation or supervision . . . . The cage does the regulation of the person continuously, impersonally, unobtrusively until it becomes to its occupant a part of the facts of life.
>
> Spence (1981) p. 68

Others may feel that the cage has become, or is becoming, somewhat more explicit as a result of central government activity — leading to an emphasis upon the direct controls which would have appeared as unthinkable only a decade ago. This begins to face education managers with a fundamental dilemma — are they inside the cage with the teaching profession or are they to be on the outside exercising a more explicit control function than ever before? Alternatively, is it possible to find another way altogether, a way which does not simply resolve the dilemma, but one which transforms the problem into a solution?

The general critique of bureaucratic management theory, as applied in the context of education, has long suggested that:

> organisational structure and decision making are considerably modified . . . when there are large numbers of professionals . . .

and that:

> the bureaucratic–professional dimension exists as a variable for organisational structure within organisations as well as between organisations.
>
> Morgan (1976) p. 22

Hughes summarises the position being outlined here:

> It must be granted that there are inevitable managerial problems for an educational system . . .

because the educational professional using his trained judgement is

> . . . liable to come into conflict with the organisational hierarchy and at least to give the impression that he is only conditionally loyal . . .
>
> Hughes (1980) p. 243

If abstractions such as 'bureaucracy' and 'classical management' theories provide some ways of thinking about the management ideology at work in our schools, what *practical* evidence do we have?

Within the schools, examples can be easily identified — they may be transitory in some cases, but they reappear in other forms at other times. They too have in common the notion of control.

One example which springs to mind very powerfully at the moment is the notion of organisation charts and the ubiquitous phrase 'senior management team'. This latter idea could lay claim to a basis in ideas of collegiality — but only of a limited nature. The team would do what the individual could no longer do because the organisation was becoming too large and/or complex. Collegiality in this form is still predicated upon the idea of control over the organisation. Genuine collegiality is something essentially different. From the organisation chart and the senior management team stems the absolute need for detailed job descriptions for all members of the organisation. An interesting point is that these often become more detailed the lower down the 'hierarchy' we look. Their purpose of course is to 'get things done'; but what are these 'things' and who decides?

Here we need to ask ourselves a whole range of questions associated with the ways in which staff are managed in general and about the ways in which appraisal will be managed in the future — for there are choices to be made there in particular. Do we see appraisal as a process which *in itself* will lead to 'improvement' (the control model), or as something which really only makes sense in the context of a fully developed staff development process?

These examples powerfully affect the relationships between teachers in schools, but the pupils are not immune. An example in this area, and one of considerable importance, can be drawn from the much discussed academic–pastoral divide which has numerous origins, including the need to 'place' a dispossessed hierarchy during a phase of bureaucratic upheaval. The creation of formalised (specialised) pastoral systems can be seen as one of the most limiting aspects of school organisation. Such systems fundamentally imply that many teachers should deliberately restrict their level of engagement with children and that the finely woven (and seamless) web of human relationships can be rationalised, divided, timetabled and generally routinised to such an extent that it can be systemised (or bureaucratised)!

A third example can be drawn from the present fascination with evaluation — this is a particularly powerful example of the distortions which 'control' can introduce even though perfectly 'rational' or 'acceptable' from a managerial perspective. What could be more desirable than the need to evaluate the work of our schools? The great problem is that evaluation focuses upon *outcomes* rather than *processes*, and this bias is given increased emphasis in the context of National Curriculum assessment arrangements. Managers may respond by devising routines which will improve the output results but these will have a dramatic effect upon the processes of education back through the school life of every child. The massive alienation thus bred may be contained in the context of a stable economic and cultural framework, but when that stability breaks down a different picture begins to emerge. There is a great need to move the emphasis away from the outcomes of education to the processes, but this raises a whole complex of management questions. Existing management structures and knowledge bases are on the one hand inappropriate, and on the other largely inadequate, for this task and these inadequacies are very serious constraints; of the two, the lack of adequate knowledge bases for evaluation in a process sense is probably more important but it is also the point at which the greatest development could take place. It is within the capacity of existing arrangements (the in-service training system) to address the knowledge base question whereas the structural dimension is a far more complex and difficult situation. The two are not distinct — development of management knowledge bases in this area may of itself be seen as one of the prerequisites and/or pressure points leading toward structural review and change.

While not applicable in a pure form, the notion of bureaucracy provides powerful insights into the managerial processes and ideology of large parts of the education service. The management of our schools has been conditioned by both the ideology and practice of hierarchy and control to a point at which, in some cases, it must attract the pejorative term of *managerialism*, a condition under which the artificial needs of managers, organisations, systems, bureaucracies or routines assume dominance over the real needs of children. Many would look to a professional perspective to balance these developments in the interests of the clients and it is to an examination of this perspective that the chapter now turns. Are existing professional forms able to meet the danger of managerialism and how well prepared are they to do so in the future?

## A professional perspective

The great weight of evidence is that the employment of large numbers of professionals in an organisation poses 'problems' for the application of the bureaucratic or hierarchical management model. Much of this evidence is drawn from outside the educational world but nevertheless has profound implications in that context. It is to an examination of this perspective that we now turn, but it is worthwhile to start by asking ourselves why the situation is regarded as a *problem* rather than a *potential*? Part of the answer lies in the managerial perspective itself and another part in the failure to develop a viable approach to the professional dimensions of schools.

However, it must be said that this paper is not an attempt to cast management in an entirely negative light and then to oppose that with an equally 'rosy' view of professionalism — with the implication that management must recede and that professionalism should advance. Such a view would be far too simplistic for a number of reasons, but perhaps most clearly because there is indeed a powerful and growing critique of professionals in our society — and a critique which is well founded! We require not a shift in the 'balance of power and influence' but an entirely changed *modus vivendi* between the two dimensions.

At bottom, this critique revolves around the feeling that many groups of professionals (in our case teachers) are organised around professional skills rather than client needs. Wilding (1981) provides a trenchant account of this critique in the wider framework of all the social welfare professions but much of what he has to say rings many uncomfortable bells in our schools. An important qualification is that we are looking at *groups* of professionals and the manner in which they are organised rather than at individual teachers — at this latter level there can be little doubt that many individual teachers do respond to client needs despite the structure around them.

The basic failure is perceived particularly acutely in the social welfare professions, and it is based upon a wide range of features such as the failure of some services actually to deliver the goods promised, failures of responsibility and neutrality, the loss of the service ideal and, in extreme cases, the disabling effects upon clients. This critique underlies much of the 'Great Debate' which has been in progress since the Ruskin speech of 1976 and which can be seen to have resulted in the 1986 and 1988 Education Acts. Characteristically, the overt discussion has concentrated upon far more apparently neutral issues — particularly it has focused upon the curriculum — ranging from concern with 'areas of experience' to the fascination with TVEI and the whole MSC approach to 'relevance', and culminating with the National Curriculum and associated assessment proposals. The discussion is more neutral only in so far as it is assumed that the curriculum (such a global phenomenon) is no-one's responsibility in particular, and clearly this is so in an individual sense — but it is however the responsibility of the profession to take a leading role in this area and at the moment it is not fulfilling this role. The initiative clearly lies elsewhere, effectively in managerial levels outside schools; and teachers are reduced to a reactive or defensive position and should not be surprised to feel alternately frustration and cynicism about the whole process. After more than 10 years of 'debate' we seem to be little better off than before — indeed the lack of motivation is, if anything, more acute than ever. Why should this be the case? It is both unfortunate and revealing that the solutions suggested by Wilding are managerial in perspective — with more planning and more control seen as the crucial ameliorative requirements. Taking various client groups into the bureaucracy is in itself no real way forward because in that context it can only lead to professional defensiveness of the worst kind. Rather it is necessary to look at the people involved — the professionals — and understand how they relate both to their clients and to the organisations in which they work, for it is these structures that powerfully condition the primary relationships. By failing to take this holistic stance and by the adoption of a narrow perspective (the curriculum) within a managerial approach dedicated to control, standardisation and output evaluation, the 'Great Debate' has not arrived at the promised land but has been confined to endless wanderings in the wilderness of the present cr indeed the past.

The relationship between teachers and pupils is in many ways similar to the relationship between other professionals and their clients, but it is suggested here that in an ideal sense (and in many cases practically too) it does have special characteristics which are fundamentally opposed to traditional ideas of professionalism. One of these is the notion of detachment between professionals and clients which is wholly inappropriate in teaching. The clearest statement of this situation was provided by Wilson (1962) and some conclusion can be drawn from the fact that this was so long ago. Wilson argues that the teacher's role is special both in breadth and depth:

> Doctors and lawyers make *patients* out of persons and *cases* out of clients . . . for the teacher the child must, of necessity, remain a whole person.
>
> Wilson (1962) p. 24

While the whole-person approach is having powerful effects upon professional fields such as medicine, other areas such as the law and accountancy retain, possibly rightly, a 'case' approach. In some respects the process in education needs to be carried further because of the time-frame involved:

> Because a teacher is concerned with a whole person over a prolonged period of time . . . so *he* tends to become involved as a whole person.
>
> Wilson (1962) p. 25

Because this role is impossible to define in terms of its action content it leads to a lack of specificity, difficulties of time calculation and the inappropriateness of contractual obligations — all hallmarks of work in general in our society and all the tools of management and bureaucracy. If management, as usually conceived, attempts to mediate this role it will either fail utterly because it will be excluded by the people involved, or it will have distorting effects which can only be dysfunctional. A curriculum conceived in instrumental terms (i.e. as the mediator between teacher and taught) or a crisis-based pastoral system are both powerful examples of this. Wilson sums it up:

> Affection is the first language which man understands, and it becomes the lever by which all other languages can be initially learned. . . . The strictly professional attitude — to remember that clients are just cases . . . is simply not possible in teaching.
>
> Wilson (1962) p. 25

The managerial implications are profound in many ways but above all a management framework must be created which facilitates such relationships in the first place and then allows them to flourish. This approach can only be created on the basis of managerial trust in the professional skills and attitudes of teachers. Corwin says:

> because the situations dealt with by professionals are unique, the professional must be given authority to solve them and to be *responsible for the outcome.*
>
> Corwin (1965) p. 237 (author's italics)

At issue here is the central theme of professional autonomy, but as the italics emphasise, authority or autonomy (which most teachers would wish for) carries with it an *exactly equal* responsibility for outcomes (and this is something that teachers need to be much more aware of). It is a classic chicken and egg situation — autonomy and responsibility are indivisible.

The literature concerning professional–managerial relationships is reasonably clear in overall direction if not in degree. The American literature rarely speaks of 'conflict' but it does reveal a certain 'tension' within the relationship. The European literature, perhaps not surprisingly, does see the relationship more clearly in terms of conflict. The professional's tendency to resist bureaucratic control has been studied in a wide range of occupations by writers such as Drucker, Kornhauser, Wardell, Abrahamson among others, and the congruence of their findings must be accepted here (Hughes 1980). In the school situation Watson has found similar tension (1975). The state of the art in the study of professionals in schools is still represented by the work of Hoyle (1975) who suggested the notion of *professionality* as a way forward from the sterile debates of whether teaching is a profession in the 'checklist of characteristics' manner. Having disposed of the ideal type approach and the question of whether or not teachers are professionals, Hoyle asks which parts of the idea of professionality are useful in the school context and he suggests two heuristic models of *restricted* and *extended* professionality. Although Hoyle's model can be criticised on the grounds that the ideal types do not exist, or that many teachers exhibit characteristics from both sides of the model, it nevertheless exposes crucial aspects of the relationships between teachers and the organisations in which they work when used in the heuristic format for which it was intended. The value of *professionality* is that it focuses attention upon the activities of teachers in relation to pupils, each other and their organisations and it is thus a dynamic concept in opposition to the rather static 'characteristics' or 'descriptive' approach inherent in most studies of professionalism. A broad outline of the ideas can be provided in tabular form thus:

Restricted and extended models of professionality

| *Restricted professionality* | *Extended professionality* |
|---|---|
| Skills derived from experience | Skills derived from a mediation between experience and theory |
| Perspective limited to the immediate in time and place | Perspective embracing the broader social context of education |
| Classroom events perceived in isolation | Classroom event perceived in relation to schools policies and goals |
| Introspective with regard to methods | Methods compared with those of colleagues and with reports of practice |
| Value placed on autonomy | Value placed on professional collaboration |
| Limited involvement in non-teaching professional activities | High involvement in non-teaching professional activities (especially teachers' centres, subject associations, research) |

| | |
|---|---|
| Infrequent reading of professional literature | Regular reading of professional literature |
| Involvement in in-service work limited and confined to practical courses | Involvement in in-service work extensive and including courses of a theoretical nature |
| Teaching as an intuitive activity | Teaching seen as a rational activity |

Hoyle (1975) p. 318

Holye suggests that traditionally the individual teacher has enjoyed a high degree of autonomy in the essential professional activity of teaching, but that teachers have had relatively little influence over the broader aspects of school life because of a very limited involvement in decision making (management). Bearing in mind the general pattern of restricted and extended modes, certain features can be highlighted. If teachers are to assume a greater role in the control of their own organisations a far wider range of knowledge and skills is required than if they are to remain 'in the classroom' — they must move from the restricted to the extended approach. Furthermore, Hoyle suggests that there is indeed a tension between the two approaches — that restricted professionality is unlikely in practice to be capable of extension or, put another way, that extended professionality can only be achieved at the cost of effective, restricted professionality at the classroom level. This would seem to be unnecessarily pessimistic and may be a conclusion laid at the door of present organisational configurations in our schools. This pessimism may have some truth given the present management approach within our schools but it is suggested here that if that managerial frame of reference was itself to be radically re-oriented, then teachers' perceptions of their own professionality would also be powerfully affected and they may indeed come to feel that effective classroom activity was *positively* related to their performance in the wider school context.

One other feature is worthy of note in an attempt to bring together these views of professionals and those outlined above on managerialism. In the present context there is yet another source of tension, perhaps the most crucial of all. To the degree that a managerial ideology and practice has tendencies towards bureaucracy and control at the school level, then it will itself create pressure upon teachers towards the restricted view of professionality. However, there are countervailing pressures since, at the same time, broader educational needs are pulling in exactly the opposite direction and require teachers to operate in the extended dimension in many ways.

Those who would run our schools cannot have things all ways. They cannot have teachers ready to respond to the rapidly changing social milieu (the educational needs context) which requires an extended approach to professionality, and at the same time expect to manage them in a modified bureaucracy which is predicated upon a restricted view. The whole process must be based upon an unprecedented release of energy and activity at all levels. It is suggested in the final part of this chapter that a different approach to education management *is* possible. Such an approach would be centred upon the management *of* and *for* professionality and it would be based upon a relocation of the whole management process — away from a top-down managerial philosophy and practice, and towards a genuinely collegiate form which would go far beyond the traditional boundaries of delegation. In this approach to the location of education management we may begin to find a new relationship between professionality and management, and to explore in a different way the questions of who does what, where and when in the whole management process.

## The location of education management

The early part of this chapter indicated that there is already a reasonable consensus that managing schools in the future will be different — equally it suggested that a simplistic 'chief executive' model is not universally accepted as the way forward, and that such a model is indeed a profoundly conservative one. It remains however to explore alternatives to that model in the context of the sections above, concerning the nature of educational change and the managerial and professional perspectives involved. Much of what follows is set therefore in the form of questions which need to be considered by all of us. Our individual and collective responses to these questions will affect not only our understanding and interpretation of the following chapters of this book but, more importantly, the nature of the school process as experienced by teachers and pupils in the future. Firstly, it is appropriate to examine some broad themes from the commercial–industrial fields and secondly it is proposed to specify a series of inter-related questions which, taken together, will determine our approach to the location and thus the nature of education management.

While rejecting the *detailed* application of management approaches from an industrial or commercial environment into schools, we should not fall into the belief that there is nothing to be learned from such experience — for in the right conditions there is. Those conditions would appear to be obvious but they are worth stating:

1. That we examine such experience from the position of the best available practice/commentary. This means not only looking for good

practice in the present but also looking for indicators for the future.
2. That we look not for detailed application of single techniques in a piecemeal fashion, but rather that we look for the generic developments from which we can build school specific approaches which translate the experience into usable school practice.
3. That we do not, in the process, undervalue the experience that is already available to us in our own schools and those around us — in particular there is a danger that we fail to make use of the managerial ability which all teachers constantly deploy with children, or that experience which schools in different age sections from our own can give us. This last point is one which is most commonly misplaced.

Within these conditions, some of the broad themes currently exercising the minds of practitioners and commentators in commercial and industrial management are worthy of consideration.

A whole series of CBI/DTI/BIM reports summarised by Constable and McCormick (1987) has created great interest in the condition of British management, and in particular in the training provision made. The general tenor of those reports is that while much has been achieved, a very great deal remains to be done. Management development at present is seen as too little, too late and for too few. The debate, amongst both academics and practitioners, which emerged from these reports is still going on and it is this debate which is of interest to schools.

One of the polarisations which took place has centred on the question of whether management development should be focused on the provision of specific tools/skills for managers (a competency model?) — or whether it would be more appropriate to set out along a more generic path which emphasised the attitudinal and interpersonal aspects of management.

The first of these approaches has resulted in a programme called the 'Management Charter Initiative', which is currently planning a nationwide training initiative with a highly flexible approach — bringing together in-house provision with higher education provision and suggesting a laddered approach to management development throughout the whole careers of those involved.

Critics have, however, found serious flaws in the whole approach. It has been attacked on the grounds that it attempts to relate particular skills to different levels of management, or that it sectionalises/parochialises management thinking. Above all it has been criticised on the level of the 'charter' concept itself. The idea of the chartered manager is equated with that of the chartered accountant — it implies a threshold level of competence in managerial skills before the 'intern' is allowed to practise. This is very revealing for us in its underlying implications. Seen in this light, management is an activity which only some people engage in, or as something which some people do to other people — once they have been chartered/qualified to do so. It remains a conservative model, based upon control and hierarchy. In the light of what has been said above about the nature of the relationships between managerial and professional processes in schools, the competency/threshold model currently being developed would seem to have little to offer in terms of meeting the need for a move towards holistic management processes.

Moreover, the cutting edge of management thinking does not fit very easily into this way of thinking — even within the commercial–industrial sector itself. To take examples from either side of the Atlantic, both Tom Peters (1988) and Charles Handy (1989) are beginning to suggest very different approaches to management, and interestingly they are approaches which reflect far more accurately the needs for collegiate management in schools. They share a common and deeply significant trend in philosophy, and that trend is to get away from hierarchy and control and to move towards emphasis upon what Peters calls 'The Front Line People' — and we know who they are!

The major management concern according to Peters is not a concern with techniques but rather a concern with people, and with the division between management and non-management. He goes on to explore the dynamic nature of excellence and to suggest that quality is really about training and unlocking the potential of the workforce. This can only be done, he suggests, by moving away from hierarchy and towards a position in which everyone is a manager.

Handy, looking from a slightly different perspective of the whole organisation, comes to essentially similar conclusions — everyone will have to be a manager but at the same time, no one can afford to be *only* a manager. It is impossible, he suggests, to run such an organisation by command — only persuasion or consent will do.

Here we may have a glimpse of the future shape of organisation and management theory and practice which is worth on-going consideration in relation to schools. Seen in this light, management is a political activity and it is an emotional activity too because organisations are about people. Peters admits that such a sea-change in attitudes is 'scary tough' but we need to ask what the alternatives really are. This starts to look like a way of thinking which would make the task of school management part of the work of all teachers. Certainly, such views as these do not sit comfortably with *managerialism* and are equally at odds with *restricted professionality*. How do they fit with the demands of the Education Reform Acts of 1986 and 1988?

It may well be possible to find ways of dealing with the demands of the various themes of these acts by yet greater dependence upon the hierarchical/control model — indeed it almost certainly will be — but at what *level* of success in terms of the educational needs of the pupils and at what *cost* to the motivation of staff?

The local management of schools policy appears to threaten the basis of much of what we have known; and there is undoubtedly much concern about some of the 'new' skills which will be needed. We should not be panicked however into top-down/control solutions, for many of these 'new' skills which are apparently so daunting at the moment (reading a financial statement?) are easily learnt by intelligent people and in two or three years, at that level, we shall be wondering what all the fuss was about. The more enduring issues will be concerned with making decisions based upon those statements and with the wider questions of who should be making them and in what way. These behavioural questions are much more important then the merely technical issues — and so it will be with the National Curriculum and all the other baggage of 1988. The greatest problem facing schools, now as always, is how to ensure the best possible service to present pupils (this may be called the steady-state operation), while at the same time, developing the creativity which alone will allow us to continue to adapt to change in the future.

If we are panicked into yet greater depths of managerialism, a great opportunity will be lost. In particular the teaching force will not be regenerated or remotivated in the ways that are necessary (and possible), and which alone will lead to the real and sustained improvements in the quality of the service delivered to pupils.

Rather than fall back on an increased emphasis upon *managerialism* based upon hierarchy and control, the Education Reform Acts should be regarded as an opportunity to review, not just in a *coping* way but in a *maximising* way, the management structures and processes of our schools. This requires bravery — to go against the 'safety first' approach — but, paradoxically, it is possible under LMS, and working with the governing body, to structure schools and their management in ways very different from anything that would have been possible before.

It is suggested here that a new *modus vivendi* is required between the managerial and professional dimensions of school life. Within this, the traditional manager has little part to play, but *management* becomes the key to success as all teachers carry out both operational and managerial roles. This brings us closer to the meaning of a genuine collegiality — management is here seen as a holistic process — touching everything and being carried forward by all teachers as of right and duty, not because of a limited hierarchical view of 'delegation'. Only then will many of the educational tasks now being approached from a quasi-managerial perspective become the focus of properly professional processes.

## Conclusion

This chapter started with a number of questions and propositions — it must end with yet more. The questions are themselves tentative (and surely incomplete) but they are questions of a different order in that they look forward rather than backward. No answers are offered in any direct sense, rather an invitation to consider the issues in the context of particular schools or situations and to use such a consideration and further develop it as the remaining chapters of this book are read. The major questions are clearly interrelated in that the answer to any one will precondition the response to the others. What we are looking at is the development of a decentralised approach to management which by definition cannot be reduced to a few single issues, although the level of management self-awareness is critical in all of them. In general we should ask ourselves whether we are happy with our responses to the following questions:

1. Where are the processes and responsibilities of management in the school currently located?
2. Do current practices reflect a real distinction between administrative and managerial activities?
3. How do we currently balance our managerial effort between (a) steady state, and (b) development work?
4. How do we set about prioritising our change programmes? (Someone somewhere is doing it.)
5. How do we attempt to bring about a generic capacity for change amongst staff?
6. Where is the line between management and manipulation?
7. How do we ensure that management is seen as a set of empowering activities and not as a control activity? This is particularly important in the resource management context.
8. Are staff seen as part of the problem or as part of the solution?

The list could go on, and it may indeed be appropriate to add to or subtract from it, but it is to be hoped that the general point is clear enough — that our first need is to have a very clear level of self-awareness about existing management structures and processes as a precondition for undertaking a review of these elements. Responses to these questions will be varied, and each will give rise to a number of subsidiary questions. However, an overall sense of direction will be determined by the extent to which we are happy with the answers given. The following chapters may help to sharpen that sense of direction still further, but as we consider in more detail the various themes of these chapters, we need also to bear in mind the relationships between them as part of the holistic management process, and to ask further questions about the location of responsibility and action in relation to each of them.

## Note

Elements of this chapter were first published as Osborne, A. 'Professionals, Managers and Comprehensive Schools', *Educational Change and Development*, Vol. 7 No. 2 1986 and 'Professionals, Managers and Comprehensive Schools' (Part 2), *Educational Change and Development*, Vol. 8 No. 1 Summer 1987.

## References

Benn, C. 1984 'Secondary Reform: the time to move on', *Forum*, 26 (2)
Constable, J. & McCormick, R. 1987 *The Making of British Managers*, British Institute of Management — Confederation of British Industry
Corwin, R. G. 1965 *Sociology of Education*, Appleton, Century, Crofts
Fullan, M. 1982 *The Meaning of Educational Change*, OISE
Handy, C. 1989 *The Age of Unreason* Hutchinson
Hoyle, E. 1975 'Professionality, Professionalism and Control in Teaching', in Houghton, V. *et al.* (eds) (1975), *Management in Education*, Vol. 1, Ward Lock
Hughes, M. G. 1980 'Reconciling Professional and Administrative Concerns' in Bush, T. *et al.* (eds) *Approaches to School Management*, Open University
Morgan, C. 1976 *Management in Education — Dissimilar or Congruent* Course 321: 1, Open University
Peters, T. 1988 *Thriving on Chaos*, Macmillan
Spence, L. D. *et al* 1981 'Conceptualising loose coupling: the garbage can as myth and ceremony' unpublished paper presented to the American Sociological Association in 1978 and quoted in Lehming, R. & Kane, M. (1981) *Improving Schools*, Sage
Watson, L. E. 1975 'Office and Expertise in the Secondary School' in Houghton, V. *et al.* (eds) (1975) *Management in Education*, Vol. 1, Ward Lock
Wilding, P. 1981 *Socialism and Professionalism*, Fabian Tract 473
Wilson, B. R. 1962 'Teacher's Role — a sociological analysis', *British Journal of Sociology*, 12

# 2 Management information

Brent Davies and
Linda Ellison

## Introduction

This chapter reviews the basic processes that underlie the gathering and use of information for decision making in schools. It aims to establish principles and practices which underpin each of the succeeding chapters by considering a rational approach to assessing the information processes and needs of each management activity.

If decisions are to be made about the deployment of resources or the implementation of the curriculum then they should be made on accurate and reliable information. Before management can proceed it needs to understand the key elements in the information process. The alternative is to manage reactively rather than proactively. This reactive approach is exemplified by realising, at the time when problems arise, that they cannot be solved without adequate information. It is much better to evaluate information needs and establish information flows in advance of the decision-making process than to discover their omission at a later stage.

The sections which follow are not about computer-based systems and jargon but focus on the information needs and systems of schools. As such, the chapter looks at:

1. A changing environment which is generating the need for high quality information for decision making.
2. The requirements of an effective information system.
3. Information gathering and processing.
4. The relationship between information and decision making.
5. Information and the level of management activity.
6. Good management practice.

It is hoped that the reader, after assessing these areas, will have a basis for evaluating the information system in his/her own institution.

## 1. The changing environment

The dynamic environment within which educational institutions currently operate was outlined in chapter 1. A particular feature in recent years has been the polarisation of power away from local education authorities (LEAs) to the centre (government) and to the periphery (schools). Schools have been given greater autonomy and greater exposure to market forces, both of which are significantly altering their information requirements.

Schools are having to become more complex organisations in order to meet the varied responsibilities which have been devolved to them since the Education Reform Act (1988). This level of autonomy will result in a changed role for the school from one of administration of policies to one of management of local resources. For senior managers the change in role is from tactical decision making to strategic decision making, highlighting the need for a significant increase in information flows and requirements. For example, increased responsibility for school finance results in the need for forecasts of future pupil numbers so that the effect of such numbers on the school's income can be predicted.

Running parallel to the changes in the legislative framework, there is a change in the relationship between schools and their immediate environment. In the past, schools felt that they could influence this environment. However, the increase in legislation and in consumer power have altered the balance so that schools, if they are to survive and be effective, must be sensitive and responsive to the demands of the external environment. This has resulted in an increased need to have accurate localised information, both quantitative and qualitative. For example, instead of working within an LEA's planned admissions policy, managers must have information that can help them in the recruitment programme which has become possible through open enrolment legislation.

With the increased responsibility and responsiveness has come an increase in the volume of management activities. This has resulted in a growing need for a more detailed and more formalised information system. The basic principles underlying a management information system are examined in the succeeding parts of this chapter. Only by understanding these basic factors can managers appreciate the context before decisions can be made about appropriate technology and other factors that may be needed to deliver the system.

## 2. The requirements of an information system

If managerial functions are to be carried out both efficiently and effectively, then it is a prerequisite that high quality information is available to inform decision making at the various managerial levels.

Laudon and Laudon (1988 p. vii) draw attention to this dependence on the type and quality of information provided:

> The work of the organisation depends increasingly on what its information systems are capable of doing. Increasing market share, becoming the low-cost producer, developing new products, and/or increasing employee productivity depend more and more on the kinds and quality of information systems in the organisation.

An information system, therefore, should be reliable and provide:

1. the right information
2. to the right people
3. at the right time
4. in the right way
5. to achieve clear objectives.

The sections which follow will examine the way in which high quality information can be gathered and used to inform decision making at the school level.

## 3. Information gathering and processing

Information gathering should not take place until a careful assessment has been made of the management tasks and decisions which require information. It is a fallacy to think that the more information an organisation has the better will be the decisions. Information must be focused so as to serve precise management tasks. Figure 2.1 represents the stages in the information-gathering process.

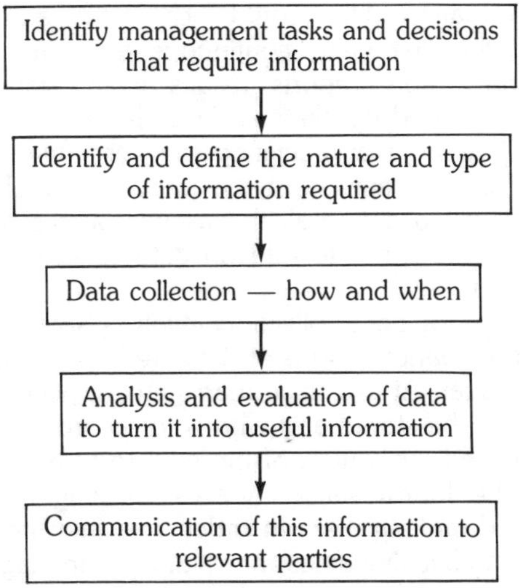


*Figure 2.1: the stages in the information-gathering process*

Once the management task has been defined then the type of information required can be identified. It is only then that the third stage comes into operation, that of the actual data collection. It is necessary, at this third stage, to define the way in which staff are to be involved and the time-scale for collection. The fourth stage involves sifting through the data and evaluating it so as to collate and analyse it in such a way as to provide useful information rather than a mass of unrelated facts or figures. Finally, it is vital that the results of the process are communicated effectively to all relevant parties in the organisation.

This process can be illustrated in the management task shown below.

| *Management Task 1: Secondary Schools* |
|---|
| 1st Year pupils are in mixed ability groups but at the start of the 2nd Year they are to be placed into three ability bands and set across the year group for Maths. |

The application of the five stages to the task illustrated would involve, firstly, the definition of the task. This is set out in the statement but clarification may be needed as to whether the bands are to be of equal size or that ability grouping determines different sized bands.

The second stage of identifying and defining the nature and type of information required would bring together both quantitative and qualitative information. This would include test and examination results during the first year, continuous assessment marks and evaluations, form tutors' reports, results of any standardised tests such as those provided by National Foundation for Education Research (NFER) and, in appreciating the continuity of education, indicators and assessments from the primary school reports. It is vital, at this stage, to define all the useful sources of data before the process starts and not to add on data collection areas as the process proceeds.

The third stage of data collection involves sequencing the collection so that the various forms of data are brought together at the end of the first year. At this stage management needs to determine how the data will be stored and who is to co-ordinate the process.

The analysis and evaluation of the data to turn it into useful information at the fourth stage involves collating the quantitative assessments and ranking them in order. It is then important to set against this the qualitative assessments and for management to discuss the relative importance of each type of information before the final decisions are made.

The communication of bands and set lists in Maths then has to take place to teachers, pupils and parents. Obviously, this needs great sensitivity when dealing with the clients in the form of pupils and the parents.

Readers may wish to apply this information-gathering process to the task shown below.

| *Management Task 2: Primary Schools* |
| --- |
| A primary school, in the light of national testing at 7 and 11, wants to provide its own profile of achievement and performance to complement and enlighten the rather crude test score approach.<br>What information will it need? |

## 4. The relationship between information and decision making

Are information and decision making separate activities or are they part of a continuum and, therefore, inter-related? This relationship has been analysed by Mason (1975) and is said to consist of: a *source*, e.g. the school and its activities, from which *data* is collected and recorded, from which managers draw *inferences and predictions* which are evaluated and the *values* and *choices* of the organisation are followed by *action*. This can be represented as shown in Figure 2.2 by Mason (1975 p. 2).

It is important for managers to assess the point at which the information system stops and the decision making begins. This is because a significant factor is the degree to which assumptions are built into the information system and thereby influence and affect the decision making. By analysing this concept it is possible to suggest four alternative decision-making systems that vary as the level of assumptions built into the information system increases.

A basic information system merely classifies and stores data. This is called a *data-bank system* and a good example is the pupil record system which is kept in a secretary's office. This may, for example, comprise 200 pupil files in alphabetical order. If specific information about pupils' ability, eligibility for free school meals, any disabilities etc. is required, then a painstaking search is undertaken each time

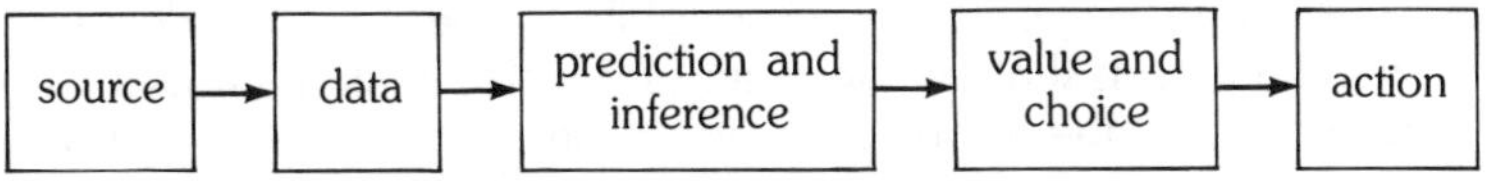


*Figure 2.2: information and decision making sequence*

for the particular piece of information required. The time consuming nature of searching through a mass of information for one factor is the main drawback of this approach, although the process can now be made more efficient by the use of electronic databases.

A second approach, *a predictive information system*, can be used where the information system may have a degree of prediction and inference built into it. Assumptions now become part of the information system and it is this aspect which must not be overlooked by the manager. Otherwise, there will be a tendency to rely on the information that the system provides without adequately reviewing the underlying assumptions upon which it is based. An example of this second approach would be the use of spreadsheets for calculating the allocation of capitation to departments within a secondary school. The spreadsheet will have built-in assumptions about weightings for age and subject needs. Any decisions made about allocations are not value-free but are now based on the original assumptions about the weightings.

A third approach is one of a *decision-making* system where the manager is simply there to approve or veto suggestions made by others. This increases the significance of the information system to that of a recommender as to what to do based on value and choices but leaves the final decision to the manager. An example of this would be the operation of a lettings policy in a school. The head, operating under powers delegated to him by the governors, would set up criteria for the policy and appoint one of the staff to run the scheme. The member of staff would make all decisions regarding letting with the head not involved in the process *but* retaining the power of final veto to be applied in sensitive cases! These decision-making systems have a considerable number of assumptions built into them and there must be an agreed value system. If this is not the case then the decision-making information system's recommendations may result in considerable problems if recommendations are consistently vetoed.

A fourth approach removes all decision taking into the information system itself and is called a *decision-taking system*. This is where management has total confidence in the assumptions and values that are built into the information system. An example of this is staff cover packages, often used in secondary schools, which allocate cover for absent staff. These allow the computer to determine who will do the cover for a particular day. While depending on assumptions being built in about priorities and free periods they relieve the manager of any responsibilities over the final decision.

It can be seen that, as the point of decision making moves more and more into the information side of the system, the significance of in-built values and assumptions expands considerably and the qualitative nature of those assumptions also changes.

In summary, when considering information and decision-making flows there are two key questions, (i) at which point does the information system stop and the decision making begin, and (ii) what is the nature of the assumptions which are incorporated in the information system? These are the critical management questions that should be asked at the outset before decisions are taken in schools.

## 5. Information and the level of management activity

A theoretical perspective which is of considerable value is put forward by Gorry and Scott Morton (1975), who draw on the work of Anthony (1965) in the area of managerial activity and Simon's (1966) analysis of decisions, to develop a sophisticated framework for management information systems.

Anthony classifies management activities into three categories: strategic planning, management control and operational control, and argues that these activities are sufficiently different to warrant different information systems. This matching of information to activity requirements is in sharp contrast to the straightforward data-bank approach. Anthony defines strategic planning as:

> the process of deciding on objectives of the organisation, on changes in these objectives, on the resources used to attain these objectives and on the policies that are to govern the acquisition, use and disposition of these resources.
>
> Anthony (1965) p. 24

This function is primarily undertaken in a school (within the parameters laid down by the LEA) by the governors, the headteacher and the deputies.

The second category, that of management control, is seen as:

> . . . the process by which managers assure that resources are obtained and used effectively and efficiently in the accomplishment of the organisation's objectives.
>
> Anthony (1965) p. 24

This relates to the middle-management area of decision and control which would be at the head of department and head of year level in a comprehensive school or the allowance holders in a primary school.

The third category, that of operational control, is 'the process of assuring that specific tasks are carried out effectively and efficiently' (Anthony 1965 p. 24). This is a situation which would equate to the teaching process and areas of curricular and programme responsibility.

Davies (1984) translates this into a school setting as shown in the diagram.

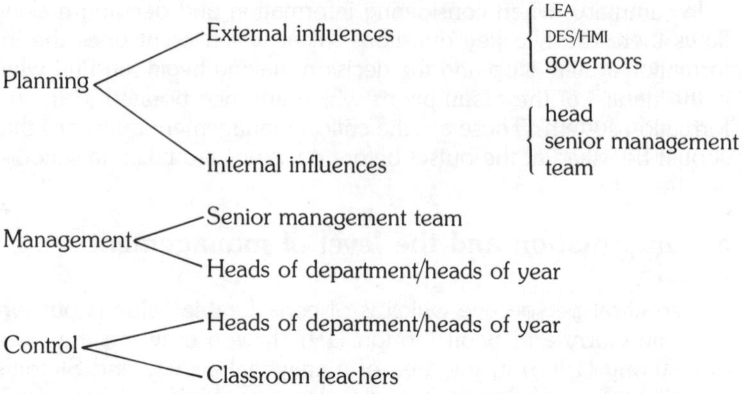


Gorry and Scott Morton (1975), despite the problems of unclear boundaries between the three categories, find this a useful approach to the analysis of information requirements for management. The type of information required at each level can now be assessed. As strategic planning is concerned with broad policies and goals it has to relate the organisation to its environment and predict the effects of any changes in that environment. The focus of information gathering will be on aggregated information to ascertain general trends so detailed accuracy will not be as important. This strategic planning process makes use of external sources for information and the non-routine nature of the process will present an irregular pattern of demand for the information. It contrasts with the information needs for operational control which are well defined, detailed and accurate. The information will be largely internally supplied and will have frequent use. The information needs of management control will be obtained through personal interaction.

This type of analysis can be summarised in Figure 2.3 by Gorry and Scott Morton (1975, p. 20).

| *Characteristics of information* | *Operational control* | *Management control* | *Strategic planning* |
|---|---|---|---|
| Source | Largely internal | → | External |
| Scope | Well defined, narrow | → | Very wide |
| Level of aggregation | Detailed | → | Aggregate |
| Time horizon | Historical | → | Future |
| Currency | Highly current | → | Quite old |
| Required accuracy | High | → | Low |
| Frequency of use | Very frequent | → | Infrequent |

*Figure 2.3: information requirements by decision category*

The areas discussed in these five sections have provided a framework which helps to understand the basic dimensions of management information. The authors now propose a checklist against which readers might evaluate the introduction of a management information system in their own institutions. This may be particularly apposite in the context of the introduction of computerised systems.

## 6. Good management practice

1. Is the introduction (or alteration) of a management information system (MIS) desirable because of changing need or is it being imposed from outside?
2. Have aims and objectives been identified in the early stages and are these goals related to managerial issues?
3. Has there been any investigation as to what the potential users want from the system?
4. Has a cost/benefit analysis, in terms of time as well as financial costs, been undertaken before implementation of the scheme?
5. Has enough attention been paid to the need for adaptability within the system, especially if it has been initiated/developed outside the institution?
6. Have staff development issues been addressed:
   (a) have managers been made adequately aware of the potential of the system and given help to use it for strategic and management control decision making?
   (b) have steps been taken to optimise the behavioural response of those affected by the change; for example, the effect of transfer of work and changes in roles between clerical staff and decision-makers?
7. Is there evidence of the scheme becoming more of a predictive tool and aid to decision making rather than working primarily in an administrative function?
8. Is there a regular review pattern established to reassess the aims and objectives, implementation processes and the changing costs and benefits of the system?

## Conclusion

It has been a mistake of many developments in MIS to concentrate on solutions in the form of computer packages such as Schools Information and Management Systems (SIMS) in the school sector or Further Education Management Information System (FEMIS) in the FE sector. Before proceeding down these lines managers should evaluate not only the technical efficiency of such systems but, more importantly, the underlying management questions outlined in this chapter. Although these basic management perspectives have been established for over 20 years, modern technology often ignores them.

## References

Anthony, R. N. 1965 *Planning and Control Systems: a Framework for Analysis*, Harvard University Press

Davies, K. B. 1984 'The purpose and functions of budgets — some theoretical perspectives for education managers', *School organisation*, vol. 4 No. 2 pp. 143–148

Gorry, G. A. & Scott Morton, M. S. 1975 'A framework for management information systems' in *Information for Decision-making*, Rappaport, A. (ed), Prentice Hall

Laudon, K. C. & Laudon, J. P. 1988 *Management Information Systems, A Contemporary Perspective*, Macmillan

Mason, R. O. 1975 'Basic concepts for designing management information systems', in *Information for Decision-making*, Rappaport, A. (ed), Prentice Hall

Simon, H. A. 1966 *The New Science of Management Decision*, Harper and Row 1966

# 3 Planning in education management

## Linda Ellison and Brent Davies

### Introduction

Chapter 1 outlined the changing environment in which schools operate today. School management will have the key task of planning how the institution is to adapt and change to meet the challenge of providing effective education for pupils and students in the 1990s. The quality of management planning will, therefore, be one of the critical determinants of a school's success.

After establishing a definition of planning, this chapter will examine the following key aspects:

- planning in the cycle of management activity
- people in the planning process
- planning aims, objectives, activities and evaluation
- rational approaches to planning
- the problems of rational planning in education
- a practical framework for school planning.

The conclusion will draw together the advantages of rational planning and provide a 'checklist' for effective planning.

### A definition of planning

Planning is the managerial process of deciding in advance *what* is to be done and *how* it is to be done. It can be applied to a range of activities which may vary in cost and scale and necessitate planning over differing time spans. This chapter defines planning as a broad process which involves the establishment of objectives and the formulation, evaluation and selection of policies, strategies and actions needed to achieve the objectives.

The planning process is, thus, one which gathers (either formally or informally), translates and communicates information so that it can be used to make decisions. In this way it brings together objectives and resources in order to meet organisational goals.

Many people see planning as one of the hard-nosed rational management tasks in organisations. However, others feel that, because of the speed of change and because of goal conflict between the professionals involved, educational planning is more difficult and has a political rather than rational dimension. This rational/political dichotomy is true in all planning activities and is discussed later in this chapter. Chapter 4 will consider a more detailed analysis of rational and political aspects and approaches in relation to the particular process of budgetary planning.

## Planning in the cycle of management activity

Figure 3.1 shows the important position which planning should occupy as a preliminary to decision making and implementation. It reflects the broad definition of planning adopted initially.

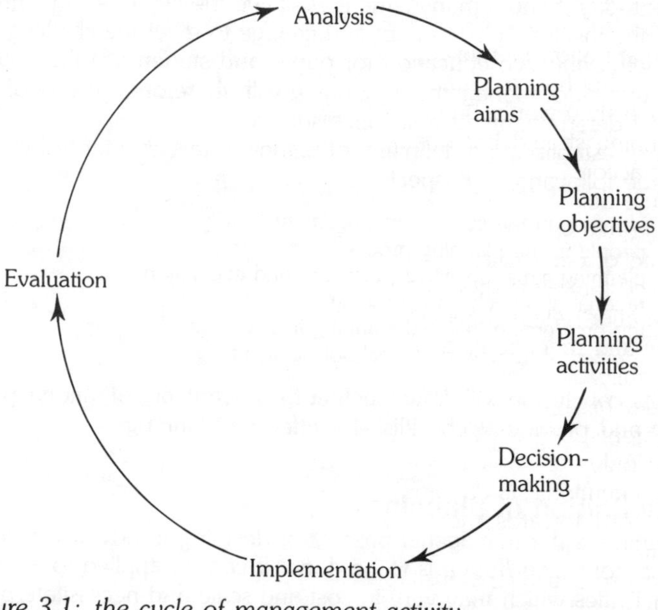


*Figure 3.1: the cycle of management activity*

The cycle demonstrates that before specific activities can be planned it is necessary to plan aims and objectives. Once these have been determined, the means of achieving them, in terms of defined programmes and activities, can be considered.

## People in the planning process

The introduction to this chapter made specific reference to the need for school management to plan the school's path through the changing environment. This was not to imply that planning is an activity which is only carried out by senior management. Everyone needs to plan and, indeed, every teacher is a manager. Even the newly qualified teacher manages time, pupils, resources and the curriculum within the classroom. Although various models are suggested in other literature, it is probably most valuable to apply the levels which were introduced on p. 27.

The planning activities at the three levels can be referred to as strategic planning, tactical planning (or 'management control') and operational planning. The features of each level are shown in Figure 3.2.

## Planning the aims of a school

The members of any organisation should have a clear idea of its general purpose which is expressed in the form of a 'mission statement' or 'corporate objective', defining the business in which the organisation is involved. This strategic role at the level of the whole school is a planning task for the governors and head, although they would be expected to consult others.

Planning should begin with an analysis of the present position taking account of both internal and external factors and a forecast of future developments, moving on to the definition of broad aims. The frequency of this planning activity will be partly determined by the rate of change in the educational environment. It is generally accepted that aims should be reviewed (even if this does not result in alteration) every four years. A school must decide how best to review and redefine its aims. Increasingly, the teaching staff participate fully, but the governors and senior management might consider broadening the process to include non-teaching staff and the parents who, after all, are the clients.

It is only when the present position has been assessed and the future intentions stated that members of the organisation can effectively plan towards the achievement of purposeful goal-directed activity.

Because educational institutions are largely staffed by professionals, there has, in the past, been a tendency to allow individuals a lot of freedom to use their professional judgement in deciding how best to achieve the aims of the organisation. Indeed, these aims may not always have been stated clearly. This has led to a situation in which individuals have either tended to pursue their own goals (deliberately) or have misinterpreted (genuinely) the aims of the school. The result may have been a conflicting programme for pupils. In the absence of planning there would be considerable frustration and pupils' activities would lack direction. If a school is to be effective, the staff should all be working in the same direction, rather than pursuing conflicting goals.

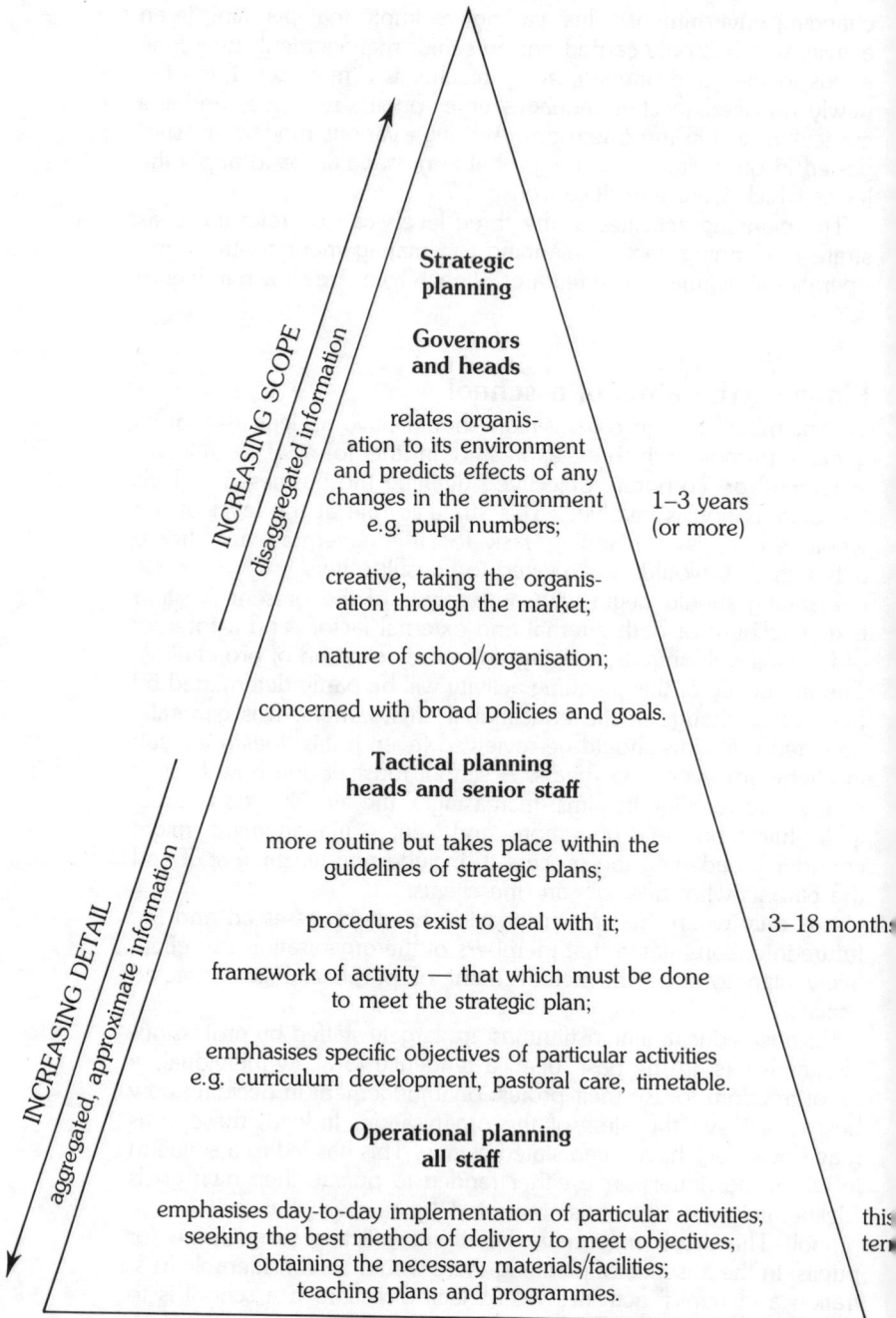

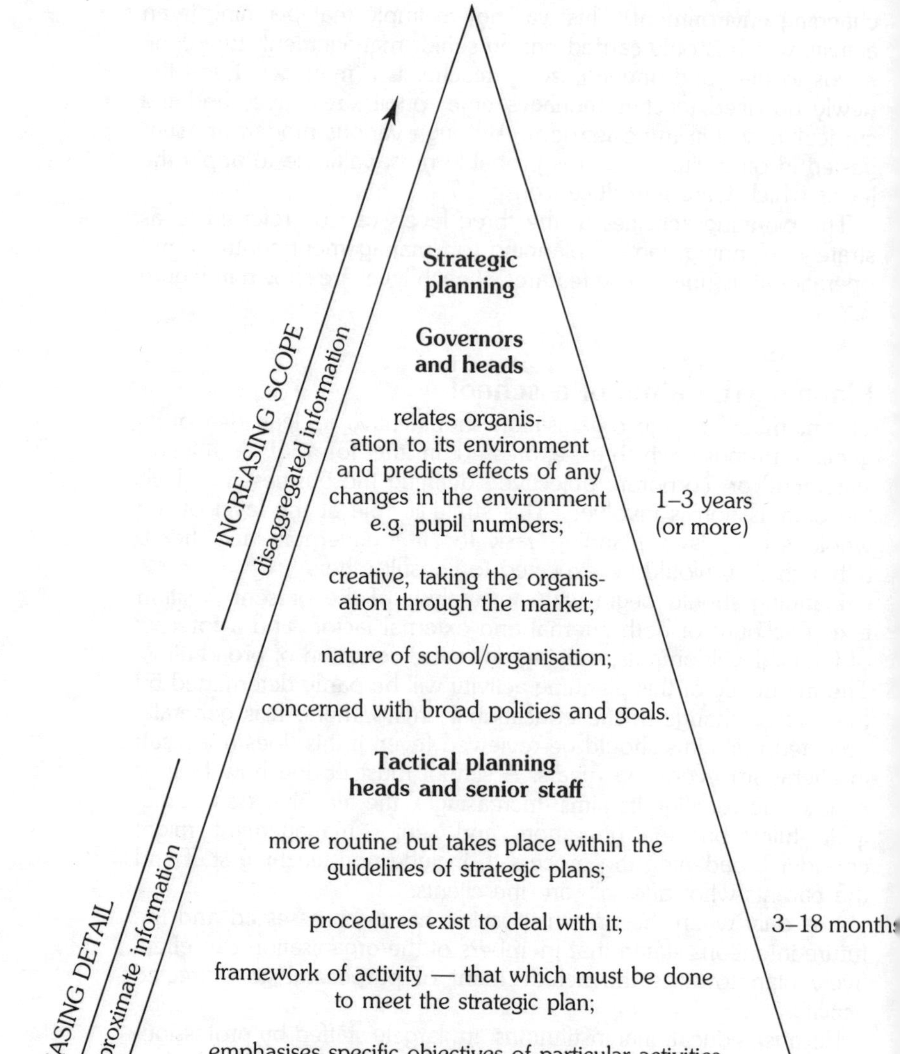
INCREASING SCOPE
disaggregated information
Strategic planning
Governors and heads
relates organisation to its environment and predicts effects of any changes in the environment e.g. pupil numbers;
1–3 years (or more)
creative, taking the organisation through the market;
nature of school/organisation;
concerned with broad policies and goals.
INCREASING DETAIL
aggregated, approximate information
Tactical planning heads and senior staff
more routine but takes place within the guidelines of strategic plans;
procedures exist to deal with it;
3–18 months
framework of activity — that which must be done to meet the strategic plan;
emphasises specific objectives of particular activities e.g. curriculum development, pastoral care, timetable.
Operational planning all staff
emphasises day-to-day implementation of particular activities; seeking the best method of delivery to meet objectives; obtaining the necessary materials/facilities; teaching plans and programmes.
this
ter

*Figure 3.2: levels of planning*

## Planning the objectives of an organisation

Once the school aims have been stated in general terms, objectives will be set at middle management level within a school and will relate to the achievement of these aims. However, at the classroom level there may be specific objectives set for a particular session or activity. These will be drawn up by the teacher and should relate to those set by middle managers. Objectives will be redefined more frequently than aims, usually at annual intervals or more regularly, following evaluation of existing activities.

If purposeful, goal-directed activity is to take place, clear objectives need to be set for all the organisation's activities. If objectives are understood by all staff in a school, they will help to form a framework on which the activities can be based. When planning objectives there are various management points to bear in mind and these will be outlined in the ensuing paragraphs.

While aims are fairly broad, objectives need to be quite *specific*. Each should be a clear, concise statement of what is to be achieved. They should be *written* so that everyone is aware of what they are. They can then be referred to and used as a tool to facilitate such activities as decision making, monitoring and evaluation. The *relevance* of the objectives should be checked. They should be appropriate to the stated aims of the organisation, rather than to an individual or sub-group's desire to maximise their own aims.

In the area of education today, much credence is given to the concept of ownership. It can be shown that individuals and groups welcome the opportunity to contribute to debate and to participate in policy making. It follows, therefore, that the formulation of objectives should, wherever possible, involve those concerned, whether they are governors, staff, pupils, parents, or outside agencies. *Agreement* with the objectives will help to ensure that they are seen to be important and that activity will be directed towards their achievement.

It is particularly because of their potential when evaluating activities that objectives should be *measurable*. If some form of quantitative criteria can be established then the evaluation process can be carried out objectively and efficiently. This highlights one of the recurring dilemmas in education, that is the difficulty of quantitatively measuring many of the desired outcomes of the education process. Although qualitative data, which are far more subjective, are usually preferred by teachers, there is still a very strong abhorrence of any attempt at output measurement because it is perceived as inaccurate or misleading. For example, under the broad aim of fostering a love of reading, an objective might be to encourage greater use of the school library. The logical quantitative measurement would be the number of books borrowed but this does not determine whether these have been read or enjoyed. The expression of output in the form of performance indicators (see chapter 10), which were to have been quantitative wherever possible, has caused considerable problems.

It is generally accepted that people are motivated by success and that it is often easier to work towards realistic short-term targets. This principle can be applied to the setting of objectives. All those concerned need to believe that the targets are being set at a level which is *achievable.* If not, there will be disenchantment because those who have framed the objectives will be perceived to be 'out of touch' with reality in the organisation. There must be a belief that, through purposeful activity, the objectives can be achieved. However, objectives should not be set which, at the outset, are demonstrably easy to achieve. If schools are fully to develop their pupils, then *challenging* activities need to be provided. Similarly, challenging objectives should motivate staff and encourage creativity.

The *time-scales* over which different objectives should be achieved may vary considerably, depending on the level at which they are applied. Nevertheless, a time by which they must be achieved should be stated. If not, those involved will be unclear about what is expected and monitoring and control will be ineffective.

To summarise, and to use an acronym which will be familiar to some readers, objectives should be challenging and:

| | |
|---|---|
| S | pecific |
| M | easurable |
| A | greed and achievable |
| R | elevant |
| T | imed |

When planning objectives, the chart in Figure 3.3 may provide a useful flowchart and checklist to ensure that they meet the criteria outlined above.

## Planning the activities

Some people may consider that only certain major activities require planning, e.g. the curriculum or the future staffing. However, it is more valuable to think of a global school development plan which

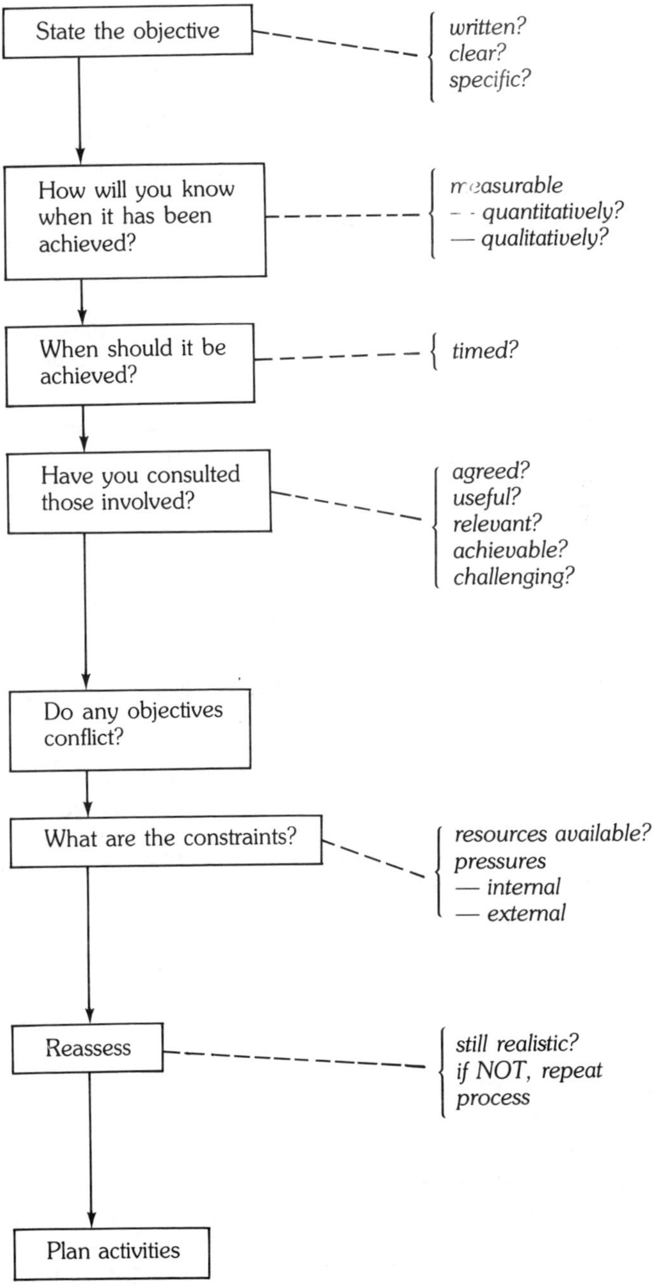


*Figure 3.3: a flowchart to summarise the process of planning objectives*

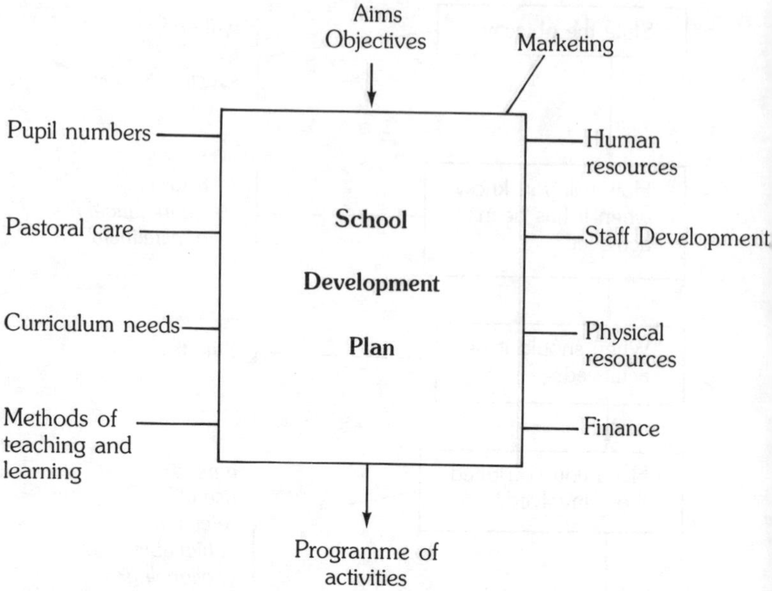


*Figure 3.4: the school development plan*

brings together all central and support activities. The components of this plan are shown in Figure 3.4.

Although there should be separate, more detailed plans for each of these areas, their integration ensures that the separate plans are complementary whereas, in the past, compartmentalised planning led to overlaps and omissions. The importance of thinking in this way is stressed by the Education Reform Act (1988) as this requires the governors to present a school development plan to the LEA annually. It is not intended that this plan should be 'cast in concrete' but, rather, that it should be flexible so that the school looks ahead but remains responsive to future changes in circumstances.

## Planning the evaluation

Because the focus of the planning process is on designing programmes to achieve objectives, it is quite common, at this stage, to neglect the mechanism for evaluation.

An organisation maintains its effectiveness by evaluating the extent to which the objectives are realised through the activities. It is important to plan the evaluation process at the outset so that it relates to the stated objectives. If the evaluation is 'bolted on' at a later date it may not be measuring the success of the original, documented plans. It is also unfair on the staff if the evaluation process is not clear in advance; it may appear that micropolitical factors are at work in order to achieve the right 'result'.

## Rational approaches to planning

Rational models of planning can be seen to fall into two distinct categories.

(a) Planning with 'precise' goals can be likened to the Tour de France in which the participants aim for A, move on to B and so on until the end is reached.

A B
Start ——— * ——— * ——— * ——— Goal

This approach may be possible if educational objectives have a very short time-scale but it does not allow for the change of direction which is often necessary in schools.

(b) The proactive, directional planning approach is usually more appropriate to the dynamic environment in which schools find themselves and to their need to react to pupils and circumstances. Goals are still identified but they are less well defined. Directional planning involves identifying barriers and potentials and choosing a course in order to overcome the former and make best use of the latter. As the dynamic environment unfolds and the planning process responds to change, it may be that the original goals are fundamentally altered. (See Figure 3.5).

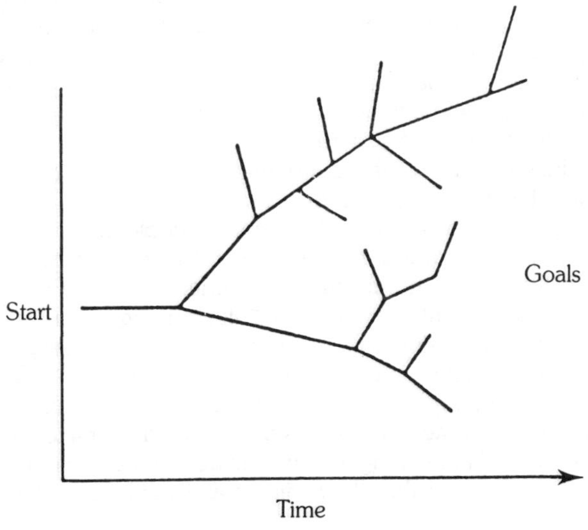


*Figure 3.5: directional planning*

As all readers will appreciate, this change of course occurs quite frequently and sometimes has to be decided upon very quickly. The ability to respond in crisis is one of the skills which all teachers must possess. It is easier to do this if one can switch course, yet still be working within the framework of broad objectives. Preactive management can be seen as a positive response to changed circumstances with plans and objectives in mind, that is it is facilitated by the directional planning approach. This structured response is preferable to reactive or crisis management which is found where objectives are unclear, plans haphazard and where the organisation lives from one day to the next.

## The problems of rational planning in education

Set against the neat rationality of these advantages must be the particular difficulties of planning in education.

There are, within the teaching profession, as well as in the community at large, diverse views about aims and goals. There is considerable debate about the value of education for its own sake, rather than as a means to an end. Even when common goals have been established, conflict may be generated during the planning process because of disagreement about the way in which these goals should be achieved. Because the business of education is largely concerned with human issues, there will be situations arising which do not fit within the rational planning model.

Because of rapidly changing circumstances, for example in policies or staff availability, there is a need for considerable flexibility in educational planning. For this reason, some people may even feel that there is little point in planning ahead. It is possible however to structure plans so that they are responsive to change, particularly when they are formed and later adjusted with the help of a suitable management information system.

The validity of some of these arguments is expressed by Hopson and Scally (1984 p. 125) as shown in Figure 3.6.

This emphasises two of the dimensions, people and time, which impinge upon the planning process. It is relatively easy to plan the immediate future for oneself but, the further away one goes from oneself and the present, the more difficult planning becomes. Many teachers have felt considerable frustration when uncertainty, for example at national level, has been used by heads as an excuse to avoid school planning beyond the immediate future. This problem has been reduced now that schools are required to make some attempt at formulating longer-term school development plans, although it is accepted that they will act as flexible guidelines.

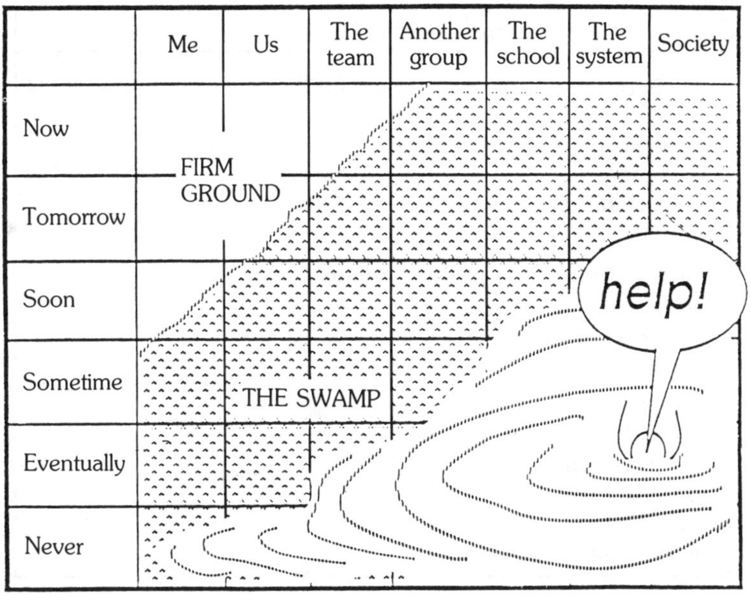


*Figure 3.6: certainty and uncertainty in planning*

## A practical framework for school planning

The nature of the planning process at the various levels needs to be different. Strategic planning tasks such as the setting of aims may be seen as essentially a people/politics-rich area where sophisticated techniques are not appropriate. At the tactical level there are planning techniques and technologies which may prove valuable, for example the use of clash tables and computerised timetable systems. It is uncommon for schools to use processes such as critical path analysis because they can be very time consuming unless used by experts, although simpler versions may be worth considering, for example stocks and flows models. These techniques can be found in a variety of texts, for example Dobson *et al.* (1985). At the operational level planning tasks will be simpler and there is less need to look for complex procedures as it would be like using a sledgehammer to crack a nut.

It is important that the planning process should define how a project is to move from the current position to the desired future position, i.e. the action needed to achieve objectives. The information could be assembled as in Blocks A, B and C.

| *BLOCK A — the current position* |
| --- |
| *Analysis* of the situation e.g. using GRIDS or a less formal audit of<br>Strengths<br>Weaknesses<br>Opportunities<br>Threats<br><br>An assessment of the present resource base<br>premises<br>equipment/supplies<br>finance<br>staff<br>training<br><br>Contacts available<br>for information<br>for assistance<br>as potential 'customers' |

| *BLOCK B — the plans* |
| --- |
| *What needs to be done?*<br>market research<br>aims and objectives<br>activity plans<br>*What will it cost?*<br>expenditure (realistic estimates of resource needs)<br>income generation<br>opportunity costs<br>(so 'PLANNING' must be closely linked to 'BUDGET')<br>this leads to financial plans<br>*When will it be done?*<br>project timetable — key dates<br>*Who will do it?*<br>there should be clear responsibilities — who will be responsible for it?<br>who will be involved with it?<br>*What will be monitored?*<br>and how?<br>and when? |

| *BLOCK B — the plans* |
|---|
| *What will be evaluated?*<br>and how?<br>what level of achievement will be acceptable?<br>how will data be collected?<br>under what situation will remedial action be needed? |

| *BLOCK C — the choices* |
|---|
| Alternative courses of action (with costs) will be generated as a result of the work in BLOCK B.<br>Criteria will then be applied to these alternatives bearing in mind the future position (defined in terms of objectives which have been prioritised).<br>A *decision* will then be taken or plans will be adjusted or alternatives will be regenerated. |

## Conclusion

The advantages of a rational approach to planning are given here and the breadth of these should alert the reader to the importance of the planning process in providing guidelines to secure organisational effectiveness.

1. It involves a review of activities and provides an opportunity for thorough examination of all aspects of the work of the school by those involved.
2. It minimises uncertainty and helps to anticipate changes for example in demography, social factors, values and employment levels.
3. By providing clear goals and objectives, it minimises frustration and wasted effort.
4. It provides a basis for action which includes setting targets and then monitoring outcomes and it motivates those involved.
5. It helps the organisation to anticipate and minimise difficulties, especially in potentially complex situations, by ensuring that careful consideration has been given to alternative courses of action.
6. It facilitates the articulation of ends and means.
7. It helps to co-ordinate resources (especially people) and processes, facilitating the optimum use of resources and time. This leads to more efficient, effective working and more enthusiastic participation so that tasks are completed and objectives are reached.
8. It gives an advantage over competitors because it provides a flexible, forward-looking framework on which to base activities.

9. It provides for greater control as it gives a framework for monitoring and evaluating.

Even the apparently rational model of planning on page 42 is, nevertheless, subject to political pressures. At the outset of the planning process, the forecasts which are taken into account may have been subjected to bias. By choosing the 'right' data source, individuals or groups may influence the outcome of the planning process. Further political pressure occurs when *generating alternatives* and when *evaluation criteria* are formulated. It can be possible to preselect the final choice by 'fiddling' the criteria.

The political model accepts that micropolitical activity can dominate the organisation so that genuine organisational objectives cannot be operationalised. When attempting a rational approach to planning it is important to be aware of these political factors.

The reader may like to reflect on his/her own planning approach and assess its validity by comparing it with the following checklist of factors which facilitate effective planning.

1. The necessary information (external and internal) is available.
2. The staff at all levels are committed to the project and its goals.
3. There are clear, precise channels of communication in all directions.
4. The level of the planning activity is clear to those who organise meetings. It is ineffective to mix strategic issues with tactical or operational ones on an agenda because it is difficult to change focus.
5. The various sections of the school function as effective teams and the objectives are clear so that they know what is required of them.
6. The evaluation process is built in during the planning stage, rather than 'bolted on' afterwards.

Although this chapter is an entity in itself , it is also a facilitating one in that the concepts and principles outlined here provide a framework to understanding the planning dimensions of the areas of management in the succeeding chapters.

## References

Dobson L., Gear T. & Westoby A. 1975 *Management in Education* 2, Open University.

Hopson B. & Scally M. 1984 *Build Your Own Rainbow*, Lifeskills Associates.

# 4 Resource management in schools

Brent Davies

The purpose of this chapter is to outline the elements involved in resource management in schools and to apply them to current practice. Initially, the changing context and framework of resource management in the 1990s will be considered. Following this a theoretical review will examine the central feature of resource management, the budgetary process, and then move on to consider two main approaches to budgeting. This will then provide an analytical background against which to review a school-focused case study.

## Resource management in the 1990s

The growth in the number of delegated schemes for school finance during the 1980s, culminating in the introduction of local management of schools (LMS) in the 1988 Education Reform Act, is leading to a revolution in resource management practice in schools.

The 1990s is an era in which schools operate with considerable financial autonomy. The polarisation of power to the centre (government) and periphery (schools) at the expense of the local education authority (LEA) will mean that schools have to adopt sophisticated resource management skills and approaches.

LMS delegates to schools control over the major part of their budgets. An analogy that is worth considering is that of a landlord and tenant relationship. The LEA acts as the landlord responsible for capital expenditure, as represented by the school building and major structural work, while the school is responsible as the tenant for everything that goes on inside. The school, therefore, has in its budget funds for teachers' salaries and other staffing costs, equipment and books, heating and lighting, rates, examination fees and all internal maintenance associated with normal 'wear and tear'. Unlike the previous financing system the school does not receive an allocation for each of these items but is allocated a lump sum and has the choice of how much to spend on each category. The amount which the schools are allocated is determined by a formula in which at least 75 per cent is based on pupil numbers 'weighted' by the age of those pupils.

The key areas of LMS as they effect resource management planning can be summarised as:

1. Financial delegation
2. Formula funding
3. Open enrolments
4. Staffing delegation
5. Performance indicators

The dynamic effect of these five factors is considerable. If parents perceive that the quality of education offered by a school is inadequate, they will move their children to another school by exercising choice through the mechanism of *open enrolments*. As pupils move around the system the funding moves with them. Thus, schools not only have to deal with financial delegation but they have to be very aware of market forces. The way in which the school is perceived by the local community may depend not only on overt *performance indicators* such as language and numeracy skills but also on covert performance indicators such as how the pupils behave on the bus going home or smoking outside the school premises. The amount of money received under *formula funding* will vary according to the number of pupils coming to the school. As the school has *staffing delegation* it will adjust the number of staff by hiring or firing according to this movement of pupils and funding. The impact of this can be assessed by the diagram in Figure 4.1 (which assumes 100 per cent funding from pupil numbers).

In the diagram 'fixed costs' include maintenance, head teacher's salary etc, while a large proportion of the variable costs will be represented by teachers and their salaries. If extra pupils come to the school the money can be spent on the variable costs, increasing teaching numbers and providing more books and equipment. This would be represented in the diagram by moving from point A to point C. The converse is true because if a school loses pupils (represented by moving from point A to point B) it is not that the school spends any more on fixed costs but because of the reduction in pupils and hence funding, fixed costs take a larger proportion of the available budget. The amount remaining for teachers, books and equipment is reduced, making the school less attractive to parents. Thus, pupils moving around the system can enhance a school's provision if it is a net gainer but cause severe problems very quickly if it is a net loser. As a result LMS rewards expanding schools and penalises contracting ones.

Financial delegation in the 1990s therefore does not only involve the school having control of its budget. It means that it has control

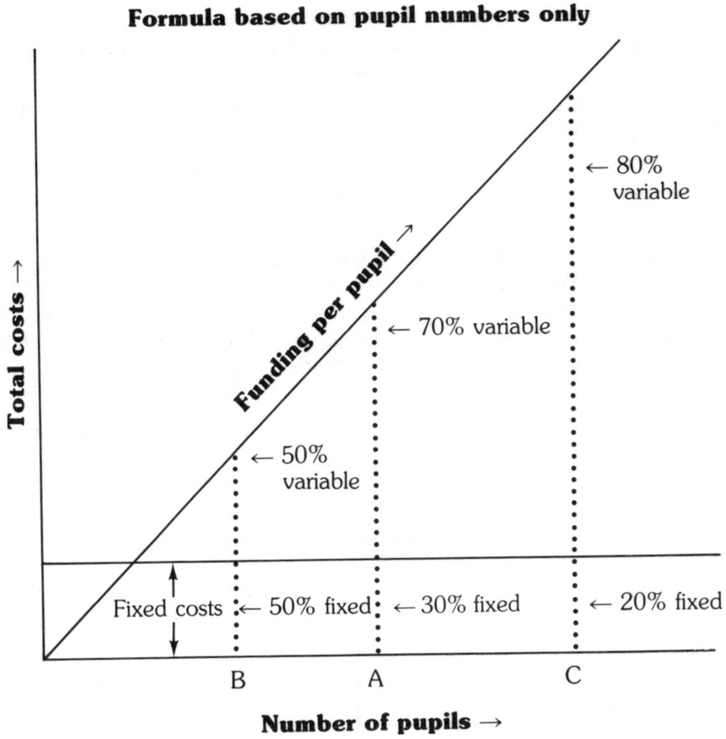


*Figure 4.1: Formula-based funding*

in the context of a market-oriented environment which has a dynamic and fundamental effect on the nature of the budgetary process.

Traditional methods of school finance have resulted in the LEA having the critical management responses for resource decisions. A school has had a restricted spending function when it came to utilising the limited amount of money available to buy books and equipment under its capitation allowance. The era of local management of schools means that the traditional spending function associated with capitation has to be replaced with a whole school budgetary process and plan. The next section of this chapter looks at the theoretical aspects which underpin this budgetary process and plan.

## Elements and dimensions of the budgetary process

What is a budget and what is the budgetary process? Schick (1972 p. 16) states that 'budgeting always has been conceived as a process for systematically relating expenditure of funds to the accomplishment of planned objectives'. Irvine (1975) sees a budget system as enabling management more effectively to plan, co-ordinate, control and evaluate the activities of an organisation. Hofstede (1968) sees the four basic functions of budgets as authorising, forecasting, planning and measuring. As can be seen, budgeting is not just a mechanical or technical exercise, a point developed by Irvine (1975 p. 74):

> A budget, as a formal set of figures written on a piece of paper, is in itself merely a quantified plan for future activities. However, when budgets are used for control, planning and motivation, they become instruments which cause functional and dysfunctional consequences both manifest and latent which determine how successful the tool will be.

Simkins and Lancaster (1987, p. 10) summarise the functions of budgets in Figure 4.2.

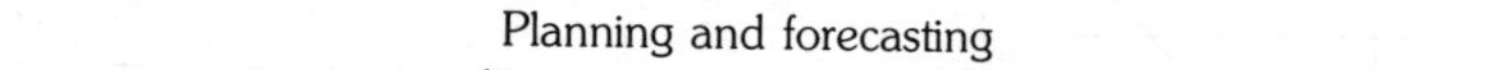

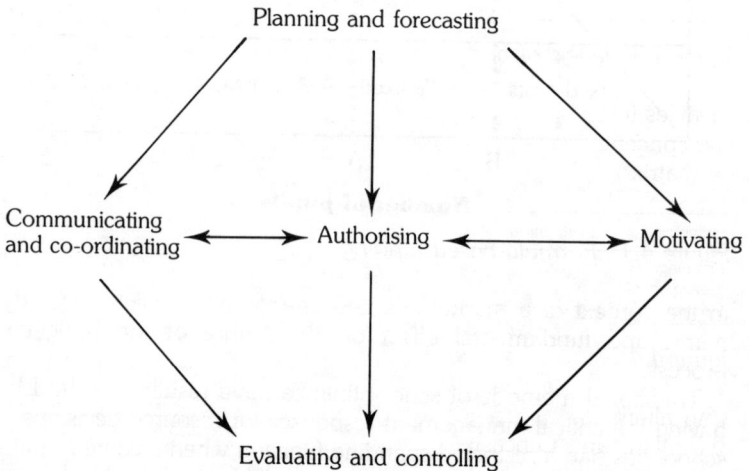


*Figure 4.2: functions of budgets*

A useful broad classification is provided by Schick (1972 p. 17) who builds on Anthony' s (1965) three-fold classification of management processes: (a) strategic planning; (b) management control; and (c) operational control; and states that 'every budget system, even rudimentary ones, comprises planning, management and control processes'. A useful analysis of the way in which different levels of management may be involved in the functions of budgeting is provided by Davies (1984) who uses Anthony's three levels of management and relates them to people in Figure 4.3.

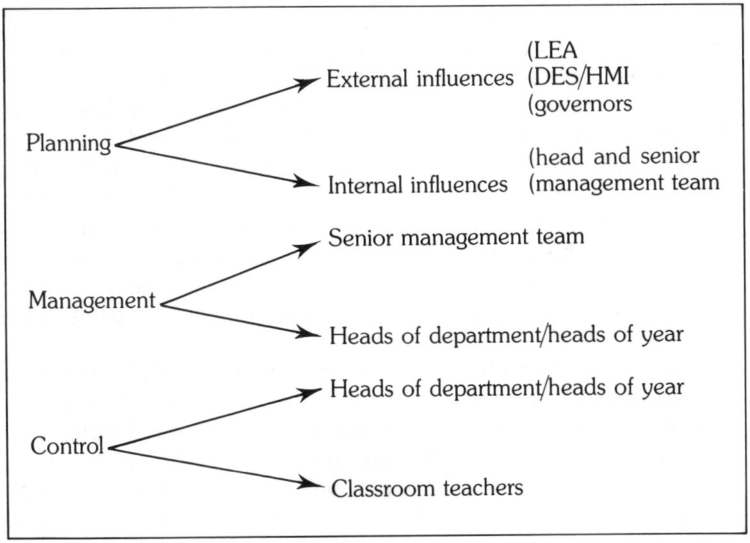


*Figure 4.3: levels of budgetary management (Davies 1984)*

Davies further suggests that these different levels of management may concentrate on different budgetary functions as represented in the matrix in Figure 4.4.

| Resource: | Generation | Allocation | Utilisation | Replenishment | Evaluation |
|---|---|---|---|---|---|
| Planning | X | X | | X | X |
| Management | | X | X | X | X |
| Control | | | X | | X |

*Figure 4.4: functions and levels of budgetary management*

An alternative grouping of the functions of budgets is provided by Simkins and Lancaster (1983). They divide these functions between operational and strategic activities, although a better categorisation could be functional and managerial activities.

The essential functional activities would be firstly, the *acquisition* of resources which involves the identification and securing of resources and then, secondly, the *allocation* of resources. This involves determination of the appropriate amount of resources to be distributed to different parts of the organisation. The third functional activity is that of *spending* when decisions are translated into action where, for example, goods are actually purchased. The fourth functional activity is that of *control* which monitors and assesses whether resources and activities are allocated as originally planned and authorised.

While these activities are fundamental to ensure that the mechanics of the budgetary process work, it is also necessary to consider the management activities which should take place. Firstly, a budget should be a *planning* document in that an organisation should clarify its goals and priorities in a forward looking way and relate them to available resources. Secondly, the budget is an important part of the *choice* process. It should provide the basis for costing alternative courses of action so that the resource implications of decisions can be assessed. In the final management function of a budget, that of *evaluation*, the analysis moves to assessing whether that type of expenditure was the best way of meeting organisational objectives.

In summary, it can be seen that there are a number of functional processes which are concerned with obtaining and distributing resources efficiently. However, reflecting back on Hofstede's definition of a budget system as enabling management more effectively to plan, co-ordinate, control and evaluate the activities of an organisation, it can be seen that there are a number of significant management elements in the budgetary process as well. The nature of delegated financial control is that decision making in these areas is moved from the LEA to the school level.

## Approaches to budgeting

Having assessed the central elements in a budgetary process, consideration will now be given to two broad frameworks into which differing budgetary processes can be categorised. The two broad categories could be considered as rational approaches, often called rational/economic approaches, and political approaches.

### *Rational/economic approaches*

Rational approaches are based on the assumption that organisations have clear objectives and resource allocation is organised in a systematic way to facilitate the achievement of those objectives.

In essence, after assessing the alternative expenditure options, spending patterns should reflect rational choices in order to maximise the achievement of the organisation's objectives. In evaluating this approach, it is possible to isolate key elements which underpin a rational budgetary approach.

The first of these elements is that budgets should be *objective* in that they relate directly to fulfilling the objectives of the organisation. Expenditure patterns should relate to outputs rather than being characterised by a list of resource inputs. The latter would be called a subjective budget and would list items in headings such as buildings, staff, rent, rates, capitation, in terms of the total spent in each category, rather than show how part of each category related to a particular programme. Hence, objective budgets are often called *output* or *programme* budgets. By using this approach it is claimed that important management processes are facilitated. These are firstly, the formulation of clear objectives and, secondly, planning, as resources must be clearly related in advance to objectives. Thirdly, the approach requires that choices are made, as assessing and opting between alternatives is necessary. Finally, evaluation takes place as criteria in the form of objectives provide a 'bench mark' against which to assess performance.

The second key element in a rational approach to budgeting is the *base* on which the range of choices is to be set. The traditional incremental approach is one in which last year's expenditure provides a base from which to make minor adjustments (disjointed incrementalism). This approach is criticised by Wildavsky (1978 p. 501–9):

> . . . traditional budgeting also has the defects of its virtues . . . comparing this year with last year may not mean much if the past was a mistake and the future is likely to be a bigger one. Quick calculation may be worse than none if it is grossly in error. There is an incremental road to disaster as well as faster roads to perdition; simplicity may become simple-mindedness.

The alternative to incrementalism provided by the rational perspective is zero-based review. With this approach there is a need to justify all expenditure and not just that expenditure at the margin or additional expenditure. As Wildavsky (1978 p. 501–9) states:

> . . . the past, as reflected in the budgetary base . . . is explicitly rejected. There is no yesterday. Nothing is taken for granted, everything at every period is subjected to searching scrutiny.

As a facilitator of management activities this imposes an opportunity–cost framework in that it encourages the reappraising of how differing expenditure patterns can best make a contribution to achieving organisational objectives. It also encourages evaluation because if choice is to be made between alternatives then evaluation of past and future spending in the alternative areas has to be assessed.

The third and final key element in a rational approach concerns the time-scale of the budget. Traditional budgets have been on an annual *time-scale*. The weakness of this is that it fails to view the implications of the spending when it makes its impact but only when the spending actually takes place. If the planning and choice possibilities are to be fully utilised then a time-scale that allows them to be fully understood has to be in operation. Therefore a multi-year time horizon budget needs to be implemented.

The rational approach has led to the development of PPBS (planning-programming-budgeting systems) and ZBB (zero-based budgeting) systems. However, despite early adoption there have been considerable doubts as to the effectiveness of such rational approaches. These doubts centre on three points. First is the difficulty in agreeing on objectives for education and translating them into programme goals. Second, the information requirements are considerable and the time taken assembling data may work against the efficiency that the organisation is trying to achieve. Finally, constant review and justification of budgets may deny managers a stable and predictable environment in which to operate effectively.

Brackett, Chambers and Parrish (1983 p. 37) state:

> Another lesson implied in the budget reform literature is the importance of simplicity and comprehensibility of the innovation. Aaron Wildavsky argued that while PPBS had many shortcomings, the fundamental reason for its demise was that no-one knew how to do programme budgeting. While the same accusation was not explicitly levelled against ZBB, the complexity of the procedures, the esoteric nature of the terminology, the potential for overwhelming paperwork and the inapplicable nature of several of the key concepts oppose acceptability.

## *Political approaches*

Because of the criticisms of rational approaches discussed above, political budgetary approaches show a remarkable capacity to persist. Wildavsky (1974 p. 13) makes the point that 'the largest determining factor of the size and content of this year's budget is last year's budget'. Why should this be so and the rational processes just described not take prominence? There are three key factors that influence the persistence of traditional budgeting processes. These can be seen as the process of incrementalism, the influence of micro-political forces and the tendency of organisations to satisfice rather than optimise goals.

The major factor in the incremental process is that the previous year's budget and level of expenditure is not challenged — there is general acceptance that it is valid. Attention is given to minor adjustments in the spending pattern or the justification of additional spending. There is no significant attempt to assess the validity of existing spending patterns. This approach provides a predictable and stable organisational climate. It also necessitates very little in terms of information and time requirements compared with zero-based approaches.

The micro-political dimension of budgeting is based on the view that budgetary decisions are not necessarily made on rational–economic grounds but that the deciding factors may be other influences such as the power base of individuals or groups and their value systems. Two useful statements which illustrate this are provided firstly by Pettigrew (1973 p. 17):

> Political behaviour is defined as behaviour by individuals, or, in collective terms, by sub-units, within an organisation that makes a claim against the resource sharing system of an organisation.

and secondly, by Wildavsky (1968 p. 193):

> If politics is regarded as conflict over whose preferences are to prevail in the determination of policy, then the budget records the outcomes of this struggle.

Therefore, gaining resources may not depend on the logic of the case but on a number of other factors. Greenwood *et al.* (1980 p. 29) express this as:

> A department's share of scarce resources depends upon the skill of its advocates in the use of essentially political tactics such as knowing how much to bid for, how far to pad estimates, how far to over/underspend, how to 'read' the political climate, how to generate and utilise public support.

The way in which the budgetary process is managed by the people involved may be as important as what is being managed as far as outcomes are concerned. Therefore, asking questions about objectives, planning, choice and evaluation may not be as important as asking questions about political forces at work if resource patterns are to be understood. Simkins and Lancaster (1983 p. 30), for example, list seven questions for consideration:

1. Which are the key groups that compete for resources in the budgetary process?
2. What differences in values and interests exist among them and how are these expressed in budgetary terms?
3. What sources of power can groups and key individuals bring to bear on the budgetary process?
4. Who controls the budgetary process itself and what means do they use to do so?
5. What political strategies and tactics are used to influence budget allocations?
6. What kind of coalitions are formed and bargains struck?
7. Who gains and who loses from the budgetary process?

These dimensions should be considered when assessing resource patterns from a political perspective.

A third concept used in understanding political approaches is the organisational process approach. In a commercial or industrial setting it is often assumed that organisations try to maximise profits as their main goal. However, the risks involved in profit maximisation may be unacceptable to managers who may prefer to safeguard their position by reducing competition through takeovers instead of maximising profits by competition. They may also aim to produce satisfactory levels of profit to keep shareholders happy and grant over-generous wage rises to avoid labour conflicts. The aim is to provide a series of acceptable solutions which meet the needs of the various constituencies that make up the organisation. Thus, the concept of an acceptable solution which satisfies the different goals and objectives in an organisation may be preferred to the most efficient one on rational grounds. In a school setting this would mean that differing objectives may be met and individual teachers supported, which would lead to overall harmony but not necessarily maximise purely educational outcomes. This satisficing element together with political and incremental forces form the key elements in political approaches to budgeting. The way in which these concepts relate to the rational perspective in resource management in practice will be analysed in the next section.

## A framework for analysing budgetary practice

It is proposed to take the seven functions of budgets on pages 49/50 as the first dimension of a matrix structure to which either the rational economic or a political model can be applied in order to form the second dimension.

Earlier in this chapter the three key elements of rational approaches were identified as: relating expenditure of funds to fulfilling organisational objectives, a zero-based approach to choice and decision making and a multi-year time horizon for budgetary decision making. Putting these central concepts together with the process indicators outlined by Bush (1986), it is proposed to use the following factors as an indicator of the existence of a rational economic decision-making process:

1. A clear perception of the choice opportunity.
2. Analysis of the choice opportunity to include data collection and evaluation of alternatives.
3. A zero-based approach to assessing alternatives.
4. Choice of expenditure alternatives to meet organisational objectives.
5. Budgetary time scale to encourage planning over a multi-year time horizon.
6. Monitoring and evaluation of the efficiency and effectiveness of differing strategies.

If these then represent key factors of the rational approach, the political approach can also draw on the perception of Bush (1986) for indicators of the political model.

The key elements of the political approach identified earlier in the chapter, those of incremental budgetary approaches, micropolitical factors and satisficing behaviour of groups, can be set in the following framework to provide factors that can be used as indicators of the existence of political decision-making processes:

1. Group activity and interest groups are the focus rather than the institution as an entity.
2. There is an incremental approach to the budgetary process.
3. Goals are seen as unstable, ambiguous and contested.
4. Decisions emerge after a complex process of bargaining and negotiation.
5. Decision making is likely to be determined, ultimately, according to the relative power of the participant individual and groups and may involve conflict between the various parties.
6. There is evidence of satisficing behaviour.

Looking at the elements in the rational and political models of resource decision making, a list of six key factors of indications of behaviour emerges for both approaches. These key factors combine with the seven functions of budgets to produce the framework shown in Figure 4.5.

| | *Rational model indicators* | *Political model indicators* |
|---|---|---|
| Acquisition<br>Allocation<br>Spending<br>Control<br>Planning<br>Choice<br>Evaluation | | |

*Figure 4.5: a framework for analysing resource management practice in schools*

In each of the seven categories the rational and political model indicators provide a framework for analysing the budgetary approach that is being used in a particular school. This analytical framework is used to assess practice in the following case study of a secondary school where the distribution of capitation allowances is a microcosm of resource behaviour.

## Case study: school capitation and its distribution

This case study by Davies and Ellison (1987) is based on a survey of all the secondary schools in Cheshire to elicit comments on their practice of capitation distribution. The aim of the survey was not to produce a set of quantified results from a pre-set questionnaire but, rather, to isolate key management issues which would prove instructive for schools establishing a formula-based scheme or modifying one and in particular in establishing a formula-based system at Alsager Comprehensive School (the case study school).

The senior management in all the survey schools were concerned with the central problem described by one school as 'any distribution of monies to departments is fraught with difficulties — each department is aware of its own pressing needs and yet the overall sum available is insufficient to meet the needs of all'. This problem is best approached by a distribution of money to departments which reflects their needs within the framework of meeting the overall school aims. Obviously, equity in the distribution of money cannot mean equal shares for all. Some subjects, for a variety of reasons, are more expensive than others. How to allow adequately for this difference presents a complicated problem. Traditionally, an approach has been used where adjustments in previous allocations have been made after qualitative assessments of changed circumstances by the senior management of the school. There are a number of weaknesses in this approach:

1. The original base figure which is adjusted annually may bear no relation to the true needs of the department. Some departments may 'cope' and be seriously underfunded! At the same time others may, through overfunding, be absorbing an unfair amount of scarce resources.
2. A situation develops in which department heads gain extra resources or prevent cuts in their allocation because of their micro-political skills, rather than because of their departmental needs.
3. Schools which operate option choices in years four and five and the sixth form may experience a considerable fluctuation in demand between courses which may not be reflected in pre-set department allocations.
4. It overlooks the need to assess and reassess the needs and changing demands made on department funds.
5. It may have a dysfunctional effect on staff motivation if figures for capitation 'appear from on high' rather than from a more open assessment of needs and available resources.

## *The experience of some Cheshire schools*

The survey schools which have, for a variety of reasons, decided to operate a formula-based approach all took a number of points into consideration when devising their own particular scheme. While it is recognised that each school may put a differing stress on the varying components in a formula system to match the school's own needs and educational philosophy, the following points seem central to developing a successful formula distribution scheme:

1. A basic acceptance that there are certain expenses common to all subjects dependent on (a) the number of pupils taught and (b) the number of periods taught.

2. A method of recognising that some age groups are more expensive to teach, for example, those at examination level which require specific books and materials.
3. A means of measuring the differing costs inherent in different subjects, such as classroom-based and workshop-based subjects.
4. Recognition that there are areas to be catered for which lie outside the subject departments and need to be kept outside the distribution mechanism, for example, administration, library, orchestra etc.
5. Provision must be made for emergencies and a degree of flexibility maintained to allow for changing circumstances, such as the introduction of a new subject or course.
6. Full and open discussion by all the participants in the scheme.
7. A review process so that 'weightings' developed for differing subjects do not become 'binding precedents' but can be changed and adjusted as experience or circumstances dictate.

The way in which these points are developed into a practical scheme can be seen by the case study school, Alsager Comprehensive School. This is how one school has used a formula-based system as a management response to a resource distribution problem.

## THE INTEREST IN CAPITATION ALLOWANCES AT ALSAGER COMPREHENSIVE SCHOOL

Alsager Comprehensive is an 11–18 school of 1,400 pupils. It is organised in year groups and faculties and has been part of the Cheshire 'Cost Centre' scheme since 1976.

Previously funds were distributed by the head after he had asked faculty heads to submit their 'bids' on behalf of the departments in their faculty and these bids had been discussed at faculty heads' meetings. While some staff felt that this system was successful, others believed it to be unfair, especially in times of contracting resources. Criticisms of the system could be summarised as:

(i) the lack of knowledge and understanding about the basis for allocation;
(ii) the perceived lack of rationality when making cuts;
(iii) the lack of a relationship between funding and pupil numbers in a subject;
(iv) the fact that an allocation could be related to the influence of individual faculty heads.

The deputy head (curriculum) proposed that a formula approach be considered by faculty heads and most were in favour of developing such a system. It was quite easy to decide on age weighting and a factor to take account of pupil numbers. During several formal and informal meetings much of the discussion centred on the following:

(a) The percentage allocated to a discretionary fund (for curriculum development, library, careers, etc.). Several people felt that this figure could determine their acceptance or rejection of the whole scheme. If the figure was too high, many future decisions could still be influenced by powerful personalities. On the other hand, faculty heads were worried that a low curriculum development fund would make it difficult to cope with future changes, especially GCSE.

(b) Subject weighting — it was agreed that Mathematics should form a base of one and figures were suggested for other subjects in order to start the discussion. Several of the proposals were accepted but, in other cases, subject staff put forward arguments for a higher weighting. This discussion gave faculty heads a chance to learn about the requirements of their colleagues and to justify their own weightings. It was agreed to incorporate most of the alterations, except that a compromise was reached on the Craft subjects. The Mathematics department felt that their allocation was being eroded as other weightings increased, so they were finally given a weighting of 1.2.

The system which was adopted is based on the chart shown in Figure 4.6.

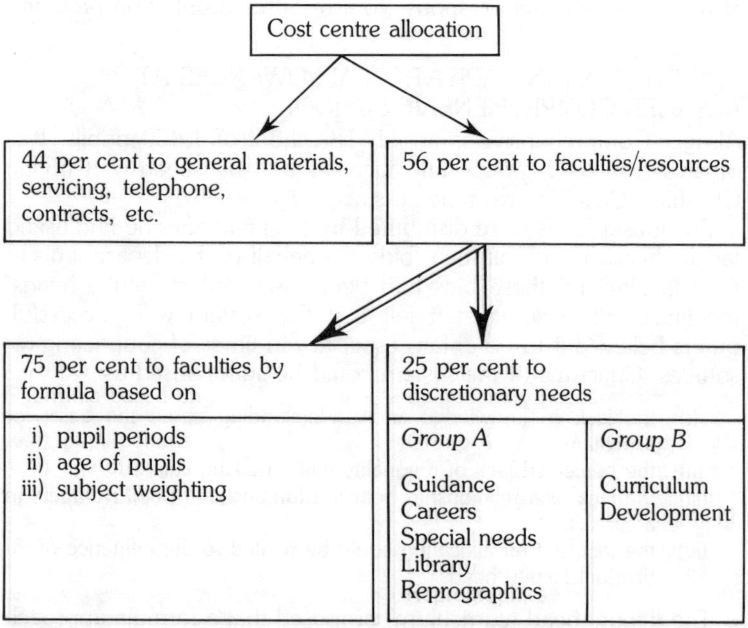


*Figure 4.6: the division of cost centre funds*

The senior management of the school had made two broad policy decisions regarding the distribution of resources. Firstly, based on past experience, they split the cost centre monies 56 per cent to capitation and 44 per cent to other expenditure headings which operate under the Cheshire 'Cost Centre' scheme.

Secondly, they retained 25 per cent of capitation monies outside the formula system for discretionary allocations. As such it can be seen that this is not a zero-based allocation system or a total formula-based system. The school is operating a formula-based system within fairly rigid parameters.

*Age and subject weightings*

The age and subject weightings agreed at Alsager were:

Age weightings:

| | |
|---|---|
| Years 1–3 | 1 |
| Years 4 and 5 | 1.5 |
| 'A'/'S' level | 2 |

Subject weightings:

| | | | |
|---|---|---|---|
| English/Drama | 1.2 | Humanities | 1.4 |
| Music | 1.5 | History | 1.4 |
| Languages | 1.2 | Geography | 1.4 |
| PE | 1 | Religious Education | 1.4 |
| Science | 2 | Local Studies | 1.4 |
| Art | 2 | Politics | 1.4 |
| Technical Drawing | 1.5 | Business Studies | 1.4 |
| Metalwork | 3.2 | Mathematics | 1.2 |
| Woodwork | 3.2 | Computer Studies | 1 |
| Design | 3.2 | General Education | 0.75 |
| Home Economics | 2 | General Studies | 1 |

The calculations are made using a spreadsheet so that alterations in data can be quickly incorporated. This is a very significant advantage as discussions about different weightings are not held up while new calculations are made. Several different scenarios can be calculated and printed out very rapidly. Figure 4.7 shows how the formula-based money was distributed in the first year of the scheme.

Most staff at Alsager feel that the new approach is a considerable improvement on the old system for several reasons:

(i) It is more open — staff can understand the basis on which allocations are made.
(ii) It has been developed to meet the particular needs of the school.
(iii) It is more rational, relating to departmental needs by taking account of demographic factors and expense.
(iv) It can be adapted as circumstances change.

This case study suggests that by moving to a more open formula system rather than the previous 'bidding' system, the school is

| *Subject* | *Subject weighting* | *Number of pupil-periods taught, years 1–3* | *Age weighting, years 1–3* | *Total number of pupil-periods, years 1–3, weighted by age and subject* | *Number of pupil-periods taught, years 4, 5 and 6, 'O' level* | *Age weighting for years 4, 5 and 6 'O' level* | *Total number of pupil-periods, weighted by age and subject, years 4, 5 and 6, 'O' level* | *Number of pupil-periods, 'A' and 'S' level* | *Age weighting for 'A' and 'S' level* | *Total number of pupil-periods, 'A' and 'S' level, weighted by age and subject* | *Total number of weighted pupil-periods* | *Total finance (£27,365) divided by total number of weighted periods, i.e. 53p per unit* | *Capitation distribution to departments (£)* |
|---|---|---|---|---|---|---|---|---|---|---|---|---|---|
| English/Drama | 1.2 | 2167 | 1 | 2602 | 1556 | 1.5 | 2801 | 181 | 2 | 435 | 5837 | 0.53 | 3093 |
| Music | 1.5 | 616 | 1 | 923 | 30 | 1.5 | 68 | 37 | 2 | 111 | 1102 | 0.53 | 584 |
| Language | 1.2 | 2259 | 1 | 2711 | 740 | 1.5 | 1332 | 220 | 2 | 528 | 4571 | 0.53 | 2423 |
| PE | 1.0 | 1446 | 1 | 1446 | 770 | 1.5 | 1155 | 0 | 2 | 0 | 2601 | 0.53 | 1379 |
| Science | 2.0 | 2265 | 1 | 4530 | 1720 | 1.5 | 5160 | 404 | 2 | 1616 | 11306 | 0.53 | 5992 |
| Art | 2.0 | 644 | 1 | 1288 | 332 | 1.5 | 996 | 48 | 2 | 192 | 2476 | 0.53 | 1312 |

| | | | | | | | | | | | | | |
|---|---|---|---|---|---|---|---|---|---|---|---|---|---|
| Technical Drawing | 1.5 | 223 | 1 | 335 | 128 | 1.5 | 288 | 0 | 2 | 0 | 623 | 0.53 | 330 |
| Metalwork | 3.2 | 406 | 1 | 1299 | 222 | 1.5 | 1066 | 0 | 2 | 0 | 2365 | 0.53 | 1253 |
| Woodwork | 3.2 | 399 | 1 | 1277 | 38 | 1.5 | 183 | 0 | 2 | 0 | 1460 | 0.53 | 774 |
| Design | 3.2 | 0 | 1 | 0 | 140 | 1.5 | 672 | 28 | 2 | 179 | 851 | 0.53 | 451 |
| Home Economics | 2.0 | 383 | 1 | 766 | 456 | 1.5 | 1368 | 44 | 2 | 176 | 2310 | 0.53 | 1224 |
| Humanities | 1.4 | 1428 | 1 | 1999 | 0 | 1.5 | 0 | 0 | 2 | 0 | 1999 | 0.53 | 1060 |
| History | 1.4 | 279 | 1 | 391 | 580 | 1.5 | 1218 | 152 | 2 | 426 | 2035 | 0.53 | 1078 |
| Geography | 1.4 | 279 | 1 | 391 | 542 | 1.5 | 1138 | 172 | 2 | 481 | 2010 | 0.53 | 1066 |
| Religious Education | 1.4 | 279 | 1 | 391 | 76 | 1.5 | 160 | 0 | 2 | 0 | 551 | 0.53 | 292 |
| Local Studies | 1.4 | 0 | 1 | 0 | 44 | 1.5 | 92 | 0 | 2 | 0 | 92 | 0.53 | 49 |
| Politics | 1.4 | 0 | 1 | 0 | 0 | 1.5 | 0 | 120 | 2 | 336 | 336 | 0.53 | 178 |
| Business Studies | 1.4 | 0 | 1 | 0 | 608 | 1.5 | 1277 | 264 | 2 | 739 | 2016 | 0.53 | 1068 |
| Mathematics | 1.2 | 2032 | 1 | 2438 | 1542 | 1.5 | 2776 | 222 | 2 | 533 | 5747 | 0.53 | 3046 |
| Computer Studies | 1.0 | 0 | 1 | 0 | 274 | 1.5 | 411 | 36 | 2 | 72 | 483 | 0.53 | 256 |
| General Education | 0.75 | 0 | 1 | 0 | 506 | 1.5 | 569 | 0 | 2 | 0 | 569 | 0.53 | 302 |
| General Studies | 1.0 | 0 | 1 | 0 | 87 | 1.5 | 131 | 81 | 2 | 162 | 293 | 0.53 | 55 |
| *Total* | | 15105 | | 22786 | 10391 | | 22861 | 2009 | | 5986 | 51633 | | 27365 |

*Figure 4.7: Formula-based distribution of capitation allowance at Alsager Comprehensive School*

adopting a more rational approach. Certainly the opening up of knowledge about finance does enable all heads of faculty to have an organisation-wide view rather than bidding behind closed doors. However, the weightings adopted may reflect individual bargaining power as well as the more rational assessment of need.

## Theory and practice combined

The case study demonstrates that resource management is a complex managerial activity. It should not consist merely of spending money, in terms of the framework established earlier. It should be seen as seven functional stages of the budgetary process which take place in a political or rational context.

In the case study, the movement to a formula-based capitation system has had a profound managerial effect. It is not only concerned with a different method of allocation. *Planning* and *choosing* between alternative systems and evaluating them takes place thus encouraging a more open approach. This, in itself, can develop a framework of trust within the school. However, it is difficult to say that it is a rational approach. The formula framework promises a rational approach but, in fact, the contrary may be the case. The initial distribution between capitation and other expenditure followed an incremental approach as it was based on previous patterns of expenditure. There is no evidence of examining outputs and relating expenditure to them. Instead it is merely an input distribution system. The weightings are based on agreement between the faculty heads and this may be a function of their power and past spending allocations rather than an objective assessment of need. The system does not take a zero-based view of needs but has an incremental approach as the formula is replicated from year to year. Therefore, it can be seen that the application of the rational and political framework is a valuable way of identifying the underlying approach to budgeting in a school. The way that schools handle this relatively small amount of the total budget can be an indicator of their management approach in the larger framework of LMS.

Schools have always been involved in issues of resource management such as the allocation of capitation allowances. They have also allocated staffing once the level had been determined by the local education authority. What LMS does is radically expand the area of school responsibility. Do schools take their small-scale budgetary approaches, built up over the years by dealing with capitation, or do they reappraise their resource management approach? The challenge is to reassess the role of resource management on two fronts. Firstly, it is important to look at the stages of budgeting and move from the functional processes of acquisition, allocation, spending and control to the more strategic resource activities of planning, choice and evaluation. Secondly, the opportunity exists to reassess the rational or political approaches to resource management practice. By not addressing these issues school management would be failing to seize the opportunity of LMS and would merely be extending the previous resource practice into the new era.

It is hoped that the reader will use these perspectives to reassess practice in his/her school to meet the challenge of the 1990s.

## References

Anthony, R. N. 1965 *Planning and Control System — a Framework for Analysis*, Harvard University Press

Brackett, Chambers & Parrish 1983 'The Legacy of Rational Budgetary Models in Education', paper presented at the Annual Meeting of the North Rocky Mountain Educational Research Association, 1st Jackson Hole, W.Y, October 13–15 1983

Bush, T. 1986 *Theories of Educational Management*, Open University Press

Davies, K. B. 1984 'The purpose and functions of budgets — some theoretical perspectives for education managers', *School Organisation*, Vol. 4 No. 2

Davies, K. B. 1987 'The key issues of financial delegation', *Education*, 30th October, p. 370

Davies, K. B. 1988 'Three steps to lift off — unfolding on LFM training strategy in Leicestershire', *Education*, 5th August, pp. 131/132

Davies, K. B. & Ellison, L. 1987 'School Capitation and its distribution: Is the Weight of Opinion Changing?', *School Organisation*, Vol. 7, No. 1, pp. 79–84

Greenwood *et al.* 1980 'Incremental budgeting and the assumption of growth: the experience of local government' in Wright, M. (ed), *Public Spending Decisions: Growth and Restraints in the 1970's*, Allen & Unwin

Hofstede, G. H. 1968 *The Game of Budget Control*, Tavistock

Irvine, V. B. 1975 'Budgeting: functional analysis and behavioural implications' in Rappaport A. (ed) *Information for Decision-making, Quantitative and Behavioural Dimensions*, 2nd edition, Prentice Hall

Pettigrew, A. 1973 *The Politics of Organisational Decision-Making*, Tavistock Press

Schick, A. 1972 'The road to PPB; the stages of budget reform' in F. J. Lyden & E. G. Miller (eds) *Planning programming budgets — a systems approach to management*, Markham Publishing 1972

Simkins, T. & Lancaster, D. 1987, 2nd ed 'Budgeting and Resource Allocation in Education Institutions', *Sheffield papers in Education Management*, No. 35, Sheffield City Polytechnic

Wildavsky, A. 1968 'Budgeting as a political process' in Sills, D. L. (ed) *International Encyclopedia of the Social Sciences, Vol. 2*, Crowell, Collier and Macmillan

Wildavsky, A. 1974 *The Politics of the Budgetary Process*, 2nd edition, Little, Brown & Co.

Wildavsky, A. 1978 'A budget for all seasons — why the traditional budget lasts', *Public Administration Review* 38: 6, pp. 501–509

# 5 Human resource management in schools

John West-Burnham

There is a need to consider the range of possible models of human resource management (HRM) drawn from outside education. The models are used here to develop principles which inform staff management in schools. These principles are identified as leadership, team management, performance management and organisational design. The potential of each perspective is considered and the chapter concludes with a summary of the factors needed for the successful implementation of human resource management in schools.

The principles, processes and skills of HRM are among the most neglected and misunderstood aspects of education management. The effective management of teaching staff has either been non-existent, regarded as a low priority or actively denied. There has been little understanding or recognition of the rights of teachers as employees let alone as adults with needs, expectations and aspirations. In essence the principles of pastoral care for children have not been extended to adults.

This raises two issues. Firstly, who cares for the carers? The demands upon teachers, reflected in concerns about stress, morale and motivation, are indicative of the lack of a supportive infrastructure and appropriate management processes and skills. Secondly, the integrity of pastoral systems and management processes is contingent upon their being reflected in all aspects of school management.

This situation is explained by a variety of factors:

1. *'No time for management'*

Schools have 'no time for management' (Handy 1984 p. 18). The technical and professional activities of teaching staff are perceived to be so important that the task predominates to the subordination or exclusion of the process. This is reinforced by Handy's view that schools have a multiplicity of purposes and these are not discriminated between or prioritised, nor do they include any reference to the management of adults.

2. *Professional status*
The aspiration to professional status is a major constraint upon effective management. The historical and social claim to professional autonomy is counterproductive in an environment where pedagogic autonomy is increasingly inhibited, entry to teaching is controlled by DES policy and not by a professional body, conditions of employment are nationally prescribed and major management initiatives, such as staff development, appraisal, recruitment and promotion, are increasingly subject to DES guidelines.

3. *Diffuse structures*
The management structures of schools generally bear little relationship to the principles of effective staff management. Structures have been used to implement pay scales rather than principles of organisational design. This is reflected in the artificially tall pyramids found in management structures in secondary schools and the often ambiguous roles of deputy heads in primary schools. Similarly, the pastoral–academic split in secondary schools reinforces the notion that, in education, form does not follow function.

4. *Organisational schizophrenia*
Handy's (1984) phrase encapsulates a major problem in the management of teaching staff. The evolution of the role of teachers and the view of the social purpose of schools have led to a multiplicity of demands on teachers which are not necessarily compatible and may be contradictory, if not actually mutually exclusive. This is best exemplified in the ambiguous, or sometimes non-existent, aims and objectives of schools. There are three issues associated with institutional aims and objectives: (i) the extent to which they are aims and objectives rather than social platitudes and/or moral aspirations; (ii) the extent to which objectives are differentiated from aims and are capable of implementation; and (iii) the extent to which they refer to teaching and non-teaching staff as well as children.

5. *Limited management perspective*
Personnel management in general has been a 'poor relation' in all organisations but particularly in education. The increasing recognition of the importance of human resource management in the industrial and commercial sectors is only now being reflected in schools. This is indicated, for example, in the absence of management training in initial teacher training, problems in responding to the demands made by Circular 6/86 and the uncertainty surrounding the introduction of teacher appraisal. The problem is further

exemplified in the limited reference to staff management issues in the preparation of teachers for middle and senior management roles.

6. *Political control*
Effective staff management in education is highly problematic because of the fragmented and diversified centres of control. Few organisations have to cope with the range of different inputs at national, LEA and institutional level. Nationally imposed conditions of employment and salary scales have to be managed at LEA level and then implemented at school level. Policy at national and LEA level is politically motivated and does not always reflect principles of effective management.

7. *Children*
There is an implicit expectation by teachers that the needs and rights of children are paramount — if necessary to the exclusion of their own. This is reflected in high levels of commitment and professionalism which may result in stress and burn-out.

The practical outcomes of these factors are illustrated in the research of Torrington and Weightman (1989). They characterise the management of secondary schools as having a number of features — many of which may be attributed to the absence of effective staff management policies. Teaching and non-teaching staff in schools are a seriously under-utilised resource. This is particularly true of women teachers and non-teaching staff. Senior and middle managers in schools often lack an explicit management role. This is due to a lack of clarity in role definition, lack of training and inappropriate deployment of non-teaching staff. Schools are often task-centred to the detriment of effective personal relationships, inevitably compromising decision-making procedures and perceptions of individual credibility.

The picture that emerges from this research is one of schools working very hard to stand still. Individuals often deploy enormous amounts of energy to relatively little effect because they are carrying out functions for which they have not been trained or which are inappropriate to their status. In essence, schools are often reactive and the individuals within them victims because of a lack of management skills, procedures and perspectives.

The changing context of educational management requires schools to adopt proactive staff management strategies in order to come to terms with a range of complex issues:

1. The introduction of performance management through appraisal-linked staff development.
2. The need to have staffing strategies appropriate to LMS and increased institutional autonomy.

3. The need to develop equal opportunities policies.
4. The recognition that institutional improvement and quality management have to be reflected in staffing policies and processes.
5. The recognition of an ageing cohort of teachers and the need to manage morale and motivation.
6. The recognition of good staff interpersonal relationships as fundamental to all management processes and important as a model for pupils.
7. The need to incorporate non-teaching staff into all aspects of effective institutional management.
8. The need to develop systematic succession planning linked to individual career development.
9. The need to develop management procedures which are understandable and credible to the institution's environment.
10. The need to recognise and treat adults as adults.

## A model for HRM in education

The term 'Personnel Management' has been widely used for 50 to 60 years to describe a range of activities, a body of knowledge and a set of skills associated with the recruitment, administration and development of staff. The culture of personnel management was essentially subordinate to the technical activities of the organisation (witness the relative status of personnel and training departments in many industrial and commercial organisations). This led to a view of people as a cost, to be controlled and administered. Equally, the growth of the personnel function tended to minimise the responsibility of *all* managers for the effectiveness of staff management, either denying the significance of skills for managing people or delegating personnel issues.

Human resource management emerged in the 1980s to compensate for these shortcomings. HRM does not invalidate the procedures and skills of personnel management but, rather, places them in a different conceptual framework. Staff become an asset in which to invest, to be developed so as to help the organisation achieve its aims and objectives. The cultural shift is, therefore, from control to enabling; to providing people with the resources, targets and opportunities to contribute to the growth of the organisation whilst enhancing themselves.

The danger in the education system is that there will be an emphasis on procedures and practices at the expense of personal growth and relationships. In Torrington and Weightman's (1989) terms the work of managers may be defined as 'agendas, lists of things to be done' which are achieved through networks — 'co-operative relationships with people who can help to get things done' (p. 112). Effective management simplifies agendas, enhances and enables networks.

Effective staff management is, therefore, as much concerned with 'why' and 'how' as 'what' and 'when'; in other words, organisational processes are as significant as organisational tasks and the one should inform the other. Handy's (1984) analysis of the education system identifies a tripartite culture: in primary schools children are 'workers', in secondary schools they are 'products' and in post-compulsory institutions 'clients'. Although dominant task orientation has particularly explicit manifestations in the management of secondary schools, it is equally significant in the relationships between adults in other sectors.

Parallel with the shift in emphasis epitomised by the concept of human resource management is the growing emphasis on 'excellence' and 'quality' as the criteria for effective management. The movement for excellence is most widely known through the work of Peters and Waterman (1982). They identified a variety of factors which were found to be held in common by a number of American companies recognised as meeting the criteria for excellence.

1. A bias for action: effective organisations are not inhibited by bureaucratic structures but are proactive in anticipating problems and generating solutions.
2. Close to the customer: ensuring that the products and services provided are those which are actually required.
3. Autonomy and entrepreneurship: the culture of effective organisations recognises and rewards creativity and initiative; failure is not penalised.
4. Productivity through people: people are seen as the sole basis for success which is developed through respect for the individual expressed through trust. Contributions from all are expected, recognised and rewarded.
5. Hands-on, value-driven: management is about the implementation of values which are explicit and form the basis for action.
6. Stick to the knitting: identifying that which is done best and ensuring that every aspect of management is geared to maintaining it.
7. Simple form, lean staff: effective and successful organisations have simple management structures, i.e. autonomous teams focused and co-ordinated by central management which is not disproportionately top-heavy.

There are obvious problems in applying principles derived from American commerce and industry to British schools but these criteria do provide a basis for analysis.

Total quality management (TQM) is an approach to management based largely on the works of Crosby (1979) and Deming (1982). The principles were first applied in Japanese industry but are now finding increasing acceptance in the UK. The essence of TQM is the process of reducing costs by improving quality, so enhancing customer satisfaction. A crucial contribution of TQM theory is the redefinition of the concept of the customer. Although, traditionally, customers are perceived as external to the organisation, TQM defines all working relationships in terms of customer satisfaction and quality is defined in terms of conformity to customer requirements.

The notion of quality is encapsulated in the related principles of conformance to requirements and fitness for purpose. This presupposes detailed definition by customers of their requirements and the development of processes to ensure that those requirements are met. It is these processes which provide the principles for staff management and enhance the quality of working relationships within the organisation.

Crosby (1979) proposes 14 steps to quality improvement and these are complemented by Deming's four points. Although there are some significant variations between these writers, they do identify a number of implications for staff management. Firstly, quality is the primary responsibility of senior management who must transmit quality values to all but must also build quality into managerial relationships, notably through communication, commitment, recognition and providing facilitating structures in the context of explicit objectives. Secondly, quality is achieved through effective teams where the outcomes of inter- and intra-team relationships are as significant as the technical functions of the teams.

Thirdly, quality is only possible where every component of the organisation's needs is defined and appropriate training procedures are identified and implemented in order to improve the staff selection process. Fourthly, detailed evaluation and monitoring procedures must exist which are used as the basis for managing change. Finally, there needs to be a commitment to continuous improvement through development.

Drawing on the insights identified above — combining the principles of human resource management, management of excellence and total quality management — it becomes possible to propose four principles for human resource management in education (see Figure 5.1).

1. Leadership: concerned with vision and growth rather than sustaining systems.
2. Team management: concerned with task and process and the quality of personal relationships.
3. Performance management: providing the means to enhance competency and stimulate development in order to achieve organisational objectives.
4. Organisational design: establishing a structure where form follows function and which contributes directly to institutional purposes and processes.

It is not possible to discriminate between the components of each category. All are interdependent and each principle in turn depends

| **Principle** | **Processes** | **Skills/qualities** |
|---|---|---|
| 1 *Leadership* | | |
| | Appointment procedures | Assertiveness |
| | Appraisal systems | Conflict management |
| 2 *Team management* | Career development | Counselling |
| | Consultative procedures | Decision-making |
| | Effective communication | Delegation |
| | Employee services | Innovations |
| | Equal opportunities policies | Interpersonal skills |
| | Evaluation procedures | Management of change |
| | Health and safety | Negotiating |
| | Industrial relations | Planning |
| | Job analysis | Prioritising |
| 3 *Performance* management | Managing information | Problem solving |
| | Organisational development | Stress management |
| | Record keeping | Target setting |
| | Succession planning | Time management |
| | Training design | Vision |
| | Welfare systems | |
| 4 *Organisational design* | | |

*Figure 5.1: the components of human resource management*

upon the effective management of appropriate processes which require relevant skills and qualities.

## Leadership

Leadership is central to the effective management of educational institutions. Successive HMI reports have identified the quality of leadership as the crucial determinant in creating an ethos which allows a school to operate to maximum effect. Leadership is axiomatic to human resource management and it is impossible to draw neat boundaries between the various principles identified in this chapter. Leadership is about vision, motivating, managing teams, creating appropriate structures and being as concerned with the people as the tasks.

The centrality of leadership has led to a significant body of literature which analyses leadership styles, the nature of power and authority and the relationship of the leader to the organisation and external bodies. At the same time there has been an uncertain analysis of the relationship between management and leadership. Classical theories of management have tended to see leadership as a sub-set or function of 'management' as an entity. The full implication of this approach will be discussed below but in the education system this has led to leadership being confused with technical competence (the headteacher as leading professional) or with implementation (the headteacher as administrator). In the context of HRM neither of these approaches is appropriate or effective.

In essence, the conceptual change involved is encapsulated in the formula that leadership provides the context in which management takes place and that leadership is about people while management is about resources. There is an inevitable tension in applying this maxim to schools — the notion of collegiality based on a community of professionals may inhibit the scope for individual leadership. In direct contradistinction to this is the legal/administrative role of headteachers which, combined with the lack of time, compels a focus on routine procedures as is demonstrated in the research of Morgan, Hall and McKay (1986) and Torrington and Weightman (1989). Both pieces of research stress how little time is spent with adults and how much time is spent either teaching or in fragmented and relatively trivial administration at the expense of creating effective personal relationships and articulating a sense of common purpose.

There is clearly no general agreement within the education system as to what the functions of the headteacher are; it therefore becomes difficult, if not impossible, to generate criteria for effectiveness. An analysis of the traditional functions of heads might produce the following list:

1. Leading professional: the 'expert' practitioner providing examples of good practice as teacher/academic and carer.
2. Boundary manager: controlling the relationships between the school and its environment, acting as focal point and figurehead.
3. Manager: co-ordinating and controlling, decision making and monitoring implementation, setting structures and deploying staff.
4. Administrator: carrying out routine procedures.
5. Policy maker and planner: determining values, establishing aims and objectives, prioritising and communicating them.
6. Conflict manager: resolving disputes, acting as a mediator.
7. Facilitator: providing guidance, advice and acting as a resource for personal and team development, i.e. facilitating motivation, stimulating effective communication and providing recognition and feedback.

The empirical work of Morgan *et al.* and Torrington and Weightman would seem to indicate a significant emphasis on 1, 2 3 and 4 with substantially less stress on 5, 6 and 7. This goes to the heart of the issue of implementing HRM in educational institutions. An emphasis on technical activities and on what is often, essentially, administration implicitly denies that staff are an asset. Leadership in the context of HRM requires an emphasis on policy making and managing interpersonal relationships and the effective delegation of other functions.

The problem is further exacerbated by the prevailing view as to the nature and constituents of leadership in schools. There are a number of models which seek to explain the components and implications of different approaches to leadership which may actually serve to compound the problem:

- trait theories
- style theories
- contingency theories

Trait theories stress the personality of the leader above all other factors — leadership requires a range of inherited characteristics or personality traits which are given priority over the job nature and demands of the job itself. Selection for senior posts is therefore more important than training; if people who display the appropriate qualities are placed in the correct context then they will flourish.

There is no consensus view as to what constitutes the most desirable traits but qualities such as intelligence, initiative, self-confidence, enthusiasm are regularly featured in studies. There are obvious problems with this approach: there is no common definition as to the components of these qualities, there is no reliable method of identifying them and a list of qualities may well include contradictory elements. In spite of these qualifications, this approach has dominated the selection of leaders in the education system. Selection methods based on references and panel interviews, without systematic job and person specification, give preference to intuitive judgements which inevitably focus on traits. Academically the traits approach has been very largely discredited, partly because of its lack of precision and partly because it has demonstrably not worked in identifying the most effective leaders, yet it is still the most commonly used approach.

Style theories are a much more sophisticated means of analysing the implications of different types of leadership. Blake and Mouton (1978) developed a model which allows a comparison in terms of the relative significance attached to the dimensions of concern for *production* and concern for *people*. Concern with production is defined in terms of task completion while concern with people is related to the emphasis on the needs of the individual, i.e. a process orientation. By examining the two dimensions, it becomes possible to identify a range of leadership styles and their practical implications:

- 'The impoverished manager' has low concern for task and people, minimum effort for production and minimum involvement with staff.

- 'The authority – obedience manager' has high concern for production and minimal regard for people who are essentially means to achieve the task. Results are obtained but at the cost of personal relationships and the outcomes are not necessarily the optimum possible.
- 'The Country Club manager' has high concern for people, low concern for production. Achievement of the task is secondary to the avoidance of conflict and the maintenance of social equilibrium. However, this may generate stress by inhibiting innovation and creativity.
- 'The organisation manager' has moderate concern for both people and production; he/she is likely to stress high concern for ethos but, under pressure, is more likely to opt for a production orientation.
- 'the team manager' has high concern for both production and people and works to integrate both by helping individuals to meet their own needs through the organisation.

The team approach balances task and process, optimising both and seeing people and production as being inextricably linked — high output depends on high personal satisfaction and commitment. Blake and Mouton argue that although the team approach is an ideal it can be worked towards by a process of diagnosis and training.

Blake and Mouton's analysis is effectively complemented by the best known of the contingency models — Adair's (1983) model of action-centred leadership. Adair argues that any working situation produces three sets of needs for the people involved and therefore effective leadership is determined by the variables operating in a given situation:

1. Task achievement: attaining objectives, planning the work, allocating resources and monitoring progress.
2. Team development: creating a cohesive unit, enhancing morale and team consciousness, improving communication and setting and monitoring standards.
3. Individual needs: giving praise and recognition, resolving conflict and facilitating individual growth and development.

Effective leadership seeks to integrate these three elements so that each is optimised and enhances the other two. As with Blake and Mouton, there is a clear emphasis on the importance of people as well as task. The components of Adair's three elements indicate the factors that are relevant to effective leadership. However, there is still a need to discriminate between the management skills appropriate to completing the task and the leadership qualities relevant to meeting individual and team needs. What is important is the relative significance to be attributed to task and process and the extent to which leadership is concerned with the minutiae of institutional administration or the vision and mission of the school.

The principles of human resource management (seeing people as an asset) and TQM (stressing the importance of integrity in all relationships) lead to a definition of leadership as a facilitating and empowering function. If leadership is linked to motivation theory and the notions of expectancy and valence accepted, then leadership becomes a creative and enabling function. The role of the leader is to facilitate motivation and, in practical terms, this means:

1. Creating and sustaining a vision that is communicated and lived.
2. Negotiating targets to help individuals to achieve organisational goals.
3. Providing resources to ensure that targets can be met.
4. Ensuring that individuals have the knowledge and skills to work effectively.
5. Providing explicit guidance on standards and levels of performance.
6. Giving recognition, feedback and reward where appropriate.

Hodgson (1987) provides a useful synthesis of this approach in distinguishing between leadership and management:

| *Leadership* | *Management* |
|---|---|
| Doing the right things | Doing things right |
| Path finding | Path following |
| Learning from the organisation | Being taught by the organisation |

The components of leadership are, therefore, seen in terms of effective skills and qualities rather than cognitive technical knowledge. The traditional approach to the training and selection of headteachers has been on the basis of technical competence reinforced by practical experience. Selection procedures have thus been largely exercises in historical data gathering, confirming the ability of candidates to do their present job rather than the one for which they have applied.

If the leadership of educational institutions is to be effective then a number of fundamental changes are needed. There must be systematic and detailed definition of the qualities appropriate to a particular post which recognise the leadership content of the role. Secondly, it is necessary to identify the leadership function which permeates all levels of the institution and thus develops a culture of creativity that discriminates between leadership and management, so enhancing both. Thirdly, appropriate training and development strategies must be established which are based on analysis and creating the capability to act; such training is thus confrontational and enabling. Within schools, structures and procedures must be created which discriminate between management and leadership and allow each to function appropriately. Fifthly, selection procedures must be introduced which are based on accurate and relevant person and job specifications and which are predictive in nature. Finally, appraisal procedures must be established which monitor and enhance the individual's ability to work to maximum effectiveness.

The practical manifestations of leadership as opposed to management in schools include:

- Communicating an explicit attainable and unique vision.
- Displaying a positive commitment to the vision, the institution and the people.
- Recruiting, reinforcing and developing talent.
- Celebrating and learning from success, establishing excellence as the basis for action.
- Delegating as much as is reasonable and appropriate, creating autonomy and responsibility.
- Building and working through teams.
- Recognising and rewarding success.
- Working through personal relationships.

## Team management

Few components of managing are as abused as the concept of the 'team'. As a label it conveys a sense of purpose and purveys an often spurious impression of coherence and integrity in working relationships. Applying the label often serves as an imprimatur of management respectability. The emergence of curriculum teams in primary schools and senior management teams in secondary schools indicates the potency of the concept.

However, the principles of effective team management are often not reflected in the practice. This is demonstrated by the research of Murgatroyd (1985) and Torrington and Weightman (1989). Amalgamating their insights produces the following factors which indicate the problematic nature of teams in schools:

1. There is too much emphasis on the tasks (agendas) of managing and not enough on the processes (networks).
2. There is insufficient emphasis on working for action and too much on the formulation and debate of principles.
3. Teams are often reactive and concerned with routine.
4. Teams are insufficiently concerned with their own social needs, i.e. they ignore their own need for development and social maturing.

The outcomes of working in such 'teams' will include: poor communication and/or high level of conflict, limited or conditional commitment, poor quality decision making with limited innovation, inhibited implementation, confused objectives and poor motivation compromising performance. These factors not only impose limitations on the ability of the team to work effectively in achieving its outcomes but detract from its credibility in its relationships with other teams. In the case of the 'task' team, its ability to complete the task effectively is constrained; for the senior management team it may lose authority and credibility, and in the case of the team-structured organisation all procedures are compromised.

There are a large number of variables influencing the effectiveness of a work-group and the extent to which they are effectively managed will determine how far groups, coalitions and regular meetings become teams. The crucial determinant of team effectiveness is the extent to which teams are deliberately created and managed to be the means by which the organisation functions as opposed to being purely symbolic structures. Effective teams must have a specific and real function, be an integral part of the organisational structure and be proactively managed as a social entity. This approach involves:

- the deliberate selection of members of the team
- the training and development of members of the team
- the development of the team itself
- managing relationships with other teams
- relating the team to the organisation as a whole in structural terms
- relating team objectives to organisational objectives.

Managing effective teams is thus a matter of achieving synergy between a variety of elements (see Figure 5.2).

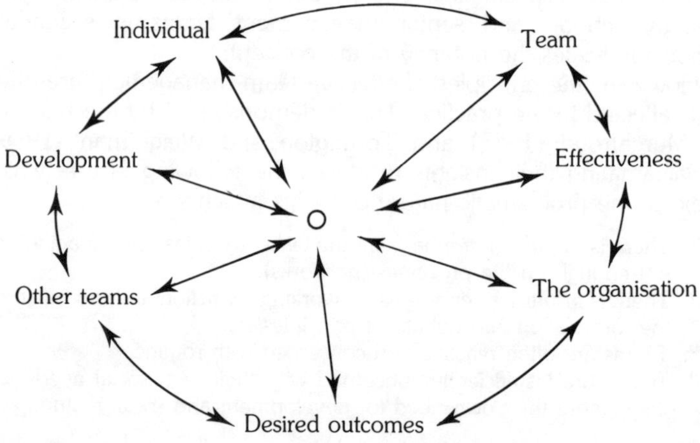


*Figure 5.2:* the components of effective teams

In order for synergy to be achieved then three elements of team management need to be addressed: building, maintenance and review.

## Team building

The composition of teams in schools is rarely the result of systematic analysis of functional needs and recruitment by logically derived criteria. The determinants are usually historical, concerned with status, the result of 'opting-in' (or 'opting-out') for a variety of motives and inappropriate delegation. The stages in the development of a team may be identified shown as in Figure 5.3.

| | |
|---|---|
| *Forming:* | identification of task, clarification of relationships |
| *Storming:* | debate over procedures and outcomes |
| *Norming:* | establishment and consolidation of working principles and interpersonal processes |
| *Performing:* | effective completion of task and enhancement of personal relationships |

*Figure 5.3 stages in team maturity*

As Figure 5.3 illustrates, it may be derived that teams which are not effectively constituted will have difficulty moving out of the forming and norming stages and that the majority of their time will be spent in these activities (see Figure 5.4a).

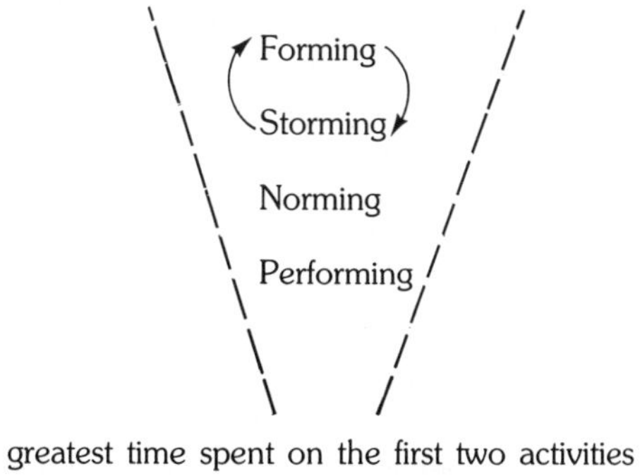


*Figure 5.4a: the performance of ineffective teams*

The outcome for such a team will either be failure to achieve the task, or the imposition of dominant leadership, or the formation of a sub-group. Whichever outcome, the credibility of the team and the motivation of its members will inevitably be compromised.

By contrast, an effectively constituted team will move through each of the stages, spending a maximum amount of time in the 'performing' stage (see Figure 5.4b).

The determinants of effective and ineffective teams include a wide range of variables, but two which are particularly relevant in this context are the basis on which the team is constituted in terms of the definition of roles and the way in which the relationship between those roles is determined.

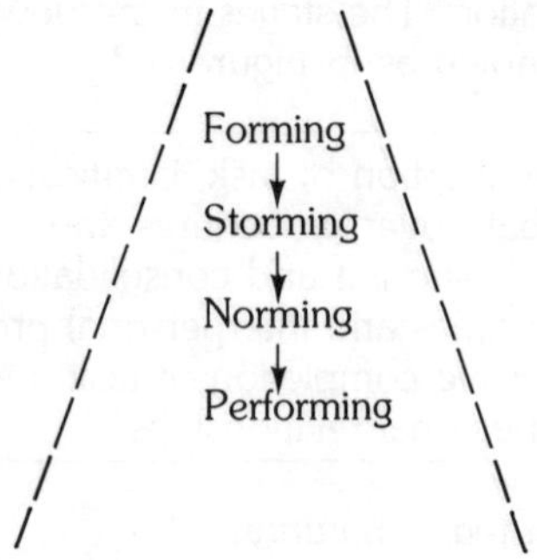


*Figure 5.4b: the performance of effective teams*

Belbin (1981) has found that one of the key determinants of a team's success is the nature of the interaction in terms of the qualities brought to completing the task. He argues that status, technical knowledge and experience are not necessarily the most significant determinants of an individual's contribution. In fact 'alpha' teams (composed of high achievers) may perform less successfully than those made up according to Belbin's criteria for effective task achievement. He identifies eight role types which refer to the potential contribution in terms of behaviour rather than knowledge or status. The types that Belbin identifies are:

| | |
|---|---|
| Company Worker: | capable of converting plans into action, working systematically and efficiently; a stable and controlled member of the team. |
| Chairman: | controls and makes best use of the team, is able to balance contributions towards an objective; stable and dominant. |
| Shaper: | pushes the team towards action, sets objectives and looks for outcomes; dominant, extrovert and anxious. |
| Plant: | innovates, generates new ideas and approaches, problem solver; dominant, intelligent and introvert. |
| Resource Investigator: | the team's contact with its environment, generates ideas and resources; intelligent, stable and introvert. |
| Monitor Evaluator: | analyses problems and evaluates contributions; intelligent, stable and introvert. |

| | |
|---|---|
| Team Worker: | supports and reinforces, improves communications, fosters team spirit; stable, extrovert and flexible. |
| Completer-Finisher: | ensures attention to detail, maintains schedules; anxious and introvert. |

There are a number of implications which may be drawn from Belbin's approach. Use of his self-analysis inventory can help an existing team to diagnose the behavioural factors which might explain its failure or success. Failure of a team might be explained by an imbalance of team types, the absence of crucial roles or a mismatch between team role and hierarchical status.

The potential of Belbin's analysis for team management includes clarifying team needs when recruiting new members, allocation of roles, identifying training and development needs, constituting new teams and serving as a basis for team review.

Although there are problems in directly transferring Belbin's analysis into educational institutions there does appear to be the basis of using it as a means of managing the issues identified at the start of this section.

## *Team maintenance*

Systematic approaches to team building can pre-empt many of the problems of effective team management but there is an equal need for Murgatroyd's (1985) notion of 'self-renewal'. Teams need to be developed in terms of their ability to interact and to make use of systematic approaches to problem solving.

In order to achieve this, teams have to work towards the situation where the knowledge and skills of all members are fully utilised. Just as it is necessary to ensure full involvement of members, so the time available has to be used to best advantage. However, the efficiency of team management has to be balanced by the effectiveness of working relationships so that the outcome reached is not only the 'best fit' decision but also enhances team relationships and generates full commitment.

The enhancement of team relationships can only be achieved if team maintenance is perceived as a learning process following the established models of action learning (see Figure 5.5).

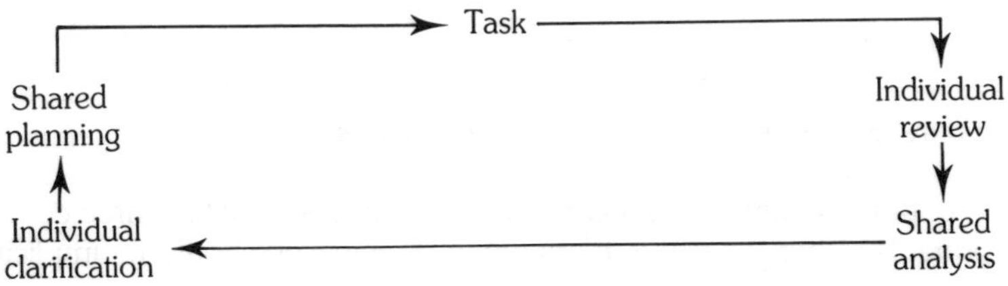


*Figure 5.5: How teams learn*

The significance of this model is that the task is one component of the team maintenance process and is relative to the evaluative, reflective and planning elements which serve to enhance interpersonal relationships whilst ensuring maximum ability to complete the task. The qualities which are required to maintain and enhance a team include:

- specific, understood and accepted objectives
- open and authentic communications
- a high level of mutual trust and reciprocated concern
- recognition of conflicts and direct resolution of them
- detailed understanding of the knowledge, skills and qualities of the team
- consensus decision making
- distributed leadership
- respect for individuality
- team relationships which are dynamic, growing and derived from personal and team learning.

In essence, effective teams spend as much time on the *how* as on the *what*.

Achieving this situation is not a random outcome but is the result of adopting a proactive process-based approach to all aspects of team working and the provision of appropriate training. Such training needs to be centred on a range of skills including: active listening, consensus decision making, conflict management, negotiating agreement, creative problem solving, self-appraisal and group dynamics. These skills not only facilitate the functioning of the team but the training process itself becomes a team maintenance activity.

## *Team review*

Review is axiomatic to the working of effective teams and is not a *post facto* activity but is implicit in every aspect of the team in terms of task and process. The place of review may be summarised as shown in Figure 5.6.

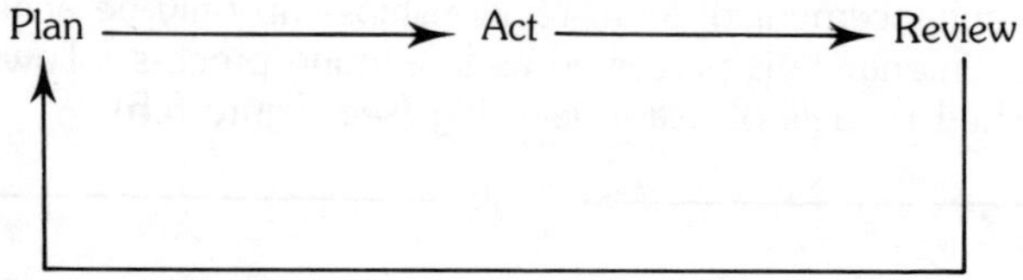


*Figure 5.6: management of team processes*

In practical terms this means that any team activity has three components rather than one. Planning and reviewing should be implicit in any team meeting — as much as the actual activity. Thus the traditional formulation of an agenda needs to be changed so that a meeting starts with clarification of purpose, agreement on timing, allocation of tasks and consolidation of process issues from previous meetings. The completion of the agenda then needs to be followed by a review process, either formal or informal, which analyses the factors contributing to a successful or unsuccessful activity in terms of the perceptions of all the individuals involved. This review process should result in an agreement of action to be taken at the next meeting to consolidate and celebrate strengths and to overcome weaknesses.

Such a process is essential to help a team to mature because it is only through reflection that a team can emerge from the forming and storming stages. The major inhibitions to this process are a natural reserve, the fact that people may not be used to being open about their feelings, a lack of trust caused by limited understanding and, finally, reserve brought about by the relative status of team members, personality and gender issues and a lack of training. These difficulties may be overcome in a number of ways:

1. The use of active learning, experiential training techniques so that skills are developed in a non-threatening environment.
2. The use of a facilitator to lead analytical review sessions and to provide data on team behaviour.
3. The use of an analytical inventory to provide a focus for review sessions.

Effective teams are one of the most powerful tools for effective management of institutions. Much of what has been discussed in this section applies as much to children as it does to teaching staff. However, team development is not a substitute for individual development — the team is only as effective as its individual members in terms of their qualities and skills and their ability to use these in conjunction with others.

## Performance management

One of the most significant indications of the lack of importance attached to staff management in education is the low priority attached to motivation and development. A cursory study of motivation in education reveals a multitude of studies of pupil motivation but virtually none of teaching staff, let alone non-teaching staff. The concept of professional autonomy could be seen as militating against recognition of the need to manage motivation or to engage in systematic development.

There is no clear theoretical model to explain the relationship between motivation, job satisfaction and performance. A number of models exist which can help to develop a conceptual framework to explain motivation at work. All human behaviour may be characterised as being subject to drives aimed at achieving a goal in order to satisfy a need. The achievement of a goal will serve to reinforce the behaviour and so establish a causal connection between needs and goals.

Much of the rhetoric surrounding motivation is based upon a number of misapprehensions, each of which may be answered:

1. Morale and motivation are the same — motivation is an individual, unique and subjective phenomenon.
2. Managers can motivate staff — motivation is at the control of the individual, therefore management policies can only support, reinforce or enhance the individual.
3. Motivation is an 'event' in itself — motivation is made up of a number of factors of which the most important are the perceived value of the outcome to the individual and the correlation between that outcome and the effort necessary to achieve it. Motivation is therefore about action.
4. Motivation is a product of determination — it is also a product of ability and performance.

For the manager the critical relationship to understand is that between the potential 'drive' of an individual and the nature of needs. There are a number of classifications of needs but three broad categories are generally adopted:

(a) *Economic* — pay, security and external factors.
(b) *Social* — relationships and involvement in the organisation.
(c) *Personal* — a subjective response to work and how it meets needs for growth and satisfaction.

The way in which these needs might be managed is considered in two contrasting theoretical models — content theories and process theories. Content theories are concerned with explaining those things which actually motivate people at work arising from needs, expectations and goals. If content theories are concerned with what motivates then process theories are concerned with how motivation works. They are therefore concerned with the variables which influence the initiation, direction and continuance of behaviour.

The most widely used content models are those of Maslow and Herzberg. Maslow suggests that human needs operate in a hierarchy, that people are always wanting and expecting and so the satisfaction of one level of the hierarchy stimulates demand for the next level. Maslow's hierarchy has been traditionally represented as a pyramid (see Figure 5.7).

There is a clear distinction between what might be termed 'lower order' needs and 'higher order' needs and the strength of the

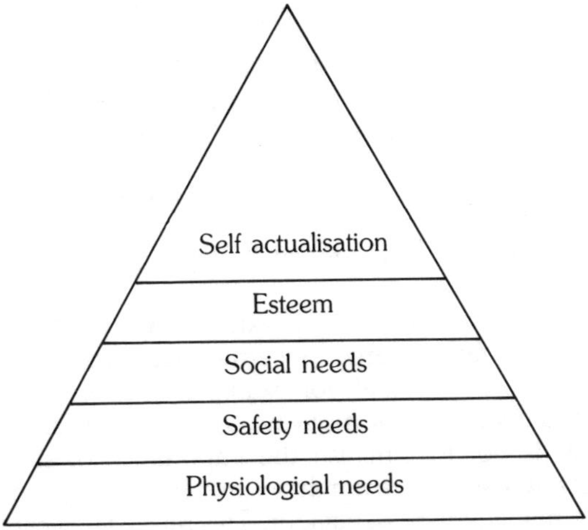


*Figure 5.7: Maslow's hierarchy of needs*

model is based upon one level becoming dominant as the subordinate need is satisfied. Thus, only unsatisfied needs motivate, although the relative levels of satisfaction may be variable. Maslow's model is obviously not empirically based but, even as the basis of a conceptual framework for managing staff, it has severe limitations:

1. It ignores the possibility of altruistic behaviour which may reject subordinate levels in favour of self-actualisation.
2. For some individuals self-esteem may be more important than social needs.
3. In some instances the imperatives of lower order needs may preclude the possibility of following higher order needs.
4. Self-actualisation is too vague a concept to usefully inform managers.
5. Continued satisfaction of a need may lead to its relative significance being diminished.
6. Satisfaction of higher order needs may well change the perception as to what constitutes satisfaction of lower order needs.
7. Work is only one of a potential range of sources of satisfaction.
8. It is not possible to assume a homogeneous workforce.
9. There is no conceptual link in this model between satisfaction and performance.

Subsequent theories (notably the work of Herzberg (1974) ) have attempted to overcome these problems. Herzberg developed a more sophisticated analysis of the significance of higher and lower order needs. His analysis of attitudes to motivation and work developed a distinction between two elements, hygiene factors and motivators — dissatisfiers and satisfiers (see Figure 5.7a).

| *Hygiene factors* | *Motivators* |
|---|---|
| Company policy and administration | Achievement |
| Supervision | Recognition |
| Salary | Nature of the work |
| Interpersonal relations | Responsibility |
| Working conditions | Advancement |

*Figure 5.7a: Herzberg's two-factor theory*

Hygiene factors are essentially extrinsic and motivators are intrinsic. Hygiene factors are concerned with dissatisfaction with environmental issues so that, for example, improvement of pay or working conditions will not motivate but will only remove dissatisfaction. This is not to diminish the importance or significance of these factors; workers have a right to proper working conditions and appropriate management behaviour. This raises significant problems in the education system where, historically, responsibility for hygiene factors has been fragmented and of disputed significance.

Equally, the management of motivation in education has been problematic — for many of the reasons identified at the start of this chapter. Herzberg stresses the importance for motivation of the organisation of work, the quality of personal relationships and the potential for development. This leads to two significant practical outcomes of Herzberg's work, job design and job enrichment. Both are concerned with an explicit recognition in managing a workforce that the way in which the organisation is structured, work is delegated and responsibility apportioned have direct relevance to managing performance. However, concentration on what motivates, as in the content theories, ignores three substantial issues:

- The fact that an individual's perception of his or her needs will change over time and context.
- Management practices based on hierarchical/satisfier/dissatisfier approaches ignore the complexity of human behaviour.
- it is not just what motivates so much as what motivates *and* how it might be achieved.

In response to these issues, process models of motivation have emerged which recognise the complexity of the relationship between the what and the how. Process or expectancy theories of motivation are based on the premise that people are motivated by the expected outcomes of their actions. Motivation is therefore a causal relationship between effort expended, the performance attained and the reward related to the performance. The potential of a factor to motivate is, therefore, contingent upon the perceived relationship between the value attributed to the outcome, the likelihood of performance leading to the outcome and the existence of the skills, knowledge and capability necessary to achieve the performance. A person's behaviour is determined by a subjective evaluation of the strength of the correlation between:

Effort ⟶ Performance ⟶ Outcome

This approach differs from content theories in a number of significant ways:

- There is no hierarchy of needs — what motivates is the individual perception of what is significant at a given moment.
- There is no classification of outcomes — individuals are motivated by their dominant value system.
- It becomes impossible to have a macro approach — motivation is a subjective phenomenon.

Porter and Lawler (1968) developed an expectancy model which identified the causal relationships between the various factors influencing behaviour. The strength of motivation depends on, firstly, the VALUE attached to outcomes and the perceived EFFORT-REWARD relationship and, secondly, on the amount of EFFORT expended. However, managing these principles has to take into account the fact that:

- effort alone will not necessarily produce performance. ABILITIES and TRAITS and ROLE PERCEPTION will determine how effective effort is;
- if effort, abilities and traits and the role perception are right then PERFORMANCE will result;
- rewards are the outcomes which are deemed appropriate by the individual; they may be intrinsic or extrinsic. For motivation to be sustained there must be PERCEIVED EQUITABLE REWARDS which will then engender SATISFACTION. Lack of such satisfaction will compromise the value placed on the outcome and so diminish motivation.

Expectancy theory stresses the complexity of managing motivation and helps to place the emphasis on working with the individual's self-perception and perception of their job. It stresses the significance of the outcome to the individual and the correlation between the outcome and the effort necessary to achieve it. Motivation is therefore about action.

## Implications for managers

1. Rewards need to be appropriate to the individual, i.e. valued and possible.
2. The causal link between effort, performance and outcome has to be viewed in individual and subjective terms.

3. Outcomes have to be negotiated, not set arbitrarily.
4. Managing motivation is concerned with understanding the individual and managing the variables.
5. Managers therefore need the interpersonal skills to identify and understand individual perceptions.
6. Job design, appraisal, target-setting, feedback and review are the practical activities associated with managing motivation.

Managers cannot motivate; they have to operate procedures which allow them to identify, support and reinforce individual perception and this is best done through appraisal linked to professional and personal development.

The appraisal of staff in the context of development and motivation is concerned with managing individual perceptions and relating them to organisational needs. Appraisal is therefore not about identifying individuals for financial reward or promotion nor is it about penalising 'poor' performance — they are separate management processes. In order to improve and enhance performance, appraisal must conform to the following criteria:

- It is developmental, being the diagnostic component of a structured and systematic approach to the management of training and development.
- It is formative as it is based on qualitative judgements which are the basis for future action.
- It is negotiated, i.e. it is based on shared perceptions of performance relative to agreed criteria.
- It is continuous, since it is a long-term strategy to enhance individual performance in the context of institutional objectives.
- It is hierarchical, i.e. it is the process by which the managerial relationships of the institution are expressed and developed.
- It is internal, because it is concerned with the institution's performance and the quality of its internal relationships.

Appraisal is thus a process of negotiating individual targets in order to improve personal performance and so enhance the quality of educational provision. If appraisal meets the criteria outlined above then a number of benefits accrue: more systematic identification of agendas for staff development, improved communication, enhanced self-awareness and improved self-analysis, improved management of learning and greater opportunities for recognition and praise.

However, these outcomes are contingent upon a supportive infrastructure of values, processes and skills which integrate what the school exists to do with appropriate management strategies which are carried out by individuals with relevant skills and personal qualities.

The structure for managing performance in educational institutions can be illustrated as shown in Figure 5.8.

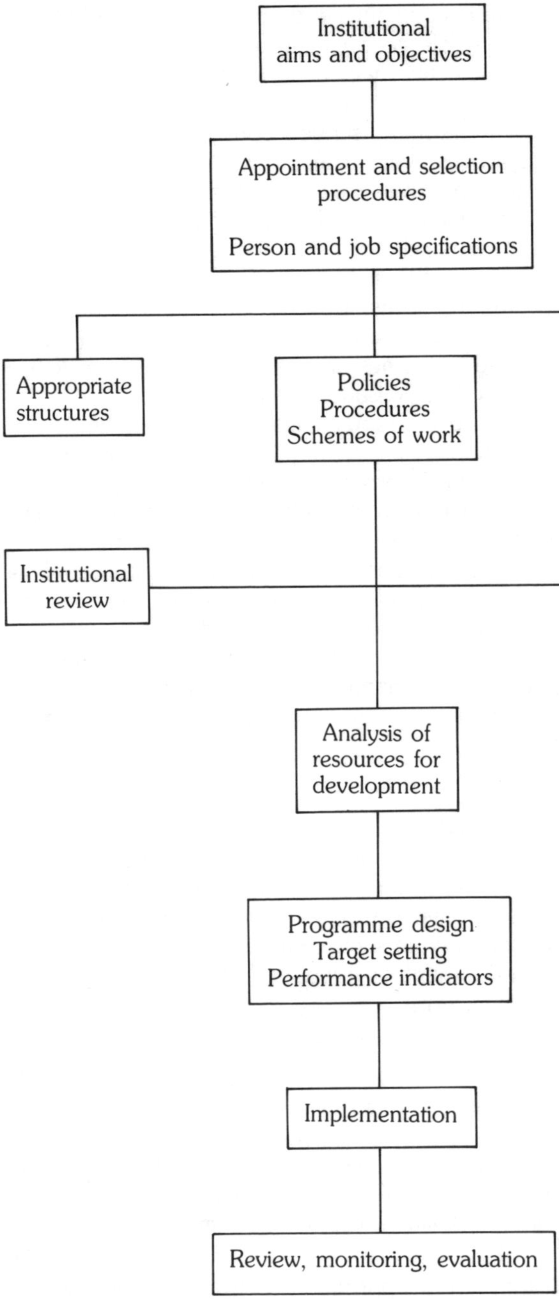


*Figure 5.8:* performance management in schools

Such a structure requires that aims and objectives are explicit and differentiated. Many schools produce aims which are essentially vague aspirations and objectives which are unattainable as they are not translatable into actions nor can their achievement be measured. By these criteria many schools consistently 'fail' as they publish the same objectives every year.

Once initial aims and objectives are established then all other processes and outcomes are functions of, and subordinate to, them. Thus the skills, knowledge and qualities of individuals appointed to the institution are formulated in such a way as to contribute to the achievement of institutional aims. Equally, training and development is based on the formulation of the current situation being diagnosed against stated outcomes and used as a vehicle to 'close the gap' in individual and organisational terms.

In order to work this process requires leadership in the terms discussed earlier in this chapter; it also requires 'open' management expressed through consultative procedures, effective delegation and a climate conducive to review, target setting, monitoring and evaluation. It is also contingent upon the avoidance of the rationalistic fallacy that there is only one correct view of the institution. This implies significant negotiating skills in order to diagnose, manage and reinforce the outcomes of individual motivation.

However close the match of management behaviour to the criteria described, performance management can only work in the broader context of managing change through learning (see chapter 6).

## Organisational design

The relationship between effective management of staff and organisational design is essentially that of form and function. No amount of leadership, motivation or team development will work unless the school is structured in such a way as to support, reinforce and facilitate the development of people. Urwick (1947) summarises this in the following terms:

> Lack of design is illogical, cruel, wasteful and inefficient.
>
> (p. 38)

Drucker (1968) reinforces this point even more emphatically:

> Good organization structure does not of itself produce good performance .... But a poor organization structure makes good perform-ance impossible, however good the managers .... improving organization structure will always improve performance.
>
> (p. 273)

An organisation that is not appropriately structured can experience the following problems:

- low motivation and morale and in extreme cases, anomie
- poor quality decision making
- ineffectual co-ordination
- potential conflict
- inability to convert principles into action
- role conflict
- inflexibility when faced with change
- inhibition of potential
- a waste of the resources of talent, money and time.

It is difficult to establish the precise rationale for the traditional hierarchical model which pervades the educational system. From the smallest primary school to the largest secondary school, the dominant model is the hierarchy expressed in terms of line management with the division of work into compartments with a clear span of control. There is a tension between this pseudo-rational structure and the notion of schools as professional communities.

The illogicality of the existing hierarchical model for educational institutions is highlighted by applying the following criteria:

1. Does form follow function? To what extent is the learning process of the classroom reflected in the working relationships within the institution as a whole, i.e. do schools practise in their structures what they preach in their aims?
2. Is there clear line management? Is it the right of individuals to know for what they are responsible and for whom and to whom they are accountable? Does the linear structure of schools reflect the reality of working relationships?
3. Do duties, authority, responsibility and relationships correlate? How real are many so-called management posts in schools, e.g. deputy heads in primary schools and middle managers in secondary schools? Is the notion of a 'teaching head' compatible with effective leadership?
4. How large are work teams? In most educational institutions teams are imbalanced; if they are too large or too small they will be dysfunctional.
5. How much authority is delegated? To what extent is delegated responsibility matched by authority and discretion?
6. Is the structure balanced? What is the ratio between those who teach and those who administer and manage?
7. How are sub-units co-ordinated? For example, is the division between academic and pastoral functions appropriate and is a departmental structure appropriate to managing cross-curricular factors, especially when the pupil experience is not divided into compartments?
8. Are working relationships defined and public? Schools rarely have explicit aims and objectives which are translated into individual and specific job descriptions, targets and performance indicators.
9. On what basis are work teams established? Are the criteria managerial or are they historic, incremental, random and *ad-hoc*?

10. Does the structure facilitate development? To what extent is the structure capable of change, adaptation and development, allowing for individual development and sensitivity to the external environment?

In many cases schools manifestly do not meet these criteria. The movement away from a tall hierarchy to a flat hierarchy, a matrix model or a team-based structure will always be artificial if the infrastructure of pay, delegation and management roles is not amended. Equally significant is the extent to which traditional structures are appropriate and relevant to the changing demands upon schools. The implementation of local management of schools, the national curriculum, appraisal and the need for marketing all impose demands upon institutions which will be impossible to meet if existing structures are retained. The challenges facing schools are considered in detail throughout this book but in essence they require a management response. The practical components of such a response are discussed below but one perspective is crucial with regard to organisational structure; it should reflect the integrity of relationships and be a vehicle for effective management. Simplistic hierarchies do not meet this criterion.

Handy (1989) has developed a model which might serve as the basis for determining the future structure of schools. The Shamrock organisation is made up of three (or possibly four) elements. The first is the professional core who are essential to the organisation and who manage its professional knowledge, giving the organisation its distinctive character. Work which is not central to the organisation should be contracted out to the second element which provides specialist services which increase expertise and diminish costs. The third element is the flexible labour force, part-time and temporary employees who provide expertise and skills in response to changing needs. The fourth leaf of Handy's Shamrock is the client or customer. He points out that in many areas, especially service industries, organisations have improved their efficiency and effectiveness and increased the perception of quality by getting the clients to do the work — self-service outlets are an obvious example.

Although Handy's model is essentially abstract it does assume significance when schools are placed in the context of local management of schools and the National curriculum. The Shamrock organisation offers some interesting implications for the future organisational design of schools:

1. A genuinely professional core can be created which has a specific focus: the delivery of the national curriculum.
2. It is necessary to question the extent to which such a core needs to be organised in terms of hierarchies or fragmented by function.

3. Teachers should not seek to be involved in every aspect of the school — administrative/clerical, catering and many aspects of the pastoral function should be contracted out to specialist providers.
4. LMS may well increase the use of part-time and short-term contracts and these will need to be managed in such a way as to enhance and support the core.
5. The core will need to recognise that it does not have a monopoly of expertise and knowledge. The community, parents and pupils themselves have significant contributions to make. For example, a major constraint upon effective management of human resources in secondary schools is the notion that the curriculum can only be delivered by one teacher in one classroom teaching one subject to one class. The use of pupil-managed learning has profound implications for the more effective deployment of skilled resources.

## Conclusion

This chapter offers a number of critical insights into the introduction of human resource management in schools. The movement from theory into practice raises two main issues. The first is a recognition that much of what has been described above already exists, but needs to be made explicit and systematic; and secondly, there must be a recognition that partial attempts to change are almost inevitably doomed to fail in that they will always be compromised and administered by the history and culture of many schools.

Human resource management in schools requires a total approach which has the following components:

1. Headteachers being leaders and not teachers with 'extra jobs'.
2. Senior staff and middle managers having an explicit management role and being trained and developed to do it.
3. A vision which is translated into genuine aims and attainable objectives that inform job design, delegation, the creation of work teams and operating procedures.
4. Recognising that management structures and procedures exist to facilitate action and are not ends in themselves.
5. Making time and releasing creative energy by incorporating the community and children into management processes so that they can contribute to, rather than be subjects of, school management.
6. Recognising that the integrity of the learning process applies as much to adults in schools as it does to children.

## References

Adair, J. 1983 *Effective Leadership*, Pan Books

Belbin, R. M. 1981 *Management Teams: why they succeed or fail*, Heinemann

Blake, R. R. & Mouton, J. S. 1978 *The New Managerial Grid*, Gulf Publishing Co.

Crosby, P. B. 1979 *Quality is Free*, McGraw Hill
Deming, W. E. 1982 *Quality, Productivity and Competetive Position*, MIT Center for Advanced Engineering Study, Cambridge, Mass.
Drucker, P. F. 1968 *The Practice of Management*, Pan Books
Handy, C. 1984 *Taken for Granted?*, Longman
Handy, C. 1989 *The Age of Unreason*, Hutchinson
Herzberg, F. 1974 *Work and the Nature of Man*, Granada Publishing Ltd
Hodgson, P. 1987 'Managers Can Be Taught But Leaders Have to Learn; *ICT* Nov/Dec
Maslow, A. H. 1954 *Motivation and Personality*, Harper and Row
Morgan, C. & Hall, V. 1986 *Headteachers at Work*, Open University Press
Murgatroyd, S. 1985 'Management Teams and the Promotion of Well-being', *School Organisation* Vol. 6 No. 1
Peters, T. J. & Waterman, R. H. 1982 *In Search of Excellence*, Harper and Row
Porter, L. W. & Lawler, E. E. 1968 *Managerial Attitudes and Performance*, Irwin
Torrington, D. & Weightman, J. 1989 *The Reality of School Management*, Blackwell
Urwick, L. 1947 *The Elements of Administration*, Pitman

# 6 The management of change

John West-Burnham

This chapter argues that the issue is not to manage change so much as to change management. The reason why educational changes are often perceived as being so problematic is not the nature of the change itself but the nature of the knowledge, skills and attitudes of those involved and the way that these are expressed in action. This book is essentially about the management of change in that each chapter argues for an approach to one aspect of management which, if adopted comprehensively, would lead to a fundamental alteration in the ways in which schools move from organisational immaturity to organisational maturity where the incorporation of new challenges and demands is a norm. Change is axiomatic to organisational life, and an organisation that ceases to respond effectively is balanced on the fine line between stability and stagnation. Neither state is appropriate to an educational institution.

The problem is essentially one of a 'category mistake'; schools have problems in responding to new demands because those demands are viewed as being additional to, to be done 'as well as', existing activities. Equally, new developments are often dealt with in the context of traditional structures and behaviour. The mistake is in seeing change as a distinctive phenomenon rather than a natural and inevitable social process to which organisational and individual behaviour should be attuned.

What is surprising is that schools, as learning institutions, should find change so difficult to manage. Two factors would appear to militate against this; firstly, the educational system is concerned with one of the most dynamic change processes in society — the education of young people. Secondly, the social context of education has never been static; reference to a golden age of stability is probably more symptomatic of current stress than historical reality.

This chapter argues that traditional approaches to the management of change have misunderstood the relationship between managing organisations and the need to incorporate new procedures, practices or value systems. Managing change is seen as a highly complex and sensitive area and a significant number of models and approaches have emerged in order to facilitate the introduction of change. However, in the context of the education system, these have patently not worked. The frequently expressed and genuine concerns about the problems in implementing the 1988 Education Act indicate the inadequacy of many existing practices.

There are many barriers to creating schools which are able to incorporate new demands as part of the normal processes of organisational life. It is important to try and identify these barriers in such a way as to help develop the appropriate strategies for overcoming them. The most significant barriers are the conservatism of schools, concern about resources, the volume of demands for change and inappropriate management styles.

## 1. Conservativism

Schools are naturally conservative places. Teachers have a tremendous capacity to assimilate changes in such a way as to perpetuate existing modes of working. This applies as much to individual classrooms as it does to schools as a whole. This reluctance to engage in fundamental rethinking is not necessarily negative. The historical stress on individual and institutional autonomy and the legal and contractual status of headteachers generates natural suspicion of external demands for change. Equally, such demands are an implicit challenge to everything that has happened in the classroom or school. There is always going to be a 'high investment in the *status quo*' because it represents years of involvement and success. A challenge to established ways of working may be legitimately perceived as a rejection of all that has been done hitherto and, subjectively, the work and commitment involved with it. Those imposing change may be implicitly rejecting a lifetime's work.

## 2. Resources

A frequent complaint in education is that demands for change are rarely accompanied by what is perceived to be appropriate resourcing. Most commonly the concern is about money and time but, increasingly, it centres upon the numbers of appropriately qualified and experienced staff. These responses are understandable from a system that is not used to planning, prioritising, budgeting and focusing training and development on the ability to respond, as well as the content of the response. As Torrington and Weightman (1989) express it:

> Many schools do not think about the use they make of, and their organisational attitudes towards, the resources available to them, and can be tempted to blame lack of resources for deficiencies in their operation.
>
> (p. 67)

The problem is compounded by the lack of clarity in what the school actually exists to do, inappropriate methods of resource management and the political perspective that often dominates resource allocation. The situation is further exacerbated by a lack of training in institutional and personal resource management.

## 3. *Volume of demands*

The issue here is the number and range of demands which emanate from the 1986 and 1988 Education Acts, in particular the national curriculum, local management of schools and teacher appraisal. Any organisation would be stretched if it had to deal with such a fundamental restructuring of practice. However, the volume of change is a relative perception and schools have dealt with equally profound measures in the past; for example, the raising of the school leaving age to 16 and comprehensive reorganisation. A lack of planning, resources and appropriate skills can only make the feeling of overload stronger.

## 4. *Inappropriate management*

This is probably the most significant of the four elements. The fact is that some schools have come to terms with the changes, able to absorb new initiatives with minimum stress or disruption and have used change to enhance and strengthen themselves.

Schools which have not been able to respond effectively will probably display one or more of the following characteristics:

- (i) lack of leadership, an absence of explicit goals, recognition and empowering;
- (ii) undeveloped middle managers, i.e. no infrastructure to translate principle into action, to ensure the development of individuals or to make the most efficient and effective use of resources;
- (iii) limited understanding and application of the principles of planning, budgeting, managing motivation and evaluating;
- (iv) a lack of recognition of the social side of work, failure to provide the adults in schools with an appropriate working environment;
- (v) inappropriate working procedures which are based on power relationships (and political processes) and often humiliating administrative procedures;
- (vi) immature social networks based on competition, secrecy, fear of criticism;
- (vii) lack of effective delegation and therefore, implicitly, a lack of trust and willingness to develop;
- (viii) restricted and poor quality communication, usually one-way rather than two-way;
- (ix) a deference to experience rather than knowledge, skills and the ability to act.

Almost any discussion of managing change will identify the majority of the factors above. However, traditional approaches to managing change identify them as 'barriers', 'resistors' or 'restrainers' to a specific initiative. This approach is reinforced by the use of such techniques as force field analysis which has the effect of making change discrete and separate. Change is thus treated as an illness, a virus to be endured until the immune system has come to terms with it so that it won't be a problem in the future. The problem with this piecemeal and *ad hoc* approach is that it condemns the individual to regular bouts of misery and incapacity. An emphasis on prevention rather than cure may be more appropriate.

In the context of managing change in education, 'prevention' has a number of components which centre on the ability of schools to mature through learning. Organisations only have reality through the experiences of the individuals working in them and so managing change comes down to enhancing the ability of individuals to learn and to communicate that learning within the context of the organisation as a whole. The implication of this is that managing change may be about a fundamental cultural shift which moves individuals and schools away from being victims to being in control of themselves and so able to respond in a positive and creative way rather than to react against it.

The process may be illustrated as shown in Figure 6.1.

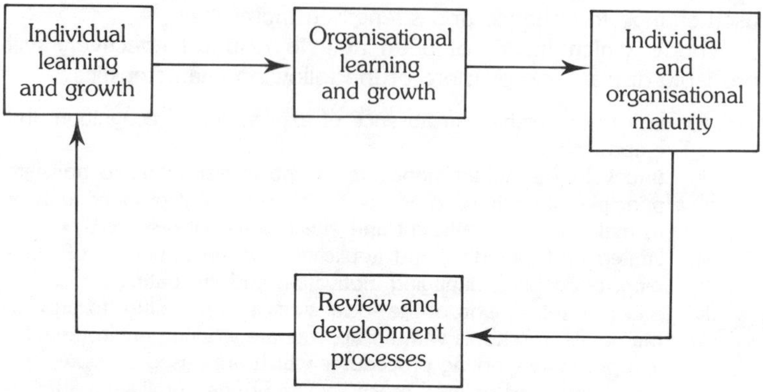


*Figure 6.1 developing the capacity to respond to change*

If institutional development is to be successful then it must begin with the individual. Thus, the process of creating a school which is capable of growing so that change is a norm begins with the individual. However, such a process assumes effective leadership (as discussed in chapter 5) because, without a clear vision and an explicit view of what the organisation is going to look like, this process is doomed from the start.

## Individual learning and growth

This whole process may be summed up in Everard's (1987) phrase:

> . . . to help people to become originators rather than pawns, to make a difference to their world by getting things to happen – a problem solved, a decision implemented, an objective attained.
>
> (p. 5)

This view raises profound questions about the nature of development and training. More importantly, it requires a fundamental shift in attitudes as to the status of, and significance attached to, training and development in the management of schools, and the nature, design, content and delivery of that training and development.

Fullan (1986) argues that any change process involves three levels of transition: the use of new resources, the existence of appropriate practices or behaviours and, finally, fundamental shifts in beliefs and understanding. He goes on to stress that working with new resources is essentially superficial, in that it is external to the individual, whereas changes in behaviour and attitudes are internal and, therefore, concerned with learning.

This perspective is reinforced by Lawrence and Lorsch (1969 p. 87 adapted) who advance the model shown in Figure 6.2.

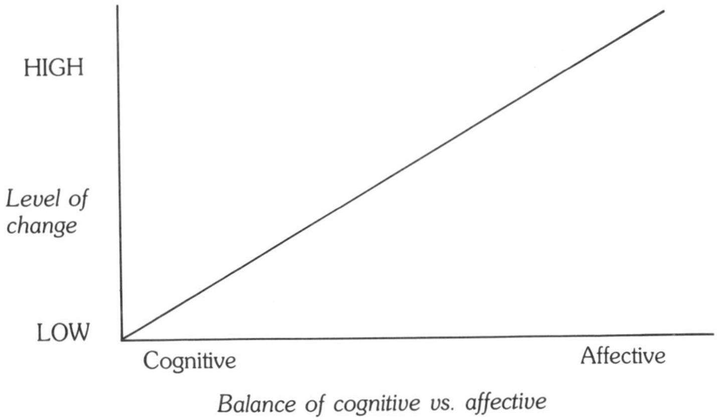


*Figure 6.2: the relationship between levels of change required and impact on the individual*

The implication of this model is that the more profound the change, the greater is the emotional impact on the individual. If the change is to be a new way of working and so create a capability to respond to new demands intuitively then it must be concerned with the affective response.

There is thus a need to help individuals to prepare for change by a process of training and development which is as much concerned with the affective as it is with the cognitive, as much concerned with process skills as with outcomes, and with personal growth as much as technical competence. There are numerous barriers to this approach; indeed the whole tradition of training and development for teachers has tended to emphasise the cognitive rather than the affective, been concerned with generic knowledge rather than specific skills, and delivered in courses without follow-up rather than integrated into a long term strategy.

A significant amount of research and experience has led to a fundamental questioning of the provision of training events. This is substantially reinforced if development is not seen in purely instrumental terms but, rather, linked to organisational growth through personal enhancement.

The first step in designing a training and development strategy to facilitate a changing school is to focus on the notion of effectiveness. If effectiveness is defined as the attainment of accepted objectives, then Mumford (1986) postulates a model which seeks to achieve synergy between three elements (p. 21), as shown in Figure 6.3.

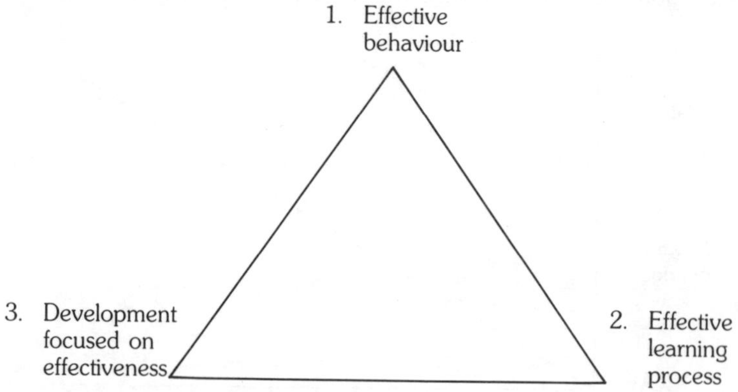


*Figure 6.3: the triangle of effectiveness*

These elements are defined by Mumford as:

1. establishing objectives and identifying the behaviour necessary to achieve them;
2. an emphasis on the appropriate learning process necessary to achieve 1;
3. an emphasis upon actions leading to the attainment of objectives rather than the acquisition of a body of knowledge.

Mumford argues (p. 24) that the emphasis in management development has been upon transmitting knowledge and expecting it to be applied rather than identifying the desired outcomes, their associated behaviours and attitudes, and then developing appropriate strategies to achieve those outcomes. Thus, learning to change is as much about personal competence as the acquisition of knowledge.

Although Mumford's discussion is concerned with management development, it is equally concerned with the professional development of teachers. In the context of managing change, the importance of this perspective is that learning is defined in terms of behaviour and outcomes. Thus, learning how to change is as much a component of learning as the change itself.

Developing the notion of the 'triangle of effectiveness' leads Mumford (p. 29) to characterise many development activities as corresponding to the 'vicious learning sequence' shown in Figure 6.4.

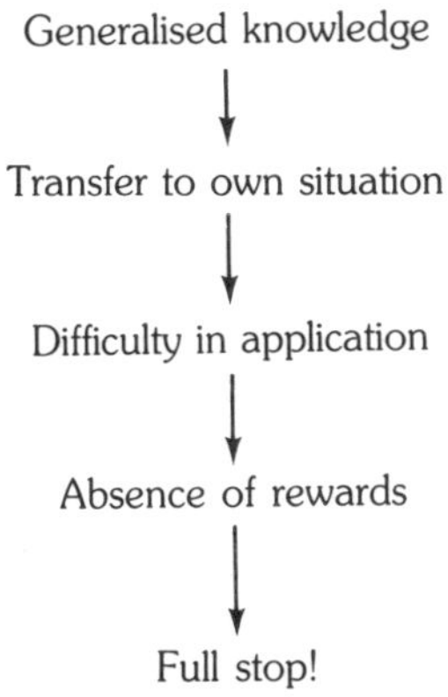


*Figure 6.4: the vicious learning sequence*

The most superficial examination of many INSET programmes will confirm the relevance of this model to the provision of professional development activities for teachers. In the educational context it might be replicated as shown in Figure 6.5.

In sharp distinction to these models Mumford (p. 28) offers the 'virtuous learning cycle' which implicitly assumes the application of principles of action learning, knowledge of motivation and proactive management of development (see Figure 6.6).

The full implications of this model are explored below, but Mumford reinforces the need to take seriously the requirements and potential for growth of individuals, i.e. the need to 'develop' rather than 'process'. This requires providers to be as concerned with implementation as with delivery. Training must, therefore, include elements which support the application of principles and pro-

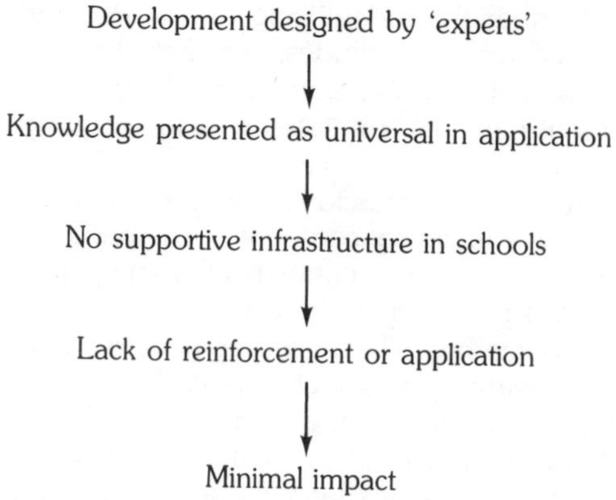


*Figure 6.5: the learning sequence in education*

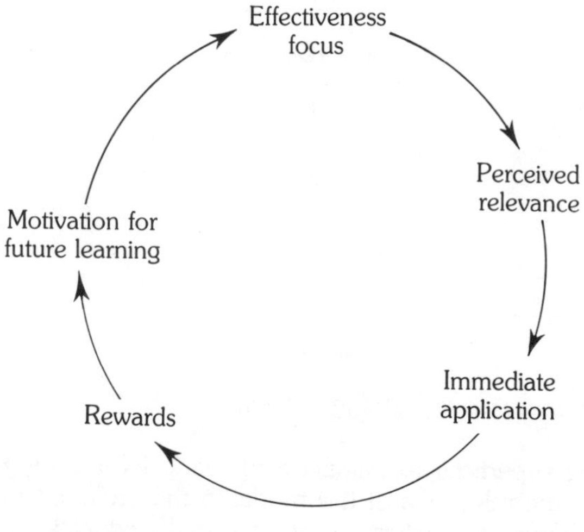


*Figure 6.6: the virtuous learning cycle*

cedures. The competencies associated with new initiatives need to be identified and incorporated into training events and such events should translate theory into practice, e.g. there should be no lectures on pupil-managed learning.

Two issues dominate this aspect of effective staff development strategies — the nature and status of the adult learner, and the identification of appropriate strategies for learning.

Knowles (1984) argues for a distinction between pedagogy, as being appropriate to some aspects of children's learning, and andragogy, which is more appropriate to adults' needs and expectations. Knowles argues that the adult learner has the following characteristics:

1. S/he is largely self-directed and requires a climate of trust, collaboration and openness to learn effectively.
2. The previous experience of the learner has to be implicit in the learning process. It is too substantial and significant to the individual to be ignored.
3. The adult learner has to accept the need to learn; i.e. it must be perceived as being of personal value.
4. S/he is biased towards problem solving as a learning activity.
5. Practical relevance will be a significant factor in obtaining commitment.
6. S/he will only internalise learning if motivated by intrinsic factors.

Andragogy therefore requires acceptance of status and self-perceptions of the individual rather than assuming common backgrounds and expectations. Mouton and Blake (1984) extend this critique of traditional approaches to adult learning by questioning the role of the provider. Their concept of synergogy emphasises the importance of learning through membership of a team which, in effect, extends and reinforces the resources available to the learner, while emphasising the importance of interaction.

In this context the most appropriate learning model is usually defined as experiential learning which stresses the importance of learning by doing, sharing, reviewing and applying. Experiential models are thus concerned with action based on changed perceptions which are achieved by a process of confrontation and exchange. The actual process of learning is as significant as the content and the outcomes affective as well as cognitive.

The implications of this approach are that for change to occur successfully in any school, then the first priority must be the personal resources and capacity for learning of individual teachers. Responding to new demands requires a range of skills and qualities, such as analysis and problem solving abilities, interpersonal skills, stress management, a sense of vision and purpose, the ability to create unique responses and detailed self-knowledge. Training has to take these factors into account and they may well be issues for training in their own right.

If the background of the participants in a developmental learning process is significant, then so is the structuring of the actual learning itself. Development implies action and the learning model adopted should reflect that. Pfeiffer and Jones (1973) view experiential learning as shown in Fig. 6.7 (top). Kolb (1984) produced a similar model as in Fig. 6.7 (bottom).

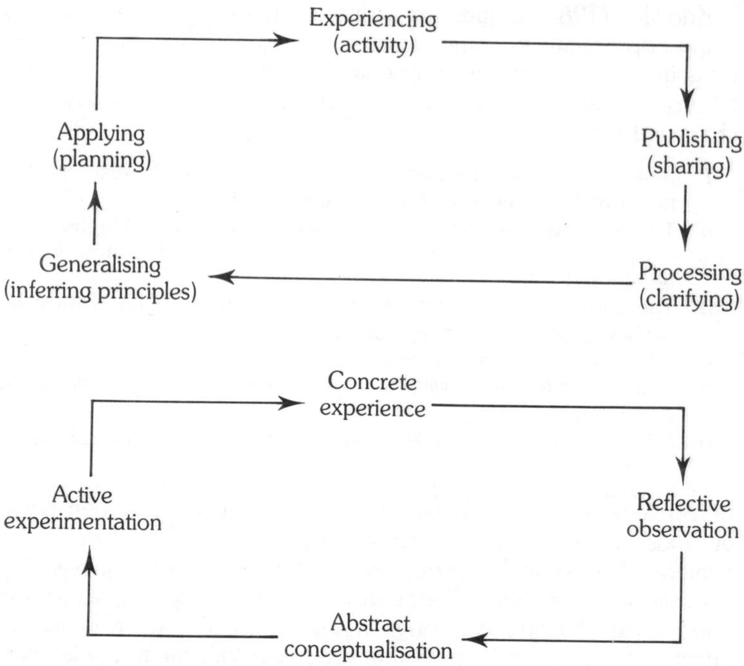


*Figure 6.7: models of experiential learning*

These models have a number of significant features in common. Learning is an active process which is reflected on and the lessons derived are immediately applied to further learning. This process is facilitated through team membership and the outcome is thus owned by the participants by virtue of being the product of shared perceptions which are applied and tested.

The theoretical perspectives discussed above, although drawn from a range of sources, may be synthesised to develop a set of criteria to inform planning, design and implementation and to provide a basis for evaluation.

1. What are the desired outcomes in terms of action *and* behaviour?
2. Is the process of delivery geared to action rather than increasing knowledge?
3. Is the learning methodology appropriate to the intended outcomes and the participants?
4. Are the perceptions of sponsors and participants included in the process of design?
5. Have the potentially varying motivations of participants been explored and taken into account?
6. Is there the potential for applying the outcomes of an activity in terms of time, resources and the credibility of teachers taking part?

7. Are there appropriate personal outcomes for individuals involved in management development activities?
8. Does the planning include provisions for further development activities in response to new needs being identified?
9. Does learning take place in groups and are those groups designed and developed?
10. Are action methods used *throughout* the training?
11. Do trainers use experiential techniques?
12. What are the mechanisms for evaluation and are they consistent with the principles established elsewhere?
13. Are there appropriate mechanisms for implementing the outcomes of the training in schools?
14. Is the training part of an overall development strategy in respect of long-term goals based on the diagnosis of LEA and school needs?

If systematically applied, these criteria have the potential to shift the balance of training and development away from the transmission of data to the enhancement of the individual.

Effective training and development is as much concerned with empowering teachers as with transmitting new demands and methods of working. However, there has to be logical correlation between the development of individuals and the development of schools.

## Organisational learning and growth

However well planned individual development strategies are, they cannot bring about the desired level of capacity for individual growth unless the school as an entity is also engaged in a process of continual review and development. The corollary of individual development is the rather amorphous concept of organisational development (OD). Although OD has a variety of interpretations, Everard (1985) proposes four distinctive components. Firstly, OD exists to improve effectiveness by increasing objectivity and, secondly, it views the school in totality, i.e. all its elements and in relation to its environment. Thirdly, it is based, as far as possible, in *objective analysis*; concerned with cause and effect. Finally, it is concerned with systematic diagnosis, generation of solutions and the *implementation* of appropriate strategies (pp. 28, 29).

There is, thus, the same emphasis on effectiveness, diagnosis and action as outlined in Mumford's model above. In order for OD to work a number of key elements must be managed. There must be a long-term perspective — changing the whole school is a complex process and the time-scale should be appropriate. A problem-solving approach is essential, the emphasis needs to be on the generation of solutions rather than the intellectualisation of difficulties; problem-solving skills are therefore a crucial attribute of those involved in OD.

Staff must be perceived as a resource — open and collaborative management is essential to maximise the generation of effective solutions and ensure commitment to their implementation. To reinforce this, the creation of a positive culture is essential. This

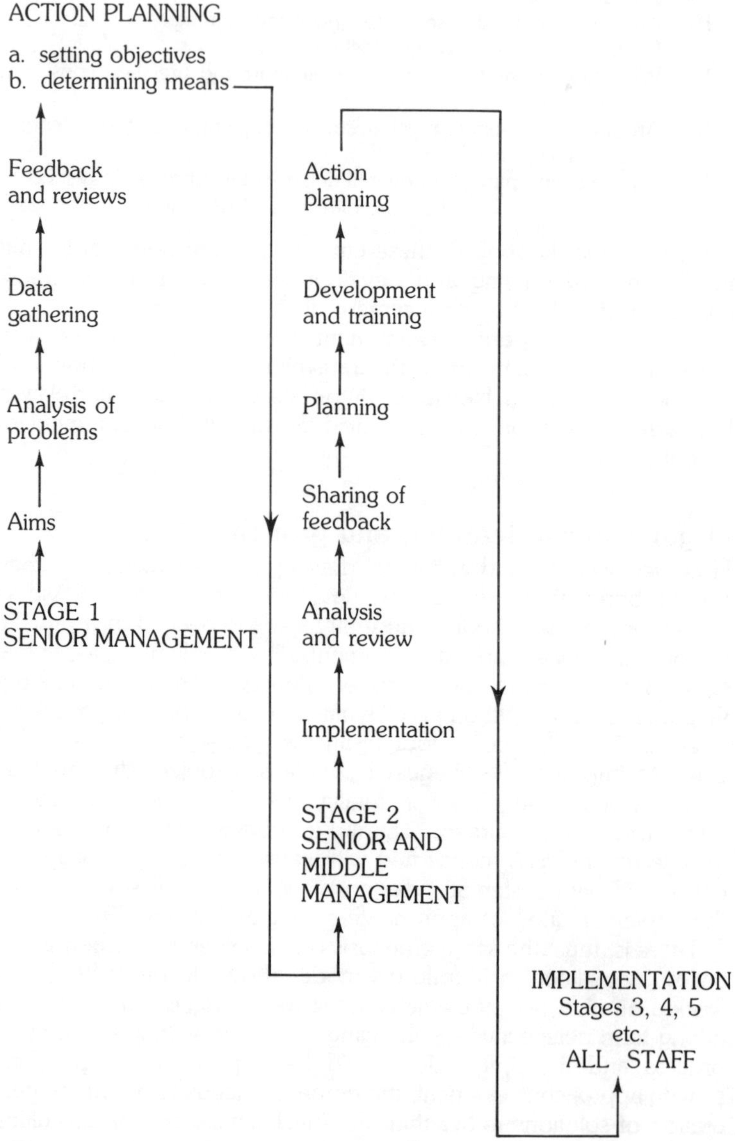


*Figure 6.8: an action research approach to managing OD*

implies explicit values and the development of strategies and procedures which are appropriate to the school. Teams are more potent in this context than coalitions of individuals — the effective team is more creative and more committed to implementation.

Organisational development is often facilitated by the use of a change manager — the identification of an individual with the qualities, skills and knowledge to facilitate the OD process. To be effective, the school must make full use of action research — combining rigorous analysis with implementation and evaluation in classrooms and the school as a whole. This must be reinforced by the testing of solutions.

OD can be as painful for schools as real development is for individuals, i.e. it forces a recognition of weaknesses and inadequacies and requires a public commitment to change — there is no turning back. Development implies a long-term, indeed a continuous process, and this is how individuals and organisations move from reacting to change to being capable of changing. The OD process has much in common with planning individual development strategies.

This model (see Figure 6.8) has a number of significant implications for school management; senior management must initiate the process, senior and middle management must go through the process focusing firstly on themselves before presuming to impose it on staff. Once started, the process sustains its momentum by a combination of shared analysis, effective planning and development to ensure action. Change management issues are thus not discrete but incorporated into a learning cycle. This provides the criterion for differentiating between organisations which react to change and those for which it is a norm — the extent to which they are immature or mature in organisational terms. Mature organisations are learning organisations and are able to implement individual and organisational development because of the relative sophistication of their management processes.

## Mature and immature organisations

It is possible to distinguish between mature and immature organisations in terms of management processes:

| | IMMATURE | MATURE |
|---|---|---|
| 1. | reinforcement of the *status quo*, deference to experience | a belief in continuous improvement, challenging traditional assumptions |
| 2. | aims and objectives not clear or differentiated | explicit aims translated into meaningful objectives and attainable personal targets. |

| | IMMATURE | MATURE |
|---|---|---|
| 3. | rigid hierarchy, work segmented by status and administrative procedures, centralised control | self-managing, task oriented teams, minimal rules, simple decentralised structure |
| 4. | top down communication, little feedback | communication open, honest direct and two-way, managers listening |
| 5. | motivation by coercion | motivation recognised, rewards in personal terms |
| 6. | leadership by exhortation and dictat, inflexible style | leadership by visible example, situational style |
| 7. | decisions announced | full consultation of all involved |
| 8. | training in functional terms only, no integration | training and development fully integrated to achieve institutional objectives |
| 9. | administrative and technical delegation to middle management | real delegation of responsibility and authority to a developed middle management |
| 10. | recruitment and selection on the basis of cloning | job and person specifications used as part of rational selection procedures |
| 11. | no definition of quality | an emphasis on quality in all relationships and procedures |
| 12. | assumption of client's needs | responsiveness to clients' perception of needs |
| 13. | deference to the authority of experience | recognition and utilisation of skills, knowledge and qualities |
| 14. | change perceived as a threat | change regarded as the norm |

*Figure 6.9: characteristics of immature and mature organisations*

derived from Kanter (1981) & Peters (1987)

Each of the three elements addressed in this chapter, individual development, organisational development and organisational maturity exist in a synergistic relationship. Each is the means of achieving the other and all contribute to a school's ability to manage change by being fundamentally committed to growth, learning and development.

The practical implications of this approach may be illustrated with reference to components of the 1986 and 1988 Education Acts. The implementation of the national curriculum and local management of schools has generally been managed by reference to the technical and resource implications rather than developing the personal qualities to facilitate the change. The same is true of teacher appraisal which is consistently viewed as another burden rather than the process of responding to the other changes.

It is symptomatic that much of the literature on teacher appraisal has emphasised the setting up of systems, creation of documentation and emphasis on the 'right' procedures. There has been significantly less emphasis on the appropriate interpersonal skills and on the resolution of existing tensions and conflicts, i.e. the task has dominated the process. In this context, appraisal is another thing to do rather than a more effective way of managing existing relationships and developing the skills and qualities which are relevant to managing the implementation of the national curriculum and LMS. Both will present enormous difficulties if they are viewed as changes to be managed, rather than schools changing the way they manage first and then addressing the practical issues of implementation.

## Note

Elements of this chapter were first published as West-Burnham, J. 1987 'Effective learning and the design of staff development activities', Educational Change and Development, Vol. 8, No. 2.

## References

Everard, K. B. 1985 'OD in Education' in Gray, H. L. *Organisation Development in Education*, Deanhouse

Everard, K. B. 1987 *Developing Management in Schools*, Blackwell

Fullan, M. G. 1986 'The Management of Change, in Hoyle, E. & Macmahon, A. (eds) *The Management of Schools*, Kogan Page

Kanter, R. M. 1981 *The Change Masters*, Allen and Unwin

Knowles, M. S. 1984 *Andragogy in Action*, McGraw Hill

Kolb D. A. 1984 *Experiential Learning: Experience as a Source of Learning and Development*, Englewood Cliffs, Prentice Hall

Lawrence, P. and Lorsch, J. 1969 *Developing Organizations: Diagnosis and Action*, Addison-Wesley

Mouton, J. S. and Blake, R. R. 1984 *Synergogy: A New Strategy for Education, Training and Development*, Jossey-Bass
Mumford, A. 1986 *Handbook of Management Development*, Gower
Peters, T. 1987 *Thriving on Chaos*, Harper and Row
Pfeiffer, J. and Jones, J. E. 1973 *Annual Handbook for Group Facilitators*, University Associates
Torrington, D. and Weightman, J. 1989 *The Reality of School Management*, Blackwell

# 7 Managing stress in schools


## Linda Ellison


Effective management of human and physical resources or of the curriculum is only possible if those concerned with managing them can operate without the dysfunctional effects resulting from excessive stress. Managers as individuals need to be able to manage their own stress but they also have a responsibility to manage the school as a whole in such a way that stress levels are reduced for all staff. The chapter starts with a review of the dimensions of stress by defining it, identifying its symptoms and causes and reflecting on who is prone to stress. It then puts forward a framework for managing stress in school and this is applied in practice by use of a case study. One of the specific causes of stress, poor time management at both individual and whole school levels, is analysed separately in the next chapter.

## Dimensions of stress

Over the last few years there has been a general recognition that many in the teaching profession are working under considerable stress. This is perceived to be a result of the pressures caused by the rapid rate of change and the increased responsibilities at the school level. Unfortunately, there has been a dangerous tendency to accept this problem without attempting to alleviate it.

### *(i) What is stress?*

Stress is the body's biochemical response to a threatening situation (stressor) and, although it is intended to ensure self-survival, the frequent changes in blood pressure caused by regular exposure to stressors can lead to cardiac (and other) illness in the future.

Kyriacou and Sutcliffe (1978 p. 2) have defined teacher stress as:

> a response of negative affect (such as anger or depression) by the teacher . . . resulting from aspects of the teacher's job . . . .

Although stress is usually seen as something which is negative and threatening, it is important to remember that it can also be stimulating, acting as a valuable human response to challenge and change. While healthy tension helps to improve performance by providing a challenge, excessive pressure can be distressing, leading to loss of effectiveness and, ultimately, to ill health and breakdown. Success in managing stress therefore depends on the ability to recognise and respond to an individual's position on this continuum. Figure 7.1 shows the relationship between pressure and performance with the conditions at the extremes being described as rustout and burnout.

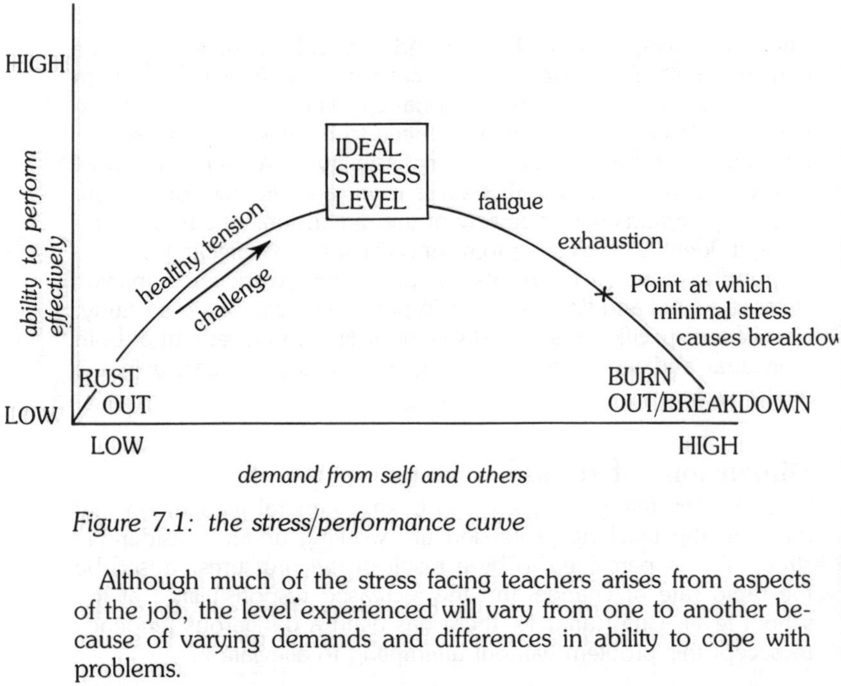


*Figure 7.1: the stress/performance curve*

Although much of the stress facing teachers arises from aspects of the job, the level experienced will vary from one to another because of varying demands and differences in ability to cope with problems.

## *(ii) The symptoms of stress*

If we accept the model described in Figure 7.1, it is important for managers in schools to be aware of the various positions which individual staff occupy on the stress and performance curve. This recognition will enable management to provide increased challenge or to reduce stress factors for individuals or the staff as a whole so that they are working at the ideal level and have the best chance of being effective.

The symptoms of 'rustout' (or tedium) could manifest themselves as boredom, fatigue, frustration and dissatisfaction. Excessive stress is currently more prevalent and has a variety of symptoms which can be divided into categories (although this is not intended as a medical guide):

| | |
|---|---|
| *Psychological* | frustration<br>tension<br>fear<br>anxiety |
| *Physiological* | |
| Short-term | edginess, faster heartbeat and breathing, need to pass water, sweaty hands, more sensitive to touch, tense muscles, cold feet, pale face, need more sleep |
| Long-term | tension resulting in headaches, backache, 'nerves', sleeping badly, loss of appetite, indigestion, ulcers, poor circulation, high blood pressure, heart disease |
| *Behavioural* | deterioration in work performance<br>irrational behaviour<br>poor problem solving and decision making<br>impaired interpersonal relationships |

Because the results of stress reveal themselves in different ways in different individuals, managers need to be on the lookout for any combination of these symptoms within the school.

If individuals are experiencing high levels of stress and moving towards 'burnout', there will be evidence of both personal and organisational symptoms. The personal symptoms will be taken from all three categories above, while the organisational ones, which will have a very detrimental effect on school effectiveness, will include:

- increased absenteeism
- lack of direction
- high levels of complaining
- lack of communication, trust and positive feedback
- increases in conflict and greater difficulty in resolving it
- difficulties in motivating staff
- lack of co-operation and unwillingness to accept change/innovation.

## *(iii) The causes of stress*

Although stress was defined earlier as a reaction to pressures, there are other factors which come into the equation such as an individual's characteristics and the existence (or otherwise) of control mechanisms. A healthy balance of pressures and these compensatory factors would keep an individual at the ideal stress level for effectiveness. On the other hand, an imbalance on one side would result in the individual moving towards rustout or burnout.

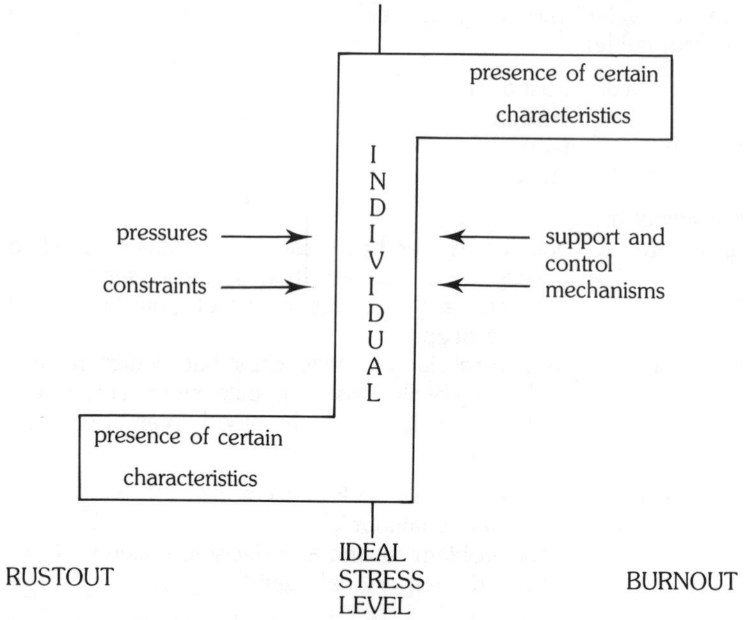


*Figure 7.2: factors which affect stress levels*

It is generally recognised that high levels of stress are caused by a life event such as the death of a spouse. Even going on holiday entails a degree of stress. People become particularly prone to ill health when a variety of these life events occurs at the same time, for example:

- changing jobs
- moving house
- increasing mortgage
- changing social life
- experiencing financial difficulties.

Such a combination is often found when teachers move to a post in another LEA.

As well as general research into the causes of stress, much has been written over the last 30 years about the specific stressors in teaching. Most of the research highlights the same stressors although they have become more widespread (and the literature more prolific) in recent years, particularly in relation to senior management. There are both core and marginal issues in creating stress. The former will comprise the basic assumptions and ways of doing things within the school while the latter includes factors related to the core issues and also more individual problems. The major stressors which have been identified (excluding personal ones) can be grouped under the following headings (which are based on the work of Rees (1989)):

(a) *Pupils*
large classes and high levels of continuous assessment work
lack of support from senior staff for those experiencing discipline problems
excessive administration for those with pastoral care responsibilities

(b) *Working environment*
poor maintenance, inadequate heating and lighting
lack of resources
overcrowded classrooms
inadequate staff facilities and ancillary support

(c) Organisational factors — management and structures
time wasted, fruitless meetings
mounting paperwork as a result of bureaucratic procedures
job ambiguity and role conflict

(d) Interpersonal relations
lack of time to maintain good social relationships
the divisive nature of the incentive allowance system

(e) External demands on the school from parents and society
changing demands causing confusion about precise responsibilities
perceived poor standing in society
lack of opportunities for career development
a largely hostile media exacerbating the situation

(f) Time i.e. work overload
(underload is not usually applicable!)
excessive workloads, hence the need for evening and weekend work at home (which can lead to family problems)
covering for colleagues on in-service training, in-service training outside the school day

It is important to remember that these potential stressors do not have the same dysfunctional effect on every teacher. Nevertheless, they are now accumulating and applying to many more people, therefore creating an increasing problem for the individuals concerned and for those who manage schools.

## *(iv) Who is prone to stress?*

The amount of stress which a person can withstand depends largely on the individual, because a problem will only be perceived if there seems to be a discrepancy between demands placed on the individual and his/her ability to cope. Some people thrive on stress and may then be viewed as ideal candidates for managerial responsibility, while the attitudes of others result in them appearing to be more slow and steady. Friedman and Rosenman (1974) have identified the former as Type A (restless, over-conscientious, workaholics) and the latter as Type B (calm, relaxed) personalities. Excessive demands (which may be self-initiated) can cause Type A people to be adversely affected by fairly low levels of stressors so that their responses become out of tune with the degree of danger and they 'blow up' at a minor inconvenience which their Type B, or less stressed, colleagues would take in their stride.

It is difficult to assess the extent of stress in teaching because of a lack of understanding of descriptions used in questionnaires and an unwillingness to admit to stress problems. Rees (1989) surveys the research on teacher stress and concludes that the various findings cannot be amalgamated in order to identify the individual characteristics, e.g. age, sex, seniority or type of school, which may cause increased predisposition to stress. Although males and females tend to identify different concerns, this could be a result of sex bias in certain roles. Some research (for example Coates and Thoresen 1976) shows that new entrants to teaching tend to experience higher levels as they have not yet developed coping skills. There is also evidence (Kyriacou 1987) that stress is seen to be connected to job satisfaction, reflecting the idea discussed earlier of positive stress as presenting a challenge.

## Managing stress

Although many in the teaching profession are experiencing undesirably high levels of stress, this manifests itself in different ways. The tendency to believe that admitting stress indicates a weak, ineffective character results in many people failing to discuss their stressors and their reactions. Wilce (TES 26 May 1989) reports that:

> One of the big problems is that there is a conspiracy of silence. You don't like to tell your colleagues you're having difficulties, so you go round holding it all in and creating more stress for yourself.

The personal nature of the problem and the varied ways in which it reveals itself demand that there is a sensitive approach to managing stress, although the possibility of difficulties should not be a reason for avoiding the issue. Because of the need for organisational and personal effectiveness, it is important that management, as well as individual, attention is given to stress reduction in the school. Although the symptoms are individual, the causes are largely organisational or school-wide and, therefore, need tackling at the level of the whole school. For example, there may be a need to improve the climate within the school.

Figure 7.3 outlines the components of a stress management plan and there follows a consideration of some of the practical approaches which can be used to identify and tackle stress in schools. These focus on overcoming high levels of stress, rather than on the

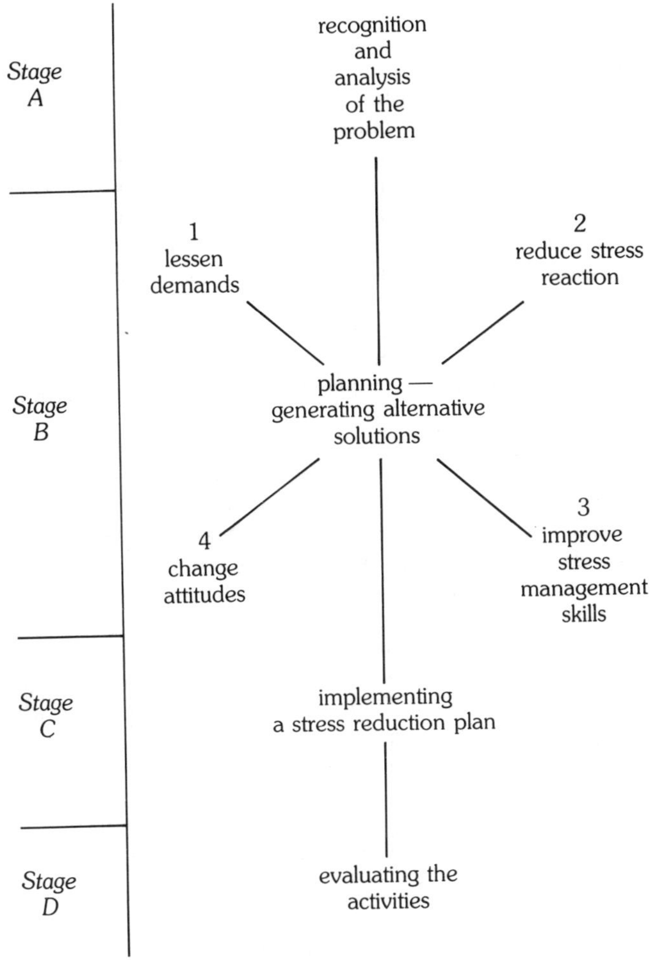


*Figure 7.3: a stress management plan*

less common cases of rustout (which could be tackled by providing more challenging work and delegating responsibilities). Although many of the ideas could be adopted at either the individual or the school level, it is the author's belief that open and supportive discussion with colleagues proves particularly valuable and that some form of whole school review can provide the opportunity for highlighting and discussing problem areas.

The stages and key elements in this plan (at either the individual or whole school level) will now be worked through in some detail.

## *Stage A — recognition and analysis of the problem*

At the individual level, it is possible to recognise the signs and causes of stress and then to manage these stressors. Gray and Freeman (1988) suggest that an individual should try to classify what he/she sees as intolerable behaviour (for example on the part of pupils, colleagues and parents). They believe that sharing this list with a colleague will improve each person's understanding of the similarities and differences in areas of tolerance. In knowing ourselves we can improve our own situation and that of our colleagues.

Although there is considerable value in this 'self-help' approach to understanding stress, the role of management is to develop a proactive strategy for stress reduction for the whole school. Recent evidence shows that if a school is well-managed, for example where staff are involved in decision making, then stress levels will be lower anyway.

In order to identify stressors, it would be possible to ask all the individuals to list the causes of stress within the school. However, this would probably mean that people would classify factors in different ways and it would produce a vast amount of data which would be difficult to analyse and to attack. There is a need to raise certain issues and to pinpoint the stressors fairly accurately without offending anyone and with some consistency over terms, descriptions etc. A specially designed questionnaire is probably the most appropriate mechanism. A well established instrument, such as DION (Elliott-Kemp and Williams 1980), could be used to identify areas which are causing concern and 'hot spots' which require immediate attention. Alternatively, a more informal questionnaire (see below) could, for example, contain statements with which each person could agree or disagree. A calculation of agreement/disagreement with the listed stressors could then take place in order to shed light on common stressors.

ANYTOWN SCHOOL

Questionnaire to be completed by individuals by ticking the appropriate column:

*Organisational structure*

| | Agree | Disagree |
|---|---|---|
| 1. New regulations frequently require me to change the way I do things. | | |
| 2. My school is very hierarchical. | | |
| etc. | | |

Individuals' responses could be summarised and an average produced for the school as a whole, although averaging in a large organisation may result in distortion of certain problems which are concentrated in only one part of the organisation.

Analysis of the data would identify the core and marginal issues in creating stress and this would help to give focus to the stress-reduction programme. The major areas of concern across the organisation could be tackled on a collaborative (organisation or group) basis, although individual variations from this norm would still need recognition and attention, for example, by individual counselling.

## *Stage B — planning: generating alternative solutions*

The first stage in dealing with common problems would ideally take the form of some sort of open forum/discussion/brainstorming session, perhaps led by an outsider such as a counsellor or educational psychologist. This has the advantages of:

using that person's skills
depersonalising some of the more contentious issues
providing a less preconceived view of things.

Alternatively, or as an extension to this, a planning team could generate solutions and propose strategies which could be implemented by individuals or the organisation. The sharing of strategies and expertise in coping can solve the problems of individuals and bring about greater cohesiveness in the organisation.

As indicated in Figure 7.3, the strategies can be divided into four categories and each of these will be examined in turn.

### 1. LESSEN THE DEMANDS

This direct approach to handling stress is the most practical and the easiest to understand. The actual cause of stress is reduced or removed and the results are clearly seen by the individual and throughout the organisation. Many of the strategies which could be employed are detailed in the next chapter.

Briefly, individuals should be helped to plan their work and to prioritise so that the most essential tasks are not overlooked. There should be more readiness to delegate, especially to others with time and expertise, and to say 'no' rather than take on too much work. Although the literature on stress suggests that only one task should be tackled at once, the author feels that, because of the complexity of roles, this would not always be practicable for teachers. At the whole school level, the establishment of realistic goals will ensure that they are attainable and staff will feel less frustrated than if there is a sense of working hard and never actually reaching the goals. Administrative procedures should be designed to suit the particular school and to support the staff in their work, rather than be based on an LEA-wide model.

There is considerable scope for a school-wide review of structures and responsibilities in order to meet changing demands in the most effective way. This may involve the redefinition of job descriptions, changes to teaching groups, the use of non-teaching assistants etc. If lack of resources (money, time, expertise etc) seems to be the root cause of the problem, this should be discussed and taken into account when planning the budget.

If the demands can be lessened there will be more time for implementing the stress-reduction strategies described in the next section.

## 2. REDUCE THE REACTION TO STRESS

This involves the use of techniques which moderate the perception of threat, not by tackling the cause but by overcoming the response. Chivers (1989) has evidence that:

> many gifted and experienced teachers are adopting personally and professionally detrimental strategies. Increased smoking, alcohol dependence or over-use . . . are all serious problems for teachers.

The aim must be to avoid such props and to seek palliative action which is not detrimental to health in the long term. Behaviour must be modified so that the individual becomes less aggressive and more able to accept crises philosophically. Approaches to raising the stress threshold can be grouped together and most of the ideas will be put into practice at the individual level, although the school may be involved in a facilitating role. Those under stress should consider adopting some of the following:

(i) Improve the diet — eat regular, healthy meals which are not too heavy; cut down on artificial stimulants such as tea, coffee and use herbal remedies instead; drink less alcohol. Relax before a meal as this prevents overeating.

(ii) Practise relaxation techniques — the art of 'letting go' — physically and mentally. This can cover simple activities like stretching, shaking, and breathing techniques, e.g. deep breathing and slow exhalation or counting to 20 when stressed. Schools can help by providing a quiet room for staff.

(iii) Practise *yoga* which teaches mental and physical control, increasing one's awareness or the inner self, or *meditation* which relaxes the mind, increasing awareness of self and potential, lowers blood pressure and decreases breathing rate. *Visualisation* (calling briefly to mind a pleasant scene) can allow control to be regained during a stressful incident, for example, a heated conversation.

(iv) Take regular exercise which releases pent up energy and improves the efficiency of the body; teachers may feel that they do quite enough of this during the school day but if it is to relieve tension, the exercise needs to be removed from the job, e.g. swimming or jogging.

(v) Develop creative rather than competitive hobbies and take an annual break from routine and the usual environment. Most teachers follow the latter piece of advice during the summer but, because of the nature of the job, they should also allow themselves a break at half-terms whereas many are involved in school trips or simply in 'catching-up' at this time.

An individual should learn to recognise his/her own stress situations and then be able to relax in order to cope. A mixture of physical and cultural activities is known to be stress-relieving but it is best if such activities take place on a regular basis and are adopted from an early age.

### 3. IMPROVE STRESS MANAGEMENT SKILLS

Staff can become better able to deal with stress if they enhance their skills in relating to others. Instead of just talking *at* colleagues, it is important to *listen* to what *they* have to say. If people can relate well to each other, they can function as groups and, through effective teamwork, develop mutual support systems. These skills, and the opportunity to benefit from them, will arise from the implementation of appraisal-led staff development.

In the case study school (see pp. 121/123) *synectics* was used as a means of sharing problems and attempting to generate solutions. This is a form of brainstorming combined with creative thinking which, briefly, involves the following:

(i) The 'owner' airs a problem, explaining its background.
(ii) The other members of the group note the situation and then generate a large number of possible solutions (all prefaced by 'I wish' or 'How to') which the 'owner' might consider. The important point is that all suggestions should be accepted and written on a board. No one should be made to believe that an idea is 'silly' as there may be the germ of a solution there.
(iii) From about 30 possible solutions, the 'owner' selects two or three for further exploration and then scores the most appropriate 'actionable idea', giving marks out of 10 for newness, appeal and feasibility (the NAF rating). An idea which scores eight or more in each of the three areas has potential.

There are various other ways to improve stress management skills:

- relax over meals and talk to friends and colleagues (not just about work) as this helps relationships as well as helping the body to reduce its reaction to stress
- get up earlier so that there is less rush; it is possible to be relaxed and to eat a meal
- adopt practical coping skills, for example when tired decide to organise things later when refreshed
- practise compartmentalisation, i.e. shutting off one aspect of life (which may be causing a problem) when dealing with another
- learn to prioritise and pace activities.

4. CHANGE ATTITUDES

A school which takes a collaborative look at stress has already begun to adopt a changed attitude to it. People are given encouragement to express their feelings with the minimum of embarrassment and without the bitterness or aggression which can accompany frustration. Just talking over a problem can help people to cope with stress, particularly when it originates outside the school and there is little which can be done to remove the cause.

*Ad hoc* or structured counselling (e.g. as part of appraisal-led staff development) may demonstrate that a person is particularly unhappy in his/her job and this may highlight the need for an internal change of role/responsibility or for a move to a different school or even outside teaching.

Gray and Freeman (1988), when discussing how colleagues can be supported, mention the value of humour. Because laughter relieves tension people should be helped to see the funny side of a stressful situation so that they rationalise the problem. There is a tendency, especially when under pressure, to worry over trivia. Not all problems are as serious as people think, and keeping a sense of proportion helps ourselves and each other. It is better if people accept in a relaxed way that certain things cannot be changed or controlled.

There is a need to consider the relative importance of being busy and successful or of being happy and to concentrate on the present rather than dwelling on the past or living for the future.

## *Stage C — implementing the plans*

The preceding sections should have demonstrated to the reader that there is a wide variety of strategies or combinations of strategies which can be adopted by individuals, groups or the organisation as a whole. The most appropriate strategies and means of operationalising them need to be chosen to suit the situation, with the aim of helping staff to take responsibility for their own lives and to solve their own problems (collaboratively if that is best). Staff may wish to consider the following as organisation-wide possibilities for tackling the stress problem:

- training day for whole staff
- on-going INSET work
- use of the Educational Psychologist, e.g. for counselling and group skills
- intervisiting (within or between schools)
- development of practical skill, e.g. through course on management or stress
- counselling, appraisal, staff development
- change in organisational structure/responsibilities/administration
- change of resource use through LMS

If the 'training day' approach is chosen, it is important to appreciate that stress reduction is an on-going process and therefore some follow-up will be necessary.

Sometimes a minor change can have a very beneficial effect. Wilce (TES 26 May 1989) reports that one primary head realised the importance to classroom teachers of a break from the children and the chance to relax with colleagues so she took over some of the break duties. This type of approach is particularly relevant in small schools where the burden of duties falls heavily on all staff.

In general, though, management of stress at the whole school level requires that the strategies are applied at a *macro* rather than a *micro* level. Effective prioritising and planning will filter out the less immediate tasks so that these can be picked up at a later date. This particular strategy was employed extensively by classroom teachers in the early stages of National Curriculum implementation when most other developments were subordinated by the need to alter the content of the curriculum.

### *Stage D — evaluating the activities*

Any activity should be evaluated in order to consider its effectiveness. While the results of a stress reduction programme should be apparent in increased organisational effectiveness, a more formal evaluation is possible. This will particularly be the case if a questionnaire approach was used at the outset; it can be repeated at a later stage and used for comparison. However, one note of caution — staff's increased awareness of stress as a result of the programme could distort their replies.

The outcome of a successful programme should be that problems are seen in a better perspective. Individuals should feel that they have retaken control of their lives and that they are able to make constructive decisions about their work. It is to be hoped that the coping strategies which are employed do actually bring about stress reduction, otherwise people will feel a sense of failure and be even more aware of their inability to cope with pressure. The case study which follows is intended to show the practical application of the key elements discussed above.

## A case study — managing stress

The following case study describes the process of attempting to alleviate stress in a large urban primary school and it provides a framework which could be adapted by any school. Although its main focus is on the individual, whole school issues are allowed to surface and can be tackled in the subsequent weeks. The stages in the process are based on the principles described in chapter 3:

1. Recognition and analysis of the problem
2. Planning the aims, objectives, activities and evaluation

3. Implementation
4. Evaluation.

## 1. Recognition and analysis of the problem

The LEA recognised the existence of teacher stress and Educational Psychologists organised a series of awareness-raising courses for representatives from the schools. (An alternative scenario could be that those within a school notice the symptoms as on pp. 110/111.)

As a result of this course, two teachers from the case study school decided to try to alleviate the problems of stress in their school, proposing to devote a training day to the topic. Because of the possibly controversial and personal nature of the subject, they first consulted all their colleagues in a staff meeting in order to develop confidence in the idea. Although apprehensive, the staff indicated a willingness to participate in a series of activities which aimed to provide positive advice for individuals and for the school.

Before setting objectives for the day, the planners needed to identify priorities by investigating the existing individual and organisational stressors. They achieved this by distributing a questionnaire to colleagues, asking a variety of questions which, when analysed, put the stressors into the rank order illustrated.

| | |
|---|---|
| Work overload<br>Environmental<br>Role conflict<br>Job ambiguity | *average scores above 50 per cent* |
| Managing people<br>Personal<br>Organisational structure<br>Interpersonal<br>Work underload | *average scores below 50 per cent* |

## 2. Planning

Having identified aims and priorities, the following objectives were developed for the day:

(i) to provide a pleasant and relaxed atmosphere so that staff could derive maximum benefit from their experiences;
(ii) to help individual staff and groups to minimise the problems of work overload;
(iii) to provide a forum for the airing of concerns such as the poor physical environment, the problems of role conflict and job ambiguity;
(iv) to provide a mechanism for evaluating the day and its subsequent impact.

The programme for the day was planned on the following lines:

relaxation techniques
time management
problem solving using synectics (see p. 119)
personal plans
evaluation

## 3. *Implementation*

Lack of funds prevented the organisers from achieving the first objective as they had wished (by using a teachers' centre) so they rearranged the school library, introducing flowers and relaxing music at the start of the day. Many staff had been worried about taking part in the relaxation techniques but found that they were not embarrassing, rather that they were soothing and calming.

The session on time management covered analysis and present use of time, and suggested ways in which this could be improved. Some of these ideas are discussed in the next chapter.

Micropolitical problems and changes in senior management meant that it was difficult to tackle some of the priorities in a direct way, so it was decided that staff should be introduced to synectics beforehand so that they could identify problems for airing on the training day. It was felt that this new approach to problem solving would be beneficial because time-wasting in meetings, accommodation problems, lack of role clarity etc. could all be tackled in this way. On the training day the staff divided into two groups for the synectics session and, in each case, many valuable ideas were put forward. However, the author felt that the most important outcome of this session was not the ideas generated, but the increased openness and sharing of problems amongst the staff. This would have many future benefits within the school.

The final sessions on personal plans and evaluation were fairly brief. Staff were left with forms which would help them to assimilate the day's experiences and to plan a stress reduction strategy for the future.

## 4. *Evaluation*

The evaluation of the day's activities produced a very encouraging response from the staff who, despite initial worries, found that they had had a worthwhile day. The organisers planned to reassess the levels and causes of stress in the school six months after the training day to see if it had any longer-term benefit. Their final evaluation may not, however, pick up the more general benefit of an increasingly open, supportive atmosphere in the school.

## Conclusion

This chapter has looked at the important area of managing stress. Its significance can be seen if one considers that effective resource management and curriculum management are only possible in an environment where individuals can cope and adapt to changed policies and respond to them effectively. Two aspects of stress management have been put forward. The first is at the individual level where self-awareness and self-discipline are improved. The second is at the level of the whole school where key strategies are applied to wider staff and pupil activities. This latter approach may involve considerable change within the school so that there is a new management culture and an improved climate.

## References

Chivers, J. 1989 'Challenging Response', *Times Educational Supplement*, 16 June

Coates, T. J. & Thoresen, C. E. 1976 'Teacher Anxiety: a review with recommendations' *Review of Educational Research* Vol. 46 No. 2

Elliott-Kemp, J. & Williams, G. L. 1980 *The DION Handbook*, Sheffield City Polytechnic

Friedman, M. & Rosenman 1974 *Type A Behaviour and Your Heart*, Knopf

Gray, H. & Freeman, A. 1988 *Teaching Without Stress*, PCP

Kyriacou, C. 1987 'Teacher Stress and Burnout: an international review', *Educational Research* Vol. 29 No. 2

Kyriacou, C. & Sutcliffe, J. 1978 'A Model of Teacher Stress', *Educational Studies* Vol. 4 No. 1 March

Rees, F. 1989 *Teacher Stress: An Exploratory Study*, NFER

Wilce, H. 1989 'Taking the Strain' *Times Educational Supplement* 26 May

# 8 Effective time management

## Linda Ellison

The case study towards the end of chapter 7 reflects national research which identifies lack of time in relation to workload as a major stressor in schools today. The concern is not only directed at teachers, but at the need to make more creative use of pupil time so as to deliver a broad curriculum within tight time constraints. This chapter develops a model of the time management process which begins by considering the existing use of time and then looks at a variety of ways in which time may be deployed more effectively. This should allow schools and individuals to reduce levels of stress and to increase organisational effectiveness.

Drucker (1970 p. 26) emphasises the importance of time:

> Time is also a unique resource . . . one cannot rent, hire, buy or otherwise obtain more time. The supply of time is totally inelastic. No matter how high the demand, the supply will not go up . . . time is totally perishable and cannot be stored. Yesterday's time is gone forever and will never come back. Time is, therefore in exceedingly short supply.

Although much attention is given to this topic in business management training, it is an issue which is often ignored in education. The main reason for this is the fact that the dual role of the teacher/manager (in whatever proportion, at whatever level) means that there is 'no time for management' (Handy 1984 p. 18). This implies that there is no spare time in which to fulfil one's management role and, indeed, many teachers see this role as a minor inconvenience. Because there is so little time to be managed, it is of paramount importance that any which is available should be used to best advantage. An additional constraint is that schools and, indeed, people in the community, have deeply entrenched, traditional views of the timing of the school day and of the divisions within it, especially at secondary level. It may be that one of the keys to improved time management in the schools of the 1990s lies in questioning the validity of such views, and that by attacking the problem at the whole school level, we can resolve the individuals' problems.

Drucker (1970) has observed that effective managers start by finding out how they use time and then they manage it, aggregating 'spare' time into usable blocks. The time management process can be seen to comprise four stages:

recording
analysing
managing
consolidating

each of which will be examined below.

## Recording the use of time

Before deciding how to improve the use of time, it is essential to consider present use. This can help to identify tasks or times of the day on which to focus. Teachers may well find it valuable to examine the whole day rather than the working day as this will give a truer picture of the way in which their burdens cross the home/school boundary.

The method chosen to record use of time will vary according to the roles and responsibilities of the individual. It is probably most effective if a rough outline is drafted, tried and then rewritten to find the most useful format. The following may be included:

time of day
task
who originated the task?
was it prescribed (fixed/compulsory), e.g. teaching at 11.00
or discretionary (voluntary/movable), e.g. tidying the filing cabinet at 12.30?
how long did it take?

Some people consider that to record everything is a waste of time, particularly in education where there is so little discretionary time. It can be more effective to concentrate on a particular problem which seems to be consuming a lot of time, such as pupil record-keeping. Other general points to bear in mind are:

- recording should be done daily for at least a week to gain a true picture
- a 'typical' week should be chosen, not the end of term or examination time (unless specifically looking at this)
- recording should be done regularly throughout the day, otherwise accuracy is lost
- there may be a need for a 'shadow' to do the recording — this is not always feasible but could be applied to a limited part of the day and there may also be a possibility of having one's use of time observed as part of the appraisal process
- it helps if specific note is made of timewasting/ unproductive activities.

Broader school issues could be examined such as the amount of time spent in meetings and the involvement of those present. Legislation requires some schools to record the use of pupils' time in respect of the national curriculum, but an occasional look at their day may reveal disproportionate amounts of time being spent, for example, on moving around the buildings.

## Analysing the use of time

Once the use of time has been recorded, it will be evident that, for the majority of teachers, much of the school day is spent carrying out prescribed activities such as teaching, registration and duties. Closer investigation of some of these activities may indicate that elements contained within them do not make the best use of time. Any discretionary time which might usefully be managed is found to be scattered throughout the day in small pockets, for example before school, breaks, lunchtime and possibly some 'non-contact' time.

The individual should begin by considering his/her job description and identifying the important responsibilities. The following questions can then be asked:

1. was the activity really necessary or could the time be better spent?
2. how successful was the outcome and are there any habitual failures?
3. how much time was spent on each of the various types of work — 'must do', 'should do', 'could do' (least important duties)?
4. where did the work come from?
   is a superior delegating too much?
   are subordinates too dependent?
   are you setting yourself too many tasks?
5. could the task be delegated?
   if yes, to whom?
   if no, why not? is it your job?
   have you made yourself indispensable?
6. was the activity planned or was it an interruption? Could it have been planned?

The author's work with teachers suggests that the following are seen to consume a disproportionate amount of time:

photocopying
trying to contact people by telephone
dealing with other teachers' discipline problems
attending poorly thought-out meetings
trying to gather management information
poor communication
reading documents especially from the LEA/DES, especially at head/deputy level and in times of great change
having to carry out routine tasks because of lack of support staff.

This highlights another contrast with the business world where research shows that frequently cited timewasters include drop-in visitors and talking on the telephone, although there are similarities such as the inability to say 'no'.

Having analysed the use of time, it will be possible to see the unproductive demands on time and these should point to what might be done by the individual or the organisation. A positive approach to managing this valuable resource can then be developed.

## Managing the use of time

Having completed the diagnosis stage, one should have some idea of which activities take a disproportionate amount of time and it would be expedient to focus on one or two of these as a first step. It is generally recognised that 80 per cent of our time is spent achieving 20 per cent of our results so, when considering how to manage time better, we should be aiming to achieve more by doing less, reflecting the view of Mackenzie (1972) that 'working smarter, not harder, is the real goal of effective management.' Possible objectives may include:

- to increase efficiency when reading documents
- to increase the opportunities for delegation
- to reorganise information systems to improve communication and decision making
- to create more time for planning and, thus, avoid crisis management
- to make meetings more worthwhile
- to allow more creativity in the use of pupil time.

Because so much of the school day involves prescribed activities, attention may fall on the use of breaks or the lunch hour. This would contrast with industry/commerce where such time would probably be considered to be outside the brief.

Figure 8.1 suggests a variety of approaches which may be adopted in order to improve the use of both 'directed' and 'discretionary' time for the individual and the organisation. A combination of approaches will usually be the most appropriate.

### *1. Developing and using basic skills*

These approaches to time management will be put into practice at the individual level.

#### (i) EFFICIENT READING

One of the stressors identified in schools is the time taken to read the large number of detailed documents which are received, particularly since schools have had increased responsibility delegated

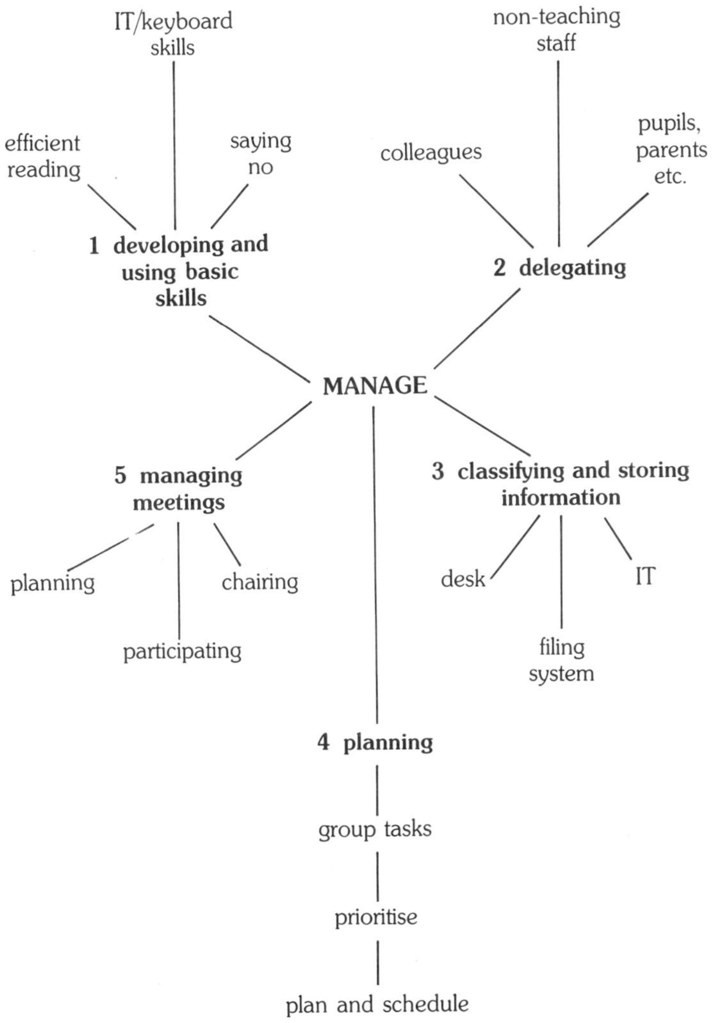


*Figure 8.1: approaches to managing the use of time*

to them. Inefficient reading can be caused by any of the following (or a combination of them):

reading word-for-word, whereas it should be done in a meaningful way
regression, i.e. allowing the eye to move backwards as well as forwards along a line of text
sub-vocalisation, i.e. saying the words silently while reading them.

Speed reading techniques can be developed such as:

scanning — to decide if the document is relevant, can be delegated or is for the bin
skimming — identifying the main sentence of each paragraph (usually the first or last) and using side headings.

It is far more effective to set aside short periods, e.g. 15 minutes when concentration will be high, rather than trying (and failing) to understand something which is read when there are distractions. Often the task of dealing with documents could be delegated to others, especially if structural changes are made in the school to facilitate this.

(ii) IT/KEYBOARD SKILLS

Many teachers have developed keyboard skills and the ability to use a microcomputer/wordprocessor. This is largely because of a lack of ancillary support and a desire to produce materials specifically tailored to their pupils. In particular, the ability to amend a document, i.e. to understand how to use a wordprocessing package, can be a great time-saver. However, it would often be a far better use of the school's resources if a clerical assistant were to do the original keyboard work.

While we acknowledge the use of computers throughout the school as a teaching aid, many people have not yet developed the ability to use them as aids to management and administration. As with curricular use, this does not require programming skills, but, simply, an understanding of the way in which software packages can store, manipulate and retrieve information for the individual teacher or for the whole school. Carefully used, IT can alleviate many of the time-linked stressors in the school. Alternatively, if it is badly applied there can be vast quantities of paperwork generated, increasing the workload with no corresponding increase in school effectiveness.

(iii) SAYING 'NO'

Many teachers admit to finding it difficult to say 'No', especially to requests from pupils or to carry out voluntary activities. The following reasons are often given for saying 'yes' when the answer should, realistically, be 'no'.

having unclear priorities
a fear of offending others
the need to be a 'good guy'
hoping to make others feel indebted to you
a desire to please superiors
the need to obtain a good reference in the future.

It should be possible to learn to say 'no', especially if one remembers that it is the way in which something is said, not just what is said, that matters. Four steps to saying 'no' are suggested here:

(a) Listen to ensure that you understand what is being requested
(b) Give a definite 'no' rather than 'maybe/perhaps'
(c) If it is appropriate, explain the reasons for your refusal
(d) If possible, suggest alternative strategies.

Failure to say 'no' to an unreasonable request may actually demonstrate weakness and cause loss of respect, rather than pleasing someone.

## 2. *Delegating*

In the business world it is accepted good practice that managers should be managing rather than carrying out menial tasks. In education there is greater role ambiguity, largely because of the dual role of teacher and manager. It is quite common to see a deputy head of a large secondary school collating and stapling hundreds of newsletters or arranging furniture. Under LMS schools have greater flexibility over staffing and it should be possible to make more effective use of time and money by employing non-teaching assistants to carry out routine clerical or technical work.

Various excuses are given for failing to delegate:

no-one else will do the job as well
it takes too long to explain it to someone else
everyone else is too busy
there isn't anyone else to whom it could be delegated
there is a need to remain responsible and accountable.

There are many reasons why delegation to colleagues can be beneficial in an organisation. There is often someone who is better able to do the job than oneself or, if not, it can form part of a staff development process and enable someone else to cope in a crisis. Delegation also helps to motivate people by giving them challenging tasks as well as mundane ones. Waters (1987) refers to the difficulties (especially in terms of staff development) experienced by primary school deputy heads when the heads do not delegate but, because of the vast increase in responsibilities which they now face, the benefits of delegation should become more apparent.

When delegating a task, the lines of accountability and responsibility must be clear and it is important to delegate the right to make mistakes. Both parties should be aware of:

(a) which items need to be *referred back up* to the delegator *before* a decision is taken;

(b) which items need to be referred back up to the delegator *after* a decision is taken;
(c) which items need *not* be referred at all;
(d) which items may be *delegated further*.

Delegation of responsibility is not limited to colleagues, but can be applied by encouraging pupils to be responsible for classroom equipment and for managing their own learning. Parents are often willing to help and, here again, care is needed so that they feel valued and are not just asked to carry out mundane jobs.

## *3. Classifying and storing information*

Chapter 2 referred to the importance of information but if this is to be of value it must be easy to find. Unfortunately the plethora of notes, documents, books etc. which a teacher receives often end up in one large pile. Mackenzie (1972) explains that 'we stack our desks with all the things we do not want to forget, but when we look at them we risk becoming sidetracked . . .'. A desk should be a place to process work, not to store it. It is the author's contention that every teacher is a manager and deserves a desk on which to work and at least part of a suitable filing system for personal use. Too many teachers are expected to operate effectively from a locker and the top of a cupboard or coffee table.

Teachers tend to hoard all sorts of things in case they are ever useful (and often they would be, if they could be found). However, paperwork clogs up the system so it is important to be ruthless and to discard or delegate as much as possible.

Each person needs to decide how to classify the important items which are received. One model offered would include boxes or files for each of the following:

IN
OUT
DO TODAY
DO THIS WEEK
TO BE FILED
FOLLOW UP (file according to when)
PROJECTS (labelled folders — leave in until needed)

Because the reading of documents is recognised as a very time-consuming activity in schools, it is important to try and generate as little paperwork as possible. This can be achieved in a variety of ways:

replying to memos by writing on them
using IT to make information accessible to those who wish to receive it but not overloading those who do not want it

using 'Plain English', lists, summaries and the underlining of keywords to improve readability
marking amendments clearly when re-issuing documents.

## 4. *Planning*

Managers must ensure that planning and target-setting at the whole school level (as discussed in chapter 3) takes account of priorities and available resources, including time and staff goodwill. There is also considerable scope for improving the way in which individuals formulate their shorter-term plans.

In order to manage time effectively, it is necessary to draw up a list of tasks and projects, attempting to group them in a meaningful way. At the individual level such lists will probably be compiled on a weekly and daily basis with the latter, by virtue of immediacy, being more detailed and less flexible. Priorities need to be considered and the standard approach is to classify tasks as follows:

Priority A —those things which must be done
Priority B —those things which should be done
Priority C —those things which could be done, i.e. which we would like to do

The next stage is to decide what needs to be done, when and by whom. It may well be feasible to delegate some of the tasks, especially the more routine aspects of category A, in order to create time for development. Having produced a list of tasks, it is now possible to plan and schedule. The aims should be to produce plans which can be adapted if circumstances change and to spend as much time as possible on activities which lead to goal achievement.

There are many personal planning aids available for purchase or suggested in the literature on time management (see for example Noon 1983, Garratt 1985). These may be inappropriate in schools because of their emphasis on appointments throughout the day but teachers could adapt them and include appropriate categories such as 'write to', 'short task' and 'don't forget'.

While deciding how best to plan the use of time, it is important to bear in mind the points which emerged from the diagnosis of the current use of time and attempt to devise a system which can help to remedy the weaknesses. It is good for morale to start the day or term with a task or project where maximum results can be achieved fairly easily and then to move on to those tasks on which one seems to spend a lot of time, yet sees few results. Particular consideration should be given as to when and where it is possible to achieve the most effective span of concentration. One of the problems in schools is that important matters, such as meetings, are left until the end of the day when a block of time is available but when staff are tired.

## 5. *Managing meetings*

The effective use of meetings is a prerequisite of effective time management in schools. Purposeful, 'limited time' meetings which achieve objectives can increase motivation and commitment whereas long, unstructured, time-wasting meetings can demotivate staff and increase stress.

Holding meetings is just one of the many ways in which members of a school communicate so that they are all working effectively towards its goals. Meetings are often informal, held over coffee in a staff room or departmental office but, nevertheless, they can still fulfil their purpose and act as a mechanism for consultation and the generation of ideas.

With the concept of 'directed time' it is now possible for senior management to require teachers to attend meetings outside the teaching day and this has often resulted in a more formalised meetings pattern. Benefits are seen because full attendance is assured so that everyone is well aware of developments but, sometimes, meetings are being held as a matter of routine, with little thought given to their purpose or composition.

The following sections are in the form of checklists to facilitate good practice, both for those who organise meetings and for the participants. They cover the types of meetings which might occur during the school year, the criteria for success and the causes of failure.

### (i) CLASSIFICATION OF MEETINGS

The type of meeting determines its size and composition as well as the way in which it is conducted. The categorisation shown may be helpful when planning a meeting.

| *Type* | | *Features* |
|---|---|---|
| 1. Informing, briefing, exchanging information | 'tells' | these meetings can be very large, yet still effective; they usually take the form of 'presentations' |
| 2. Persuading | 'sells' | |
| 3. Problem-solving, collect views, generate ideas, brainstorm | 'consults' | these tend to be more effective if there is a smaller group involved, preferably not more than twelve; they usually involve sitting round in 'boardroom' style |
| 4. Deciding | 'involves' in decision making | |

Quite often there will be a mixed agenda, involving elements of all four types, although problem solving and decision making with large groups may well result in very poor use of many people's time. It is also difficult to switch from one type of meeting to another unless there is a break, for example for coffee.

Participants in a meeting should be aware of the type of meeting in advance. This may not always be clear from the agenda. For example, an item such as 'allocation of teachers to classrooms' does not make it clear whether this allocation is to be discussed or whether the allocations have been decided and are to be announced. Such lack of understanding may result in participants wasting time preparing points for discussion when there is to be no debate. Conversely, if staff do not realise that an issue is for debate, they may not have the necessary information ready so as to present and substantiate their arguments.

### (ii) EFFECTIVE MEETINGS

Successful meetings usually have certain characteristics in common. They have a distinct purpose, they involve communication and there is a controlled situation. The right people are present and the timing is right in terms of frequency, start and finish. On the other hand, failure of a meeting to make best use of time or to achieve its purpose is usually the result of one of the following:

- too many meetings held
- unclear purpose or lack of purpose
- agenda badly prepared — order wrong
- unclear agenda or late agenda — participants therefore not prepared
- late start, meeting too long or too short
- time not divided carefully, therefore urgent/important matters not given priority/adequate consideration
- agenda not kept to, uncontrolled – side discussion etc., repetition
- interruptions
- lack of balance of skills, wrong people there — key person missing/too many people
- uninformed chair
- indecision, lack of conclusions
- unminuted, therefore decisions are unclear, not communicated, not carried out
- poor minutes or too late after event
- lack of follow-up.

Figure 8.2 provides a checklist to assist the chair and participants of meetings. Greater detail can be found in a wide variety of books which have been written on the subject (see for example Warwick 1982, Allan 1989 ch. 9), most of which are intended as general management texts but are directly applicable to management in education.

| AS CHAIR | AS A PARTICIPANT |
|---|---|
| *Before the meeting* | |
| 1. Set the objectives i.e. decide what is to be achieved. | 1. Read the agenda and consider whether you have anything to add. |
| 2. Check that a meeting is the best way to achieve this. | 2. Brief yourself, collecting opinions and documentation which may be required. Consider the arguments and alternatives which you might put forward. |
| 3. Be clear about what sort of meeting it is to be. | 3. Be prompt. |
| 4. Draw up the agenda, listing each item unambiguously. It should tell people why they are to be there and be a plan of the meeting time. | |
| 5. Decide who should attend. Beware of having too many present or having the key person missing. Numbers can be kept down by receiving reports from working parties and by attendance for only part of the meeting. | |
| 6. Decide when and where to hold the meeting. Start and finish times should be clear. Consider the most effective time of the week. | |
| 7. Send out the agenda in good time. | |
| 8. Brief someone to take the minutes. | |
| 9. Brief yourself thoroughly on the issues to be discussed. Collect the necessary documentation and background information which may be required. Work out approximate time limits for each item on the agenda so as to reflect priorities. | |

*Figure 8.2: meetings checklist*

| AS CHAIR | AS A PARTICIPANT |
|---|---|
| *During the meeting* | |
| 1. Start promptly, follow the agenda, keep to time and finish on time.<br>2. Avoid a hidden agenda.<br>3. Control the meeting — do not allow sidetracking, side discussions or over-domination by certain individuals.<br>4. Listen carefully and summarise at intervals so that everyone is clear about what is intended.<br>5. Do not allow AOB to become more than a few very quick points. | 1. Listen to what others have to say.<br>2. Be concise when speaking.<br>3. Do not become side-tracked or involved in side discussions. Avoid a hidden agenda.<br>4. Stick to the agenda.<br>5. Be supportive and positive, rather than destructive and critical.<br>6. Keep a note of any follow-up which is required of you. |
| *After the meeting* | |
| 1. Ensure that accurate minutes are sent out as soon as possible and displayed for other interested parties, e.g. the whole staff.<br>2. Take any action which you agreed to take.<br>3. Evaluate the organisation and operation of the meeting. | 1. If appropriate, inform your team of the issues and outcome of the meeting and make the minutes available to them.<br>2. Check that you carry out any actions which you agreed to carry out and that you take action according to the minutes. |

Fig. 8.2 (cont'd)

The main activities can be summarised as:

| | |
|---|---|
| Before the meeting | Planning<br>Pre-notification<br>Preparation |
| During the meeting | Processing |
| After the meeting | Putting 'actions' into practice |

## Consolidating the use of time

The aim should be to consolidate discretionary time into the largest possible continuing units so that worthwhile tasks can be carried out. For senior management this may mean an increased emphasis on diary management as there is a tendency to fit appointments round those requiring them giving fragmentation of one's time. Because of the large number of prescribed 'slots', it is difficult for most teachers to group their discretionary time in this way. Secondary schools may wish to give greater consideration to grouping non-teaching periods so as to provide worthwhile blocks. The desirability of non-contact time for primary teachers has, at last, been realised and, in many schools, LMS can provide the opportunity to adjust the staffing in order to facilitate this. It is possible to go even further than the ideas put forward here. Osborne (1986) believes that there is even greater scope if pupil groups are kept large and time is blocked, delegating to groups of staff the power to manage those pupils and that time and thus be creative.

## Conclusion

This chapter has made various proposals regarding the analysis and improved use of time in schools in order to increase effectiveness. Managers must apply them to the organisation as a whole and must facilitate their implementation by individuals. The following rules summarise the main ideas.

1. Have a 'flying start' — get going first thing with something which can be accomplished.
2. If the maximum amount of brain work is needed, carry out the task when at one's best.
3. Prioritise, putting off the less important tasks but do not put off important matters.
4. Learn to say 'No'.
5. Do it, delegate it or ditch it.
6. Collect all information in one accessible place.
7. Do things well enough — avoid exaggerated perfectionism.
8. Finish a job if possible.
9. Make a habit of completing a task which is over and above the daily routine.
10. Regularly check the use of time.

## References

Allan, J. 1989 *How to Develop Your Personal Management Skills*, Kogan Page

Drucker, P. 1970 *The Effective Executive*, Pan

Garratt, S. 1985 *Manage Your Time*, Fontana

Handy, C. 1984 *Taken for Granted? Understanding Schools as Organisations*, Longman
Mackenzie, R. A. 1972 *The Time Trap*, AMACON
Noon, J. 1983 *Time for Success*, ITPL
Osborne, A. 1986 'A Comprehensive Approach to the Management of Time' *School Organisation* Vol. 6 No. 2
Warwick, D. 1982 *Effective Meetings*, Education for the Industrial Society
Waters, D. 1987 'Delegation: The Big 'D' ' *Management in Education* Vol. 1 No. 2

# 9 Marketing schools

## Brent Davies and John West-Burnham

Every school has a reputation and that reputation has to be managed. All schools in the 1990s have to consider how they relate the service they provide to the needs of their clients. A great deal has been written about processes or techniques of marketing. This chapter seeks not to replicate these but to establish a management perspective on five key issues in marketing a school. It is hoped that the reader will then be able to apply them to analysing his/her own school marketing strategy. This chapter is divided into the following sections to achieve this:

1. What is marketing? — an overview
2. The who, what and why of marketing
3. The place of marketing in the organisation
4. The marketing cycle
5. Establishing a marketing culture in a school.

## 1. What is marketing? — an overview

Marketing as a management process is the most recent addition to the field of education management. Its rise in significance is largely attributable to the impact of the 1988 Education Act, introducing as it does the central notion of choice. If parents have a choice then schools will need to be more sensitive and responsive to them. These notions of sensitivity and responsiveness are the essence of marketing. The majority of effective schools have been operating a marketing strategy for years although the label has not always been used. Many of the components of marketing have been discussed in previous texts but usually in the academic and political context of accountability. This chapter argues for the professionalism of the ways in which schools manage their relationships with their clients.

There are two common misapprehensions about marketing, firstly, that it is synonymous with advertising and, secondly, that it is concerned with external relationships. Advertising is one possible outcome of a marketing strategy, however it is not that strategy. Equally, marketing is as much about internal as it is about external relationships. Marketing is about managing relationships through effective communication and, by definition, such communication is a two-way process. Any successful transaction is concerned with the achievement of mutually desired outcomes. It is equally important that the message is delivered consistently and that it is fundamental to internal working relationships. Marketing in education therefore involves diagnosing needs and values, developing appropriate responses and then ensuring that those responses are meeting the needs identified. Marketing is not just about 'selling a product'; it is about identifying the nature of the product required and ensuring that it is delivered and that every facet of the organisation contributes to the quality of the product.

Therefore, marketing is implicit in every component of effective management. It provides the basis for integrating schools' aims, the data for planning and decision making, the criteria for resource allocation and thereby the budget. It will also inform staff selection criteria and help to generate training and development programmes. Equally, marketing will serve to focus monitoring and evaluation procedures. Marketing is implicit in effective management because if effectiveness is about the attainment of goals then marketing helps to ensure that the 'right' goals are being pursued, identifies the extent to which goals are attained and is as much concerned with the processes involved as the outcomes.

It can be stated that marketing is about conformity to client needs. In the context of schools it means the systematic analysis of those needs, the development of strategies to meet them and the deployment of resources to allow such strategies to be implemented effectively. Like all management techniques, marketing is about action but it is specifically about deciding direction and being capable of responding to changing needs. Glossy advertising and good public relations techniques are peripheral outcomes of marketing, skills which have to be based on professional integrity.

Marketing relationships are extremely complex and multi-dimensional. It is not just a matter of the 'school and its environment'. The possible permutations are substantial but may include the following: senior management team and teaching staff, teaching and non-teaching staff, school staff and governing body, staff and pupils, school and parents, school and employers, higher education, etc., school and external agencies, school and LEA. Each of these relationships is distinct, each has its own marketing needs and procedures; all are interdependent in order to achieve their desired outcomes. Each relationship, to be successful, depends upon effective communication and the analysis and meeting of needs.

Most commercial organisations have few problems in identifying the customer/client and the product. For service industries, and education in particular, the issue is more acute notably in the context of defining both the client and the product let alone securing agreement as to the nature of outcomes. These issues will now be explored and developed in more detail in the succeeding sections.

## 2. The who, what and why of marketing

This section looks at three questions about marketing schools:

(i) WHO are the clients the school is marketing to?
(ii) WHAT is the school marketing?
(iii) WHY is the school marketing?

It is hoped that the reader will reflect on these basic questions before becoming involved in the 'technique' side of marketing in terms of brochures and publicity handouts.

### *(i) Who are the clients the school is marketing to?*

This presents a difficult problem of definition and prioritising for the school. In the primary school most teachers would consider that the pupils are the clients and, therefore, the first priority of the teacher. Secondary teachers often consider that the parents are the clients and that they are responsible/accountable to them. There is also a responsibility to the wider community which funds the school through local business rates and the community charge.

However, the child/parent dimension of who is the client is the key one for schools to explore. The thrust of government action during the 1980s and the underpinning of the 1988 Education Reform Act is to reduce the power of monopoly suppliers and to put power in the hands of the consumers. This certainly has been true of a number of reforms, for example, the reform of trade union legislation. In the education service the legislative and other government action has definitely been to reduce the power of the suppliers of education — the teachers. This can be seen in terms of the very significant reduction in teacher control of the curriculum in favour of centrally determined and controlled developments in GCSE examining and, more latterly, the National Curriculum.

As was seen in chapter 4, one of the key elements in LMS is open enrolments. This gives the power to parents to send their child to the school of their choice, providing the school has the physical space to accommodate that child and the child meets any pre-existing entrance requirements, for example, religious affiliations. This choice depends on two crucial factors, firstly, that there are sufficient schools locally for the choice to be exercised and, secondly, that the parents have the resources (time and finance) to transport the child from the immediate catchment area school.

What impact does this have on a school? Certain schools will still retain a near monopoly position because if there are no other local schools conveniently available parents have no effective choice. The nature of the catchment area may also mean that, even where choice exists, the convenience of a local school may overcome broader educational factors. However, whether schools, because of their near monopoly position, are only affected at the margin or are in a much more competitive position, relating to the client is a prime factor in a school's success.

The younger the child the more dominant is the parent in making the choice of school. Children at the age of five exercise very little choice as to the school they attend. This is ironic as primary teachers often see the pupils as 'their children' and put their professional views as being of greater importance than those of the parents. Teachers' perceptions of this relationship often change when their own children go to school and they sit on the opposite side of the teacher's desk on parents' evenings. As children get older and attend secondary school and, more significantly, when they transfer to Sixth Form College, Tertiary or Further Education College, the pupils play a more dominant role in the choice process.

It would be wrong, however, to take the simplistic view that the parent is the client with an increasing role being undertaken by the child as he/she gets older. At stages the child and parent influence each other as to the value and esteem in which the school is held. When the child comes home and relates good or bad experiences about the school this influences parental opinion, and the parental response influences the child's perception of the school.

Viewing the parent/child as the client is not fudging the issue but is the fine balance which schools need to achieve in effective relationships with their customers. Schools do not exist to provide teachers with jobs; they exist to provide effective education to their clients. Reflecting on the changing importance, power and definition of who is the client/customer in education is the essential prerequisite for effective marketing of schools.

Outside the immediate consumer is a broader set of clients, the local community who fund the school and who are also significant in marketing terms.

## *(ii) What is the school marketing?*

That which follows will not be a discussion of the different values and attainments which a school puts across, such as examination results or sports achievements, important as these undoubtedly are. Instead it will consider whether the school is concerned with marketing perceptions or marketing reality. Another dimension of this can be expressed by asking if it is paying attention to overt or covert performance indicators.

Do the clients choose a school because of its examination results and other quantifiable factors like this? Certainly they are major factors but the reputation of a school is made up of a series of complex and inter-related factors. When a child is five the quality of education may not be assessed by the parents in any meaningful way. Overt factors such as test scores may not be as important as covert factors or perceptions. Wearing school uniform, which parents associate with good discipline, and the taking home of their reading books by five-year-olds, which parents associate with homework and academic standards, may be very significant. These determinants of the perceptions which parents have of the school may be more important than the reality of what is actually going on to deliver effective education. The reputation of many secondary schools may be enhanced by the overt reality of good staff/pupil relationships, high academic standards, etc. This reputation may be undone by the behaviour of pupils in the local town at lunchtime, smoking outside the school gates and the behaviour of pupils travelling to and returning from school on school buses.

A useful management exercise for school staff to undertake is to list the four strengths and weaknesses of the school as they perceive them. Secondly, drawing on the knowledge from the interaction they have with parents at parents' evenings, etc., to list the strengths and weaknesses as perceived by parents. The key management information comes in comparing the two lists. It is not the internal educationists who set the criteria; there may be significant factors in the perceptions of parents that determine the reputation of a school which have little to do with its core educational activities.

Schools, therefore, have to decide whether they are marketing a set of values which is taken for granted but ignoring a number of factors that parents perceive as being key indicators of a 'good' school. While the authors would not suggest that fundamental educational values are ignored at the expense of marketing pragmatism, it is vital that schools do not assume they know what parents want. It is important that if schools are to fulfil their educational mission, they address the concerns of their clients and respond to them. The only way to do this is to sample parental opinion to find out what they consider is significant and not to rely on the existing teacher perceptions based within the internal culture of the school.

### *(iii) Why is the school marketing itself?*

This can be summed up by stating that, in the modern world, 'virtue does not of necessity bring its own reward' while virtue with a good marketing strategy may! Whatever the good attributes of a school are they will not, of themselves, ensure continued success and survival unless the wider community understands, values and, above all, knows about them.

Marketing a school is basically a process of relating the school's aims, objectives and achievements to the needs and wishes of the community. This is the prime accountability dimension of marketing in an educational institution. This has been given tremendous power by the overt introduction of market forces through the 1988 Education Reform Act. In chapter 4, and earlier in this chapter, reference was made to LMS and, in particular, to two specific aspects of it; formula funding and open enrolments. As was seen in the diagram on p. 47, increasing or decreasing pupil numbers as a result of parents operating their power of choice under the open enrolment entitlement has, through the formula-funding mechanism, a direct effect on the financial viability of schools and, hence, on teachers jobs.

While the main reason that a school *should* be marketing is a desire to improve its service and relationship with its clients, the main reason why it *has* to market itself is that, in the 1990s, economic realities make this a precondition of its future survival.

## 3. The place of marketing in the organisation

It would be very easy for schools to appear to be responding to the need for marketing. As with all management activities it would be possible to establish roles and procedures which appear to indicate the acceptance of the principle. Thus the appointment of a member of staff with responsibility for 'marketing', the setting up of a working party, the introduction of the marketing approach outlined below and the production of professionally designed brochures might be interpreted as a school having come to terms with marketing. The reality will probably be completely different.

The messages and images projected by a marketing strategy need to be integral to all parts of the school and every individual must become a 'marketing manager'. The headteacher, teaching and non-teaching staff and every pupil are all essential components of the marketing 'team' and what they say and do will determine the impact of the school's message. In essence marketing is about managing an image and behaviour will always be a more important determinant of that image than statements and promises. The problem for schools to come to terms with is that, in managing their image in the community, they have to deal with subjective impressions and these are formulated on a selective basis which may have nothing to do with systems and designated roles. The work of the marketing manager can be totally undermined by one disaffected member of the school. The glossiest brochure can be negated by an incomprehensible letter, the finest art displays invalidated by an attack of graffiti.

For a marketing strategy to work it is therefore necessary to address fundamental issues about the school. In their study of successful British companies, McBurnie and Clutterbuck (1987) identify what they describe as the 'marketing edge' — the qualities which allow those companies to dominate in their respective sectors. They distil the special qualities of these companies into the '3 Cs' — culture, creativity and commitment; but permeating all three is responsiveness to the customer or client and it is therefore proposed to add a fourth 'C' — the client. Every organisation — company or school — is unique and there is no magic formula or panacea which can be taken 'off the shelf' and imposed. The crucial thing is that organisations evaluate themselves against these criteria and then formulate their own response which is appropriate to their history and context.

## *(i) Culture*

This is the least tangible and most problematic aspect of managing any organisation. However, if practical outcomes and activities are used as the basis for analysis then a number of factors emerge. The single most important determinant of the culture of any organisation is the quality of leadership. In essence, culture is a function of leadership and the qualities of the leader will be reflected throughout the organisation. This has been well documented in industry and commerce and, equally so, in education. The values, attitudes and behaviour of headteachers will be the crucial determinant in deciding the extent to which a school is able to project itself to its community.

Positive leadership will help to ensure that the single most important component of effective marketing — awareness of the primary function of the school — is continually at the forefront of all planning and decision making and is fundamental to all aspects of school life. This is in turn reflected in the clarity of a school's aims and objectives and the extent to which they are the basis for action and evaluation.

These values, aims and objectives are derived from a further important aspect of organisational culture — a sensitivity to the environment and a willingness to change in response to it. This in turn involves an openness and honesty in assessing strengths and weaknesses; the school is aware of and celebrates its strengths but is equally conscious of its weaknesses.

It is no coincidence that the principles identified above are very closely related to the notion of the changing school discussed in chapter 6. The first component of a successful marketing strategy is for the school to be clear and explicit about what it exists to do, for leadership to constantly reiterate that mission and to be constantly aware of changing needs and the school's ability to respond to them. Without such a culture a marketing strategy will be superficial, vulnerable and lacking integrity.

## *(ii) Creativity*

Creativity refers to the ability of any organisation to develop a unique, positive and effective response to changing circumstances which solves problems by improving services. One of the fundamental components of successful marketing in education is that schools are perceived as solving problems. In order to do this two qualities are required. The first is the ability to diagnose the components of any problem accurately and in response to the perceptions of those involved. The second is the ability to formulate imaginative responses which resolve the issue to the mutual satisfaction of those involved and yet do not become a new orthodoxy.

Marketing is therefore about anticipating changing needs, being sensitive to economic and social changes and preparing strategies which move the school forward. However, creative solutions need to be creatively communicated. One of the major weaknesses of many schools is that they have been able to generate highly effective responses to new challenges but these have failed because the creativity in managing the curriculum was not matched by creativity in communication. Schools often concentrate on the product to the detriment of the clients. Creativity is needed to develop the most appropriate means of informing clients about the validity of the product — working from their needs rather than assuming that all educational changes are coherent, understandable and self-legitimating.

## *(iii) Commitment*

Organisations which are successful in marketing their products and services set out to create commitment rather than simply assuming it by virtue of the employment contract. There is therefore an emphasis on communicating a constant reiteration of the values of the organisation and, crucially, the rationale behind them. All those involved in marketing therefore know what the organisation exists to do and, equally, why particular policies and strategies are adopted.

Commitment is thus obtained through communication and explanation. However, this has to be reinforced by selecting people who display the qualities necessary to advance the organisation and by ensuring that the motivation of those involved is understood and appropriately managed. In schools this has obvious implications for the selection, appraisal and development of teachers. However it is equally significant for non-teaching staff and, in the context of rationalisation, for pupils. Commitment is often a function of understanding and this implies that everyone lives the school's values, mission and specific objectives. This means that they have to be understandable, that the means of attaining them are available and that everyone understands their role in achieving them.

## *(iv) Clients*

Marketing is about responding to clients' needs and these are best defined not in terms of specifics but, rather, as 'conformity to requirements' or 'fitness for purpose'. In other words, marketing is about demonstrating the extent to which clients' needs have been identified and then met. Thus the components of meeting a specific set of client needs will vary according to the client as will the appropriate vehicle for communication. Equally, it is impossible to draw a neat line between the school and its environment and argue that marketing starts after the line (see Figure 9.1) — numerous individuals will be involved in the generation of a policy or service and they are therefore all part of the marketing relationship.

It is unfortunate therefore that the marketing relationship is too often seen as a one-way process whereby a school tries to sell itself and its services to a perceived external market. This very simplistic view needs to be replaced by a multi-dimensional approach which sees marketing in terms of a continuous process of interaction between the different client groups within the total school framework as seen in Figure 9.2. Here clients' groups are identified as sources of ideas and information rather than simply as 'customers'.

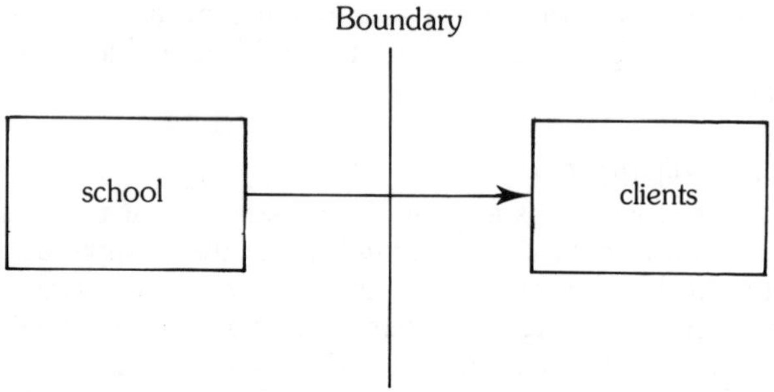


*Figure 9.1: traditional marketing relationships*

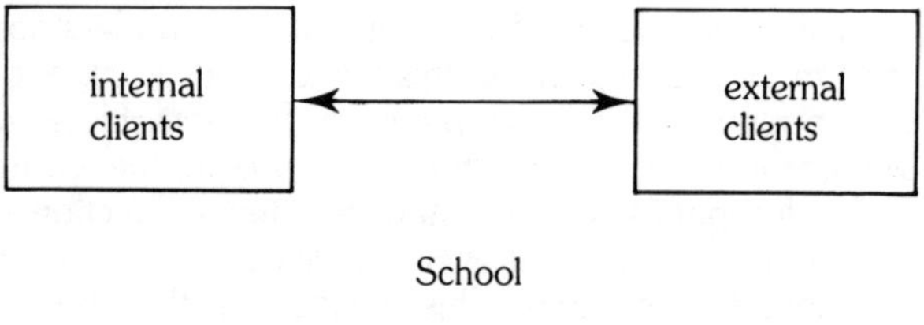


*Figure 9.2: quality marketing relationships*

## 4. The marketing cycle

Managers in schools should not be seduced into looking at one aspect of marketing in isolation from an overall management approach. Figure 9.3 shows an outline of the seven key stages in the marketing process or cycle.

*Figure 9.3: the marketing cycle*

### *(i) Market research*

This activity involves defining who is the client to be served and what the product is that the client wants. This, from the earlier discussion in the chapter, involves assessing the parents' and child's relative needs from education and defining what influences them in educational decisions. The earlier discussion of perceived and actual values and outputs is a valuable concept here.

### *(ii) Analyse your product*

Product analysis can be carried out using a SWOT analysis, that is, an examination of Strengths, Weaknesses, Opportunities and Threats to an organisation. It needs to be applied to all aspects of the school. A useful checklist approach to this is provided by Dennison (1989). The analysis can reveal areas which the school can market but, also, areas which will present serious weaknesses unless the school devotes managerial resources to overcoming them.

## *(iii) Develop a marketing strategy*

This stage involves laying down the aims of the marketing strategy and the objectives which are to be achieved. It should look forward at least two to three years and not just be concerned with short-term initiatives. Most importantly, the strategy should not be bolted on to other management plans. It should be an integrated part of the whole School Management Development Plan for school improvement (see chapter 3). While this strategic view is necessary, it is also vital that objectives can be achieved and that there is a clearly defined implementation schedule detailing the tactics to be employed.

## *(iv) Define and re-define the product that the school is offering*

All staff should have a clearly articulated view of what the school stands for and what strengths and opportunities it is offering to its clients. Some sort of 'corporate identity' or 'image' is necessary if clients are to get a clear picture of what the school is offering.

## *(v) Marketing and promotion*

The first distinction to be made here is between internal and external markets. Internal markets consist of governors, teaching and non-teaching staff, pupils and parents of existing pupils. All these individuals need to have a clear view of the school's aims and objectives and its current plans for the education of the children in its care. They can only be effective in communicating this to the wider community if they *realise* that they are all ambassadors of the school and are kept informed of and participate in school activities, achievements and plans. Making this key market satisfied and enthusiastic about the school is a prerequisite for concentrating on external markets. Otherwise any success with the wider community will be offset as soon as they talk to individuals within the school community.

External markets consist of people or organisations with little or no knowledge of the school. These are the people that you have to influence, perhaps for the first time. These could include feeder schools, estate agents, removal firms, Citizens' Advice Bureaux, public libraries, local employers, local organisations that use the school buildings, local media, etc. All need to have relevant up-to-date information and promotional literature about the school as they all influence potential parents and children who live locally or are moving to the area.

### *(vi) Quality control and performance indicators*

Schools are working on a series of performance indicators to assess whether they have achieved their objectives. Schools may be able to 'sell themselves' in the short run, but will only retain pupils in the long run if they deliver what they promised they would. These performance indicators can be short-term and tactical, as perceived by parents, or longer-term and more strategic. An example of the former would be setting up a homework timetable. If teachers are not setting the homework then this is a clear indicator to parents of a failed performance indicator. While there are broader indicators such as long-term improvement in language skills, schools should work on both levels to ensure client satisfaction.

### *(vii) Monitoring (after sales service)*

This is to assess how effective the *marketing process* has been. Did all the parents get the right information before choosing the school? Did they get adequate information during the child's educational career about education choices that had to be made? A key area could be to explore parental attitudes about things they would want to see remedied or changed. This can be sought by informal methods such as discussions with parents or local members of the community. A valuable formal method is to send follow-up questionnaires to past pupils and ex-parents. An example of this is provided by Thompson (1989).

## 5. Establishing a marketing culture within a school

The main thrust of this chapter has been that of taking a strategic view of marketing rather than adopting *ad hoc* responses to immediate marketing needs. It is clear that marketing should not be a 'bolt on' activity but an integral part of school management. To this end, it is vital that school managers create a culture in which all members of the school community help to define, design and implement a coherent strategy of relating the school to its clients.

## Conclusion

The practical components of a marketing strategy have to balance the need to manage the image of the school and to be the vehicle by which accountability is made explicit. The role of the headteacher and senior management is therefore central in generating the values and principles to be marketed and in providing an example of marketing in practice.

This has fundamental implications for the nature of working relationships within the school which can then be extended to external clients. For example, the quality of internal communications is a vital component both in terms of what is expressed and how it is expressed. The marketing relationship demands constant checking that information is being provided in the most appropriate manner and that it is information which is needed. Equally the conduct of meetings says as much about values and perceptions as the actual contents of the agenda.

This relationship must be extended to all staff and therefore be a fundamental component of the school's accountability and permeate all working relationships. Unless staff have ownership of this concept of marketing then it is unlikely to be successful.

## References

Dennison, B. 1989 'The Competitive Edge — attracting more pupils' in *School Organisation*, Vol. 9, No. 2

McBurnie, T. and Clutterbuck 1987 *The Marketing Edge*, Penguin

Thompson, C. 1989 'Monitoring Client satisfaction in schools — a marketing activity' *School Organisation*, Vol. 9, No. 2

# 10 Managing the evaluation of schools

Allan Osborne

A great deal of evaluation goes on in schools every day, for an evaluative element is hidden in almost any decision-making activity at whatever level — the individual teacher deciding upon the *best* approach to a particular group or topic, the head of department and colleagues choosing the *most suitable* courses for particular groups, or the headteacher managing responsibilities in the *most appropriate* manner. All of these examples would inevitably involve those concerned in a process of making evaluative judgements against more or less explicit criteria for choice, and of course parents and pupils are involved too. Obvious examples here are parental choice of school in the context of open enrolment under the 1988 Act, or the choice of option pathways at 14+ in the secondary sector. However, in many of these situations, the evaluative element is often very undefined and/or very subjective — it is often referred to as 'informal evaluation'. This should not, however, lead us to detract from the merit or power of this level of activity.

At the other extreme there is a range of activities which can be characterised as 'formal evaluation'. These examples may include formal inspections by HMI, or Local Authority Inspectors/Advisers, reports to Governors or, more importantly, significant evaluation projects undertaken by staff within the school to investigate the effectiveness of a particular area of activity, either at the level of the whole school or at the level of a sub-unit within the school. For the individual teacher some forms of appraisal, too, may fit into this category. Formal evaluations are usually well documented in terms of the evidence collected and the conclusions drawn, whereas informal evaluations are not.

At various points along this informal/formal continuum a number of issues arise. Firstly, all evaluation is (or should be) concerned with doing things better, both now and in the future: although better can be described either in terms of effectiveness ('doing the right things' is the frequently used phrase), or in terms of efficiency ('doing things right'). We should make no bones about the relative significance of these two dimensions — of this, more later. There may also be further, related distinctions to draw between those evaluations where the major purpose is accountability rather than improvement *per se*, and between summative (output) and formative (process) styles of evaluation.

Secondly, we need to be careful about pushing too far the distinction between formal and informal evaluations. This is particularly the case when we consider the management of how we move from evaluation into the action or change stage. It may initially appear as strange that the 'weaker' end of the continuum (informal evaluation) is more successful in bridging this evaluation/action gap than is the 'stronger' end of a more formal evaluation. This is in part the case because there is a type of syllogistic thinking which afflicts much formal evaluation, and which represents a significant problem for managers of the process. This thinking would suggest that evaluation leads to an awareness of problems, that such awareness then guides remedial action and that, therefore, evaluation leads to improvement. Bollen and Hopkins (1987) report on this problem but our own experience also tells us that this is not always true — especially in relation to accountability-based evaluations. Sometimes, and perhaps quite often, we learn instead to live with the 'problem' rather than attempt to really solve it. We survive by 'managing the ambiguity' because the costs of doing otherwise are too great — another level of evaluation has intervened upon the first and over-ridden it, in this case an informal evaluation of the opportunity costs involved in a choice between solving the problem and living with it. In this sense, any attempt at formal evaluation contains within it the possibility of further layers of informal evaluations, which are never articulated but which can (often with great ease) over-ride the carefully documented and structured path of the formal programme. Those who would manage formal evaluation procedures forget this at their peril. Actually, of course, this means that if we draw too rigid a distinction between the formal and informal approaches then we inherently run the risk outlined above. Moreover, we also fail to learn the great lesson that can be drawn from the informal dimension — how to translate the evaluation into action.

There is no great secret here, just a ton of common sense. People undertake informal evaluations on issues which are important to them as individuals or groups — important in that they feel an issue or a problem in a real way — real in the sense that something has to be done about it in their working situation. Consequently, they are predisposed to action at the point at which they *begin* to evaluate — first the evidence and then the alternative courses of action — in however 'ramshackle' a way. It is this prior commitment to action which should be the starting point, too, for the more formal evaluations with which we are involved and with which this chapter is mainly concerned.

The third feature of note at this stage is indeed more specifically concerned with the processes of formal evaluations, and it can be called the Cinderella Paradox. Of all the tasks facing managers and/or teachers in schools none has been more frequently (and formally) invited to the management ball in the last decade than evaluation — and none is so often obliged to leave early. After being saved from neglect or abuse, just at the point at which the real benefit of her attendance should become clear, time, energy or commitment runs out and her chance seems to be lost. This could be called the Cinderella phenomenon — the paradox element arises since this is so despite major efforts to the contrary.

The volume of literature which has been produced upon the subject of school evaluation and accountability, and the attempts by both central and local authorities to promote practice-led initiatives, have both been considerable. Centrally-led initiatives (as represented by *Better Schools* (1985), the work of the Assessment of Performance Unit or the GRIDS project) or local authority initiatives (for example the Sussex Accountability Project or the Oxfordshire School Report), have apparently had considerable impacts locally and for certain periods of time; but neither they, nor the flood of books, articles and LEA-generated guidelines seem to have created a self-sustaining process of formal evaluation in our schools. We need to ask why this is the case.

The answer to this Cinderella Paradox is important to those who would wish to develop such a self-sustaining process in the schools in which they work, and for which they are responsible as managers, for in that understanding lies the way forward. It is a situation which is broken down here into three parts, although they interact in a highly complex manner in the real world of education management. The following concentrates on the third of the elements as being that which is of underpinning importance but this should not lead to an underestimation of the value of exploring the first two elements more fully; and to that end a selective bibliography is provided for those who wish to pursue those avenues in greater detail. The three elements to be explored are:

(1) The nature of existing literature and practice
(2) Managing the process
(3) Evaluation design at school level.

## 1. *The nature of existing literature and practice*

There is a great deal of literature on the subject(s) of school evaluation and/or accountability and much of it is good in an isolated sense, but not in a comprehensive or integrated sense, although there are notable exceptions such as Hoyle's (1979) contribution. Seen as a whole the literature, whether from academic or practice-led origins, is fragmented and non-cumulative. This can lead to a situation where it is sometimes actually confusing or contradictory.

In part this is due to the origins of the whole area of interest in the latter part of the 1970s when it was part of the knee-jerk reaction to the emerging consumerism being applied to education on a wide front, but which is usually symbolised by the 'Great Debate' established by Prime Minister Callaghan's Ruskin Speech of 1976. As these forces gathered momentum, they gave rise to an unfortunate emphasis upon the accountability function of evaluation, at the expense of the feedback or improvement function internal to the schools. This emphasis has conditioned the response of the profession to the whole process.

This early accountability focus was well represented by the work of McCormick (1982) or Lacey and Lawton (1981) and there is a continuous thread of development from these concerns into the Education Acts of 1986 and 1988. At its maximum this strand to the process resulted in the appearance, in the mid and late 1980s, of a number of publications which brought to the surface the concept of performance indicators, and did so in such a way as to relate them very strongly, if not exclusively, to the accountability context. Notable amongst these publications was the Audit Commission's (1986) *Towards Better Management of Secondary Education*, the Coopers and Lybrand Report (1988) *Local Management of Schools*, and the Chartered Institute of Public Finance and Accountancy's (CIPFA 1988) *Performance Indicators in Schools*. By the time of the appearance of the last two in particular, the accountability context was also being heavily reinforced, and yet modified, by the emergence of the local management of schools concept and, within that, by the financial delegation aspects.

The CIPFA document in particular is interesting. It identified the following as those areas in which both quantitative and qualitative performance indicators should be explored:

1. Management of staff and the quality of teaching
2. Management of the quality of learning and of the curriculum
3. Pastoral management
4. Financial management
5. Liaison with other agencies and the community
6. Management of information

Although the report attempted to explain the nature of its proposals as a framework from which schools and/or LEAs should develop their own performance indicators, the climate of the time, and some elements of its presentation (those indicators identified as quantifiable and some of the values expressed in the selection of indicators) did little to move the debate away from the accountability focus.

In February of 1988 eight LEAs were involved in a DES pilot exercise and by the end of 1989 the results of the pilot were published as *School Indicators for Internal Management: An Aide Memoire* (DES), although this was put forward as only a first stage document for schools to consider. The categories used in the Aide Memoire are:

1. Basic school data
2. School context
3. Pupil achievement
4. Parental involvement
5. Pupil attitudes
6. Management

It is interesting to note that in comparison with the CIPFA document, the Aide Memoire is much more reflective of an earlier tradition of LEA-based checklist approaches to effectiveness. There is less emphasis upon quantification and more upon asking questions, and also an emphasis upon context and pupils which is significantly more professional and less managerial. (The word management appears in five of six CIPFA categories and only one of the six Aide Memoire categories.)

The spectre of an imposed accountability framework had apparently been abandoned, but it is worthwhile considering why this was the case. Perhaps the voice of the profession was being listened to, or perhaps the understanding of the logistics/costs of a fully blown system had grown — or perhaps other lines of thought in the accountability tradition were emerging? One such line of thought may be seen in the context of local management of schools, when formula funding is seen alongside open enrolment provision. That line of thought may suggest that, in a consumer or market-led system, quality control is a function of the market and there is simply no need to develop formalised, structured or bureaucratised approaches to accountability. In such a context the use of performance indicators could be left more open and more concerned with the internal management of schools, as those schools sought to identify which performance areas were significant to their major constituencies.

Whatever the case, in one way or another, the accountability phenomenon has exercised an important influence both on the literature and practice of evaluation in our schools. At the former level there has been a split between that literature and research with an accountability focus, and that which has concentrated more clearly upon school-based review for the purposes of internal development and improvement — and this split has not greatly aided schools in developing a self-sustaining approach to the whole area, either in the sense of developing the skills and knowledge base required, or in setting the climate in which they could develop.

This disarray in the literature and practice is in fact compounded even when looking within the improvement tradition itself. Compare, for example, the approaches taken by Shipman (1979) and Holt (1981) in two of the major contributions to the literature:

> This book is about ways of making schools more effective and about ways of ensuring that they are seen to be effective. It is not about the ends of education . . . . The concern here is with means not ends, on how to do it more effectively rather than what to do.
>
> Shipman (1979) p. ix

> There is no need to agonise too long over philosophical matters of aims. The need is for a set of working objectives that can focus evaluation. The objectives establish a tactical position that can enable the staff to get on with evaluation.
>
> Shipman (1979) p. 11

> The choice is between leaving evaluation to impressions that have no necessarily consistent or even detectable frame of reference, or organizing it so that the criteria of success and failure are spelled out. It is a choice between casual and systematic judgement.
>
> Shipman (1979) p. 165

> Above all, the disturbing things about the fashion for school 'self-audit' or self-evaluation is the assumption that a good school is one which uses the right mechanism or routines. The value judgements seem to take second place to the functionalism of schooling.
>
> Holt (1981) p. 121

> It (Shipman's view) is based on the fallacy that, in education, means can be divorced from ends. For values are implicit in every educational act, and there is no 'objective' or 'systematic' way in which the quality of an act can be separated from the way it is performed.
>
> Holt (1981) p. 122

At issue here are fundamental differences concerning the location (input-process-output) of evaluation studies and the related differences in underlying concepts of effectiveness — these are issues which are explored in more detail in Section 3 following.

Much valuable work has, however, been undertaken within the improvement tradition, and it is possible to mention only a small selection of the available material. Notable contributions have been made from a number of sources. A wide range of the earlier LEA practice-led initiatives are reviewed by Clift (1982) in a brief but useful way, and Glatter (1986) outlines the background to school-based review in the framework of the International School Improvement Project. A particular example of the latter is the GRIDS project which will be familiar in outline to all readers but a useful review is provided by MacMahon, Holly and Steadman (1987). Bollen and Hopkins (1987) attempt to provide a mechanism or process for ensuring that the review–action gap is crossed in the context of school-based review. The brief publication from HMI, *Quality in Schools: Evaluation and Appraisal* (1985) and the DES *Better Schools* (1985) are also valuable, whilst evaluation in the context of the self-managing school is approached by Caldwell and Spinks (1988), amongst others too numerous to mention.

The problem remains, however, that these practice-led approaches, and the reporting to which they have given rise, are fragmented and non-cumulative as a whole, and may even be contradictory in quite serious ways which do not help those in schools who would attempt to get to grips with the problem. The major division, that between the accountability and the improvement traditions, remains strong, whilst in the latter area itself, there is a major failure to establish a common currency of approach or practice. This in turn is related to the failure to examine underlying principles to the evaluation of effectiveness which alone could lead towards a more useful process of evaluation design by those in schools.

In a related area of study Reynolds and Reid (1988) have already indicated the need to move to a second stage in the methods of school effectiveness studies and part of their analysis is appropriate here:

> Much of the early work in this field has been highly atheoretical . . . . Much of the British work grew out of attempts to test the hypotheses of Jencks and Coleman and therefore tended to work within the same paradigm of traditional atheoretical empiricism as they . . . .
>
> Reynolds and Reid (1988) pp. 176–177

They go on to say:

> The problems caused by our atheoreticism, however, are now numerous. No piece of work is cumulative, either set against work from the past or against other work in the present . . . a work is not testable in theoretical terms . . . is unrelated to any current theoretical position except that of 'grubby empiricism'.
>
> Reynolds and Reid (1988) p. 177

Section 3 of this chapter will attempt to outline just one way in which theoretical approaches to effectiveness can be related to the process of evaluation design in schools. For now we turn to examine briefly the organisational and micropolitical issues surrounding evaluation.

## 2. *Managing the process*

Some of the organisational and/or micropolitical factors involved in establishing more formal approaches to evaluation have already been touched upon (above). The danger of ignoring the power of informal agendas even within a formal process, the climate surrounding the different accountability/improvement approaches, the problems involved in ensuring that action follows evaluation and the possibility of wider micropolitical activities within evaluation are major issues for anyone involved in managing an evaluation process — and there are others. Few of these issues are simple in the sense that a straightforward solution is available. Indeed most of them are extremely complex in so far as they interlock, and in the sense that they are present *throughout* the evaluation in different ways. For example, building commitment to the process is not just something that has to be done before evaluation starts, but that commitment also has to be maintained throughout the process and then translated into a yet different form at the point of moving into the planning/action stage. The management of the process therefore is itself a dynamic task facing managers and one that requires the deployment of a wide range of skills — from resource management through motivation and staff development to the technical skills concerning evaluation *per se* and the whole spectrum of people management skills. Neglect of this area is the second of our reasons behind the Cinderella Paradox.

Before proceeding to a brief examination of some of these issues, there is a basic question of perspective to establish for the manager(s) involved, and this underlying 'mind-set' will undoubtedly condition responses to most of the questions to be raised here. At this point there is a close relationship to the major questions raised in chapter 1 about the location of management activities, in chapter 5 concerning staff development and chapter 6 on the management of change. The question is, do we see evaluation within the school as a management responsibility to be fulfilled by those in overtly managerial roles or is it seen as something which is a professional duty of all staff? The role of the manager in relation to the second of these perspectives is clearly very different to what it would be in the former — much more concerned with the organisational and people processes of evaluation than with the technical issues or the substantive focus of any particular evaluation. It is suggested here that such a perspective takes on board the matters now to be raised in a holistic and genuine way, whilst the alternative, top-down managerial approach would rapidly involve managers in running the risk of crossing the line between management and manipulation in such a way as to diminish greatly the opportunity of a successful outcome — the distinction revolves around the difference between the 'hard-sell' and genuine 'ownership'. This idea is neatly summed up by Holly (1987) in the context of self evaluation:

> Self-evaluation in the primary school is . . . internal as opposed to external evaluation; it is done *by* the members of staff — with appro-

> priate support — *for* the members of staff . . . it is not a case of the work being done *to* or *at* these same participants.
>
> Holly (1987) p. 208

What then are the practical implications of this underlying approach to ownership and process as it unfolds through the various stages of evaluation design, data collection, judgement of evidence, reporting and then moving into the planning/action phase?

Although it would seem to be essential to approach evaluation from a negotiated perspective, once this is begun a rich arena for micropolitical activity is created. This negotiation would need to involve all of those concerned, and should be maintained throughout the process. For example, it would not only be necessary to negotiate the why, who and what elements of the basic design but also to look forward to the data collection stage, the judgemental period, the reporting stage and the planning/action processes that may arise. At any or all of these points, the people-rich environment gives rise to the possibility of destroying the trust which is essential, or of allowing/fostering micropolitical activity which is detrimental to the eventual outcome. Obvious examples which would destroy trust occur when the reporting stage is suddenly made available to an audience which was not included initially, or if un-negotiated methods of data collection are suddenly introduced into the middle of an on-going evaluation or, very powerfully, if the basic evaluation design is altered in some way — for example from within an internal/improvement paradigm to an accountability one.

The data collection stage is also extremely sensitive. It well behoves those who would obtain reliable data to negotiate access to it as fully as possible and, again, in an on-going way. It would be foolish in the extreme for senior staff to assume that they have *droit de seigneur* access to all the data required. Certainly the documented areas of data collection should be readily available, but the more judgemental or subjective areas of data are likely to be deeply hidden within groups or even held by individuals, who will only give access to that information in conditions where they feel that it is relevant and safe to do so. In this connection the methods of collecting data can be as sensitive as the data itself. In terms of the improvement of school practice, this is exactly the sort of information which is of paramount importance — much of the more readily available and objective documentation is likely to be more appropriate to descriptive rather than explorative evaluation designs.

Negotiation also needs to take place with regard to the identification of criteria for judgement within the evaluation. This is concerned with the phenomenon of the 'moving goal posts'. Again, if the criteria for 'success' are imposed or if they are suddenly shifted during the evaluation, then trust will be lost and the value of the exercise will be seriously compromised as people start to withdraw access to information or become selective in providing only that information which conforms positively to the criteria. The danger of reductionism of highly complex activities and consequently of de-skilling is ever present.

Reporting, and then moving forward into the planning–action stage if that is appropriate, also requires careful thought and wide agreement — perhaps with an initial agreement on likely approaches but always bearing in mind the possibility of renegotiation of these elements as the evaluation nears 'completion'. It is at this point that energies may be relaxing, and if this is so it may require extra attention, particularly to bridge the evaluation–action gap. Alternatively it may be the case that no action is required, and if that is the outcome of the evaluation then the fact should be acknowledged and congratulations offered to all concerned!

These various stages are not, of course, discrete and the relationships between the various elements also require a proactive approach. For example the basic evaluation design will set parameters upon the other stages by indicating likely sources of data, methods of collection and criteria against which judgements can be made. These parameters should be made explicit to all concerned and subsequent re-negotiation should always respect those parameters too. Similarly, an awareness of the possibility of individuals or sub-groups within the body of those involved indulging in micropolitical activity should constantly be borne in mind. This is especially true if the evaluation is likely to have resource distribution implications for the future. Such strategies are possible at any point but are most likely to occur at the design stage when the broad outlines of the whole process are being forged — although *real* activists will maintain their efforts throughout, and some may even see a particular evaluation project as a micropolitical tool in a much wider campaign with which they are concerned.

For those who wish to pursue these process elements further, the literature is again rather fragmented and, at this point, quite limited, although recently more attention has been given to such issues.

The GRIDS documentation has much of an implicit nature to say about the process issues, whilst Hughes, Ribbins and Thomas (1985) develop a rather schematic approach to the relationships which can be identified within the situation. Day, Johnson and Whitaker (1985) consider questions of timing, and to some extent climate, alongside issues of the resources needed in both human and other terms for a successful evaluation to be carried out. This latter point is very important and suggests that a school should not be involved in too much formal evaluation at any particular time. Questions concerning the human resources and skills (extended professionality?) required are dealt with by Holly and Hopkins

(1988), and may of the other items identified elsewhere in this chapter contain much that is useful in terms of managing the process.

Finally, it is often suggested that any evaluation process should itself be reviewed and sometimes checklists are provided to facilitate this. It is interesting however that these checklists are usually provided in a way which sets the review as a *post hoc* exercise once the evaluation is completed. It would be much more helpful to review the process at the initiation and operating stages thus:

1. Is this the right time to be doing the evaluation?
2. How can the methods of evaluation be made explicit to all concerned?
3. Will the evaluation serve to inform decisions or judgements?
4. Who are the most appropriate people to carry out the evaluation? Are they available?
5. What information will be appropriate to the purpose of the evaluation? Where is the information and is access readily available?
6. What steps can be taken to allow for reliability and validity in the information gathered?
7. How much time will be required for each stage of the process?
8. Are the criteria by which judgements or decisions may be made clearly stated and agreed?
9. Are there any possible side-effects or micropolitical issues in terms of the school as a whole, groups or individuals which may arise?
10. What is the audience for any report and what possible forms of reporting will be undertaken?
11. How will any further development resulting from the evaluation be managed?

This checklist may be useful in relation to the process issues outlined in this section, but it is far from comprehensive in relation to the wider aspects of an evaluation programme, and particularly so in relation to the underlying process of evaluation design. It is to that task that this chapter will now turn.

## 3. *Evaluation design*

The 'atheoretical' or 'grubby empiricist' basis to much of our thinking and practice about effectiveness (a concept) and evaluation (a process) was highlighted earlier — and this weakness underpins or compounds many of the issues raised in the previous section. In order to develop a self-sustaining programme of evaluation, much greater attention needs to be given to underlying views of effectiveness and to the task of building an evaluation design which is congruent with the effectiveness concept being employed. As a starting point we need to be clear about the relative significance of effectiveness and efficiency and to think through the relationship between them.

Managers and teachers are rooted in particular schools and situations, and necessarily have a particularistic perspective which emphasises the uniqueness of that situation. Their requirement of effectiveness as a notion is that it should enable them better to understand, and then to improve, the performance of 'their' school in one or a number of ways. However, these schools are not static, they are changing in a number of ways and as these changes occur, so too does the concept of effectiveness required to monitor the new situation and yet further develop it. Effectiveness is therefore, to some degree, a shifting concept which reflects changing educational processes or priorities. Efficiency, on the other hand, is a much more static idea; always concerned with doing things in terms of the best possible use of resources — whatever those 'things' may be.

Efficiency without effectiveness is meaningless in the context of education (or anywhere else for that matter) but effectiveness without efficiency is at least a starting point for improvement. It is dangerous, of course, to push this thinking too far, because the latter situation is *only a starting point* — improved curriculum effectiveness is closely related to the way in which resources are used, and this clearly raises questions about the efficient use of those resources. The management of school-based finance could also be approached primarily from an efficiency perspective but if that were to be the case then much would indeed have been lost! Managers in schools should make no mistake then about the order of priority in the effectiveness/efficiency relationship — the latter is a subset of the former. Any evaluation design needs to be clear on this issue.

The evaluation design also needs to be clear about the location of evaluation in another sense — is it to be concerned with the evaluation of school outputs, or processes within the school, or even with using inputs as some way of judging (measuring?) success? This is often explained in terms of a simple systems theory view of organisations, with jargon attached as illustrated.

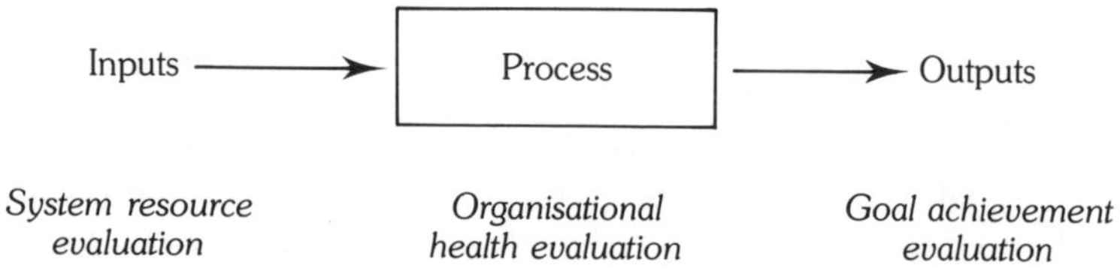


Evaluation can be carried out at any or all of the three points in the diagram. Consider for example these three statements:

(a) The school has attracted 25 per cent out-of-catchment enrolment.
(b) The staff really work as a team in the school.

(c) The school has achieved examination results 25 per cent better than the national average.

Each of these statements could be used in an evaluative sense and they represent input/process/output levels of evaluation respectively. Unfortunately, there is a tendency to select the location of the evaluation in this sense before a clear idea has been created about what it is that is actually being evaluated. The risk is then that the evaluation location (model) is not properly congruent with the area of effectiveness being investigated. We will return to this later, but for now it suggests to us that evaluation design is a two-part process — firstly, define the effectiveness concept you wish to explore and secondly select the location (input/process/output or a combination) of the evaluation which will most usefully explore that concept. It remains to unpack these issues and to suggest ways in which the task can be approached. An important contribution has been offered in this area by Cameron (1980) from within the broad field of organisation and management studies. He suggests the idea of *frameworks for assessing effectiveness* as an alternative to the search for universalistic concepts of effectiveness. This undersold idea may provide us with a way of approaching the task of evaluation design outlined here. The structure of the remainder of this chapter will therefore be to examine Cameron's idea of *frameworks*, to relate this to existing major approaches to evaluation and to suggest that this does throw up practical management perspectives and tools for use at different levels in examining the effectiveness of schools.

## Frameworks for assessing effectiveness

To clear the ground it is necessary to find an understanding of effectiveness which does not, by definition, bind us to a subsequent mode of evaluating effectiveness. This is one of the major problems associated with the existing literature whether it comes from the goals, system-resource or health schools. The most promising avenue is the notion of an *effectiveness construct* as utilised by Steers (1975) who tells us that:

> A construct is an abstract idea rather than a concrete phenomenon. It is based on the hypothesis that several variables will consistently covary or fit together to form a unified whole.
>
> Steers (1975) p. 551

Steers is, however, still looking for a 'unified whole' or a generalisable construct and concludes that:

> until the construct can be explained . . . it will be difficult to make meaningful recommendations to managers about steps to improve effectiveness in their organisations.
>
> Steers (1975) p. 551

This does not mean that the idea is not useful — indeed it is very useful seen from the vantage point of one school. It is suggested that the effectiveness construct(s) for a school should be developed within that institution or at least with reference to it. The model suggested would have both static and dynamic characteristics — that is, some aspects of it could be expected to be present over long periods (say) academic dimensions, whilst other aspects would appear to serve particular functions but may then fade from view, perhaps to be replaced by other more pressing concerns, for example the evaluation of a change from horizontal to vertical pupil organisation.

Such a view of the effectiveness construct could also handle the two basic purposes of evaluation — accountability to stakeholders and feedback aimed at improvement. The accountability end of the evaluation would most clearly be related to the static part of the model whereas the improvement function would make most use of the dynamic characteristics. These relationships would not be absolute however since there would clearly be an important traffic between the two parts of the model. For the moment, the most important point is that we have developed a view of effectiveness that has dynamic properties and we are not, therefore, tied to any particular mode of evaluation — the manager(s) can provide detail of the construct(s) and they can be guided in this by Cameron's framework. Since universalistic approaches will not work we are left with a process of *selection* and the framework approach is really, at this stage, little more than a guide to that selection.

Cameron gives us seven pointers. These are:

1. *From whose perspective is effectiveness being judged?*

One of the reasons why the universalistic criteria for school effectiveness have been so elusive is that different constituencies will have different criteria for judgement.

Whilst this remains a problem for theorists in their search for yet another 'holy grail', it is much less of a problem in the context of the individual institution where managers can make such an identification based largely upon the purpose of the evaluation exercise. This choice would not be permanent but would alter with time and changing requirements.

2. *On what domain of activity is the judgement focused?*

All schools operate in a number of domains — a simple model for schools may be: academic, pastoral, organisational and disciplinary. However, this must not be seen as prescriptive, as the real decisions must be made at the institutional levels. A significant feature is that effectiveness in one domain may be in conflict with success in another. Is it perhaps better therefore to seek *optimisation* in all domains rather than *maximisation* in any one? Again, dominant domains will change with time and perspective.

3. *What level of analysis is being used?*
Effectiveness can be judged from a number of levels — the individual, the sub-system or the school as a whole. The choice here is clearly interdependent with 1 and 2 above and with 4 below.

4. *What is the purpose of the evaluation?*
Although it may be true, as Hoyle (1979) suggests, that there are two basic answers to this question — accountability and feedback aimed at improvement — these terms cover a wide variety of different situations. To give just one example in the improvement area, the investigation may be constructed as part of an on-going evaluation exercise aimed at improvement of academic performance in departments x y and z — or it may be aimed at making the decision as to which of these departments to close because of fundamental contraction. Clearly, the effectiveness construct would be different in each of these cases.

5. *What time-frame is being employed?*
A relevant time-frame is required in order to validate any assessment since effects or outcomes may not be visible at all if the time-frame is wrong — for example it would be inappropriate to measure academic performance over a very short time-period whereas it may be appropriate to study certain organisational processes over just such a period.

6. *What type(s) of data are to be used?*
The choice here lies between objective and subjective data — each with its advantages and disadvantages. The choice made will depend upon decisions about data availability but more powerfully upon other questions raised here about building the relevant effectiveness construct(s). Perhaps most importantly, the data employed must be acceptable to the operative perspective(s) — for example, many accountability constituencies would only be satisfied by consideration of outputs.

7. *What is the referent against which effectiveness is judged?*
It is on this rubric that Cameron's work does not quite break free from existing theories of effectiveness, since one of the referents he suggests is:

> to compare organisational performance . . . against the stated goals of the organisation.
>
> Cameron and Whetton (1983) p. 273

This clearly pre-determines the approach to the goal-achievement model at a stage when the manager has not yet fully defined his effectiveness construct. Therefore, in order to maintain flexibility at this stage, an alternative is suggested — based upon the educational audit of Dennison (1978). The audit would present three possible referent points for the evaluation — judgement in terms of either (a) an absolute standard; (b) comparison within or without the institution; and (c) the direction and extent of change. Clearly, one or all three could be utilised in the light of the effectiveness construct being established.

At this point it is necessary to state forcefully the position arrived at. Cameron's framework is not being used to select a particular approach to the evaluation of effectiveness (goals, system resource or health) but rather to guide the manager(s) to a position where a *relevant effectiveness construct* can be established. Cameron suggests that the questions above be considered 'in concert'. It is suggested here, however, that although the seven factors are interdependent, two of them act as controlling influences for the operation and therefore provide the starting point for the practical task of creating the effectiveness construct. These two are clearly number one, the effectiveness perspective, and number four, the purpose of the evaluation. It is suggested therefore that domain focus, level of analysis, time-frame, type(s) of data employed and referent(s) employed will be functions of perspective and purpose if the construct is to have validity and utility. This can be expressed diagrammatically for ease of presentation as shown in Figure 10.1.

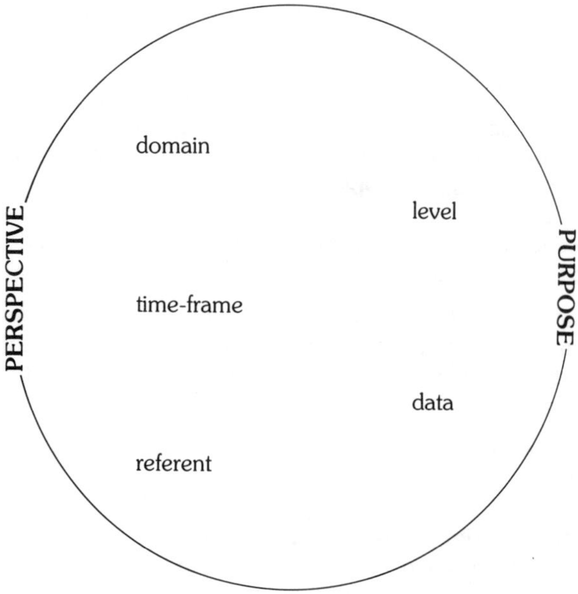


*Figure 10.1: elements of an effectiveness construct*

Working through this model allows us to create an effectiveness construct which is rooted in a particular situation and which is focused on a specific task. It remains to evaluate the construct.

## *Evaluating the construct*

Broadly speaking there are three alternative approaches available. They are discussed here in the order in which they are most commonly utilised in schools: the goal-achievement model, the systems-resource model and the organisational health model. There is sometimes a suggestion that a fourth model exists — the participant satisfaction model which defines effectiveness as the extent to which all of the organisation's strategic constituencies are at least minimally satisfied — this however seems to be a derivative of the goals model and will not be treated separately.

Each of the three models has advantages and disadvantages and choice should be made in relation to the relevant effectiveness construct, not as an *a priori* decision. What then are the salient characteristics of the three approaches and what do these characteristics indicate about the utility of each?

## *The goal-achievement model*

Perhaps the major attraction of the 'goal approach' is its conceptual simplicity or its conceptual attractiveness to those managers working in schools. Effectiveness is defined in terms of the extent to which goals are achieved. Teachers have a long experience in curriculum areas of either the setting of objectives or of working towards objectives laid down by others (perhaps by examination bodies, universities or now, the 1988 Act), and which they broadly accept as valid. This process has also been greatly developed over the last decade. Interestingly, they are involved too, either implicitly or (increasingly) explicitly, in an evaluation of their success levels relative to these goals. This alone is a powerful incentive to adopt a goal-based approach within those constructs or parts of constructs where it can be utilised.

Furthermore, the same advantages are multiplied greatly when consideration is given to acceptability of the evaluation to other constituencies, particularly non-expert or lay constituencies existing out-side the school. The evaluation can be presented in a form that is readily intelligible and which can be understood by such constituencies. The systems-resource approach and the organisational health view both have serious problems in this area of acceptability — even to those well within the boundaries of the profession.

Much of the criticism of the goal approach revolves around the whole series of problems associated with defining educational objectives. Lengthy review of these arguments is not possible here but a way forward is provided by Steers' (1975) notion of *operant* goals. Briefly, this suggests that attention should not be on goals prescribed (by senior management?) or derived (from functional theory) but rather on goals actively and actually pursued by the school (or a part of it).

This approach to the idea of goals is not tied to the search for universal meanings for effectiveness and managers at different points in the institution would see much less difficulty in defining their goals than would theorists. That they could not in every situation do this does not mean that the method should be abandoned in total. If the effectiveness construct, or a part of it, is amenable to a goal approach, there are strong reasons (above) for adopting it.

## *The systems-resource approach*

The systems-resource method of evaluating effectiveness centres upon a school's ability to acquire needed resources from its external environment. The view holds that successful schools are able to attract extra or better quality resources — and this can be measured. Price (1972) makes three major criticisms of the model from a technical perspective, but again these need not detain us here for they are essentially criticisms aimed at the model's (in)ability to provide a universal framework. From a school management perspective, other problems are evident, perhaps the most important being the 'complexity' of the concept and its level of acceptability to different constituencies. A proper use of systems-resource requires at least some understanding and (perhaps) 'belief' in the general area of systems theory, and this is very unlikely even with professional constituencies.

Another issue arises with the 'focus' of the systems-resource approach which (as stated in the literature) forces attention onto the boundary relations of the school with its environment and, furthermore, suggests that the school is in competition with others for resources. The open enrolment and local management aspects of the 1988 Act lend reality to this situation as never before.

If a (or the) major element of the effectiveness construct was designed to explore and evaluate the relationships between the school and its environment then the systems-resource approach would be applicable, within the constraints of acceptability already referred to. This does not mean however that this would be the only situation in which systems-resource would have validity — an example at a different level will illustrate this. If the construct was aimed at exploring different levels of achievement between departments or functions of a school, then the approach could be very powerful indeed if the sub-units concerned were themselves treated as systems within an overall super-system. If it could be shown that there was a relationship between the perceived success levels of (say) the departments and their abilities to attract resources from the super-system then the evaluation method would become a very powerful tool for managerial activity as a method of tackling the 'problem'. Thus, evaluation would lead to activity in a way that the goal approach would not seem to be capable of, and this is a considerable merit.

## *The organisational health approach*

The organisational health approach is also related to open-systems theory and therefore shares some of the problems of systems-resource with regard to acceptability, but not to the same degree. A cogent statement of the model is provided by Miles (1969). Successful schools are said to exhibit smooth or healthy organisational processes, with a lack of strain or conflict. At least some of the dimensions of 'health' suggested (if not all) fit very easily into the liberal democratic cultures of the west and the approach can to some extent be 'acceptable' to non-expert or non-professional constituencies. The absence of internal strain, individuals highly integrated into the system, smooth internal functioning, trust and benevolence are all *positive* features when seen from a liberal culture and it is (too) easy to make a jump from such 'cosy' views to claims of effectiveness. Indeed the very opposite may be the case.

The danger of confusing efficiency with effectiveness is perhaps greatest in the organisational health model. There are also methodological difficulties inherent in this approach. Miles suggests that one of the features of a healthy organisation is goal focus:

> In a healthy organisation, the goal (or more usually goals) of the system would be reasonably clear to the system members, and reasonably well accepted by them.
>
> Miles (1969) p. 380

*At this aggregated level* of whole school goals criticisms about the problematic nature of goals would be valid. But perhaps the major difficulty of this model is the wide-ranging characteristics it attempts to bring into the framework and the necessarily judgemental nature of many of them. This is also, in the context of the relevant effectiveness construct, its major strength for it alone can provide the holistic perspective to effectiveness which is of crucial importance at the whole school level and which can also have a direct bearing upon the performance of individual members of staff. Emphasis would therefore be placed upon those dimensions of the model which are 'people-based' and which are capable of affecting the relationships between individuals and the school as a whole.

* * * *

Each of the major approaches to evaluation thus has its own advantages and disadvantages in the evaluation process and selection can be made with reference to the effectiveness construct under consideration. The goals approach has strength in terms of acceptability at all levels but would seem to have particular strength at those levels where goals are well defined. Thus, the smaller the unit under analysis the greater its validity — i.e. at the levels of individuals or sub-units such as departments and pastoral 'teams'. It is at the level where school-wide goals are under consideration that definitional problems come into play.

The systems-resource method would be of little utility in relation to individuals but may be of considerable use at the sub-unit level. If relationships between sub-units were being studied then a powerful perspective could be created by a system-resource viewpoint. This would also be the case if the focus of attention was the relationship between sub-units and the super-system of which they formed part. Also if the focus was concerned with the relationship between the super-system (school) and its environment, the system-resource approach may be appropriate, in which situation the controlling factor would be the constituency of the evaluation. If the report was a managerial tool designed for internal 'consumption' then acceptability may be positive, but if in addition the report had to satisfy environmental constituencies it would certainly need major overhaul in terms of presentation in order to give it acceptability.

The organisational health perspective is most useful in its approach to the relationships between individuals and the organisation since it alone provides the holistic perspective which is needed even to attempt an exploration of such a complex series of webs. It is a tool likely to be useful to those most concerned with personnel management because of its emphasis on factors such as power equalisation, communication adequacy, goal acceptability, cohesiveness, autonomy and morale. This would suggest its utility for whole school issues.

If an effectiveness construct is carefully put together *at the appropriate level* and then evaluated appropriately in the terms outlined here, the results of the evaluation should possess both acceptability and utility.

## Conclusion

This brief application of the frameworks approach is of course very partial — it gives only some examples of possible features in the creation and evaluation of a construct. The fine detail could only be determined by the teachers (managers) in question working in the context of a real situation. Similarly, although it would seem that a goal-based approach to the evaluation of effectiveness would be the dominant mode of activity, for reasons given earlier, it would not be the only one — for example the health approach would have much to offer in a construct focused on the personnel domain.

The keynote of this chapter builds upon the philosophy of chapter 1 — that to some degree all teachers are managers and that they must be involved in the evaluation of effectiveness at all levels within the school. Only in this way can a series of relevant effectiveness constructs be created and only in this way can *collective* professional autonomy be preserved and even enhanced. With the present state of the art it is unrealistic to attempt to utilise universalistic approaches to evaluation in the school context — and in the context of a pluralist society this will always be the case. The framework view offers the opportunity of tailor-made constructs as an alternative to the 'blunt instruments' currently on offer — and it may help to initiate that self-generating approach to formal evaluation with which this chapter has been concerned.

## References

Audit Commission 1986 *Towards Better Management of Secondary Education*, HMSO

Bollen, R. & Hopkins, D. 1987 *School Based Review: Towards a Praxis* Leuven, Belgium: ACCO

Caldwell, B. J. & Spinks, J. M. 1988 *The Self-managing School*, Falmer Press

Cameron, K. S. 1980 'Critical Questions in Assessing Organisational Effectiveness' in *Organisational Dynamics*, Autumn

Cameron K. S. & Whetton D. A. (eds) 1983 *Organisational Effectiveness: A Comparison of Multiple Models*, Academic Press

CIPFA 1988 *Performance Indicators in Schools*, CIPFA

Clift, P. 1982 'LEA schemes for school self-evaluation; a critique' in *Educational Research* Vol. 24 No. 4

Coopers & Lybrand 1988 *Local Management of Schools*, DES

Day, C., Johnson, D. & Whitaker, P. 1985 *Managing Primary Schools — A Professional Development Approach*, PCP

Dennison, W. F. 1978 'Monitoring the Effectiveness of Educational Insitutions' in *British Journal of Educational Studies*, October

DES 1985 *Better Schools*, DES

DES 1989 *Schools Indicators for Internal Management: An Aide Memoire*, DES

Glatter 1986 'The Management of School Improvement' in Hoyle, E. & McMahon, A. (eds) *World Yearbook of Education: The Management of Schools*, Kogan Page

HMI 1985 *Quality in Schools: Evaluation and Appraisal*, HMSO

Holly, P. 1987 'Making it Count: Evaluation for the Developing Primary School' in Southworth, G. *Readings in Primary School Management*, Falmer Press

Holly, P. & Hopkins, D. 1988 'Evaluation and School Improvement' in *Cambridge Journal of Education*, Vol. 18 No. 2

Holt, M. 1981 *Evaluating the Evaluators*, Hodder and Stoughton
Hoyle, E. 1979 'Evaluation of the Effectiveness of Educational Institutions' in Watson, L. (ed) *Current Issues in the Management of Education*, Sheffield Papers in Education Management, No. 12, Sheffield City Polytechnic
Hughes, M., Ribbins, P. & Thomas, H. 1985 *Managing Education*, Holt, Rinehart & Winston
Lacey, C. & Lawton, D. (eds) 1981 *Issues in Evaluation and Accountability*, Methuen
McCormick, R. (ed) 1982 *Calling Education to Account*, Heinemann/OU
McMahon A., Holly, P. & Steadman, S. 1987 'GRIDS' in Bollen, P. & Hopkins, D. *School Based Review: Towards a Praxis*
Miles, M. B. 'Planned Change and Organisational Health: Figure and Ground' in Carver, F. D. & Sergiovanni, T. J. (eds) 1969 *Organisations and Human Behaviour*, McGraw Hill
Price, J. L. 1972 'The Study of Organisational Effectiveness' *The Sociological Quarterly*, Winter
Reynolds & Reid 1988 *Power and Culture in Educational Organisations*
Shipman M. D. 1979 *In-School Evaluation*, Heinemann
Steers, R. M. 1975 'Problems in the Measurement of Organisational Effectiveness' in *Administrative Science Quarterly*, December

# 11 Perspectives on managing the curriculum in schools


## Allan Osborne and Linda Ellison


If management in schools is significantly different to management elsewhere, it is so in large part because of the phenomenon of the curriculum, and the particular blend of management skills which the curriculum requires us to create and deploy at any given moment. This is the arena within which our information systems, planning, resource management, staff development, change management and evaluation strategies must be brought together themselves, and then further integrated with a wide range of professional skills and knowledge in order to create those learning experiences for pupils, which alone provide a rationale for the whole business of education, schools and, indeed, education management.

It may appear to readers as foolhardy, in the final chapter to a book of this scope, to attempt to deal with such a large set of interrelated issues and processes — and indeed to explore them fully would require a second volume. Nevertheless, it is possible at least to begin by exploring just some of the curriculum management issues raised by the Education Reform Act and the ways in which the processes examined in this book can be applied to the resolution of those issues.

## The curriculum management context

The creation of a legal basis for a National Curriculum in 1988 was seen by many teachers as the (inevitable?) outcome of a process which went back to 1976, and the launch of the so-called 'Great Debate' by Prime Minister Callaghan. This view was then commonly developed to suggest that the National Curriculum would settle the *what* of the curriculum, leaving with teachers much of the *how*. In this view was encapsulated a significantly changed perception of what curriculum management was to be about at the level of the individual school. It also contained something of a sop to the profession or that element of the profession which had, to date, regarded itself as being concerned with curriculum development as well as implementation. Whilst superficially attractive as an explanation (if not in real terms) for what was happening, this is a view of the situation which greatly underestimates the task of curriculum management. It does this firstly by building upon the conceptual inadequacies of the 'Great Debate' itself; secondly by adopting a segmented view of the other elements of the Education Act which surround the National Curriculum; and thirdly perhaps also by underestimating the need to harness the range of professional skills and knowledge concerning the curriculum with the management processes required.

The 'Great Debate' from 1976 concerned itself with two major themes which gave a particular and rather limited direction to curriculum management work in schools — to the detriment of other very significant avenues. The first of these themes centred on the question of what the curriculum was to consist of (content), and the second with the whole business of who controls the curriculum. The content discussion was well displayed by the emergence in the early days of the HMI-led approach to 'areas of experience' as a means of organising our thought about, and approach to the delivery of, the curriculum. Department of Education perspectives by the early 1980s were however looking significantly different, by remaining tied to an older tradition of describing the curriculum in terms of subjects. These different ways of looking at or describing the curriculum give rise to equally different ways of thinking about organising and delivering the curriculum in schools — i.e. curriculum management. The distinction between them is well displayed by comparing the DES paper *Organisation and Content of the 5–16 Curriculum* (1984) and the HMI publication *The Curriculum from 5 to 16* (1985). It is evident from the emerging National Curriculum which of these perspectives won the day.

Another, never fully developed, dimension to the debate centred upon a differentiation between narrow and broad definitions of what the curriculum comprised. In the narrow view, curriculum was discussed in content or skills-based terms as far as the classroom was concerned, in subject area terms or in relation to a content or skills-based view of educational objectives. Other major dimensions of curriculum management were either taken for granted or reduced to the position of subsidiary concerns only — for example major questions of pedagogy and the whole question of pupil grouping policies and organisation. An even broader definition was taken to include what became known as the 'hidden curriculum' as well as the more traditional elements. The totality of this view was well put by the Schools Council in 1981 as 'what each child will take away from school'. This was indeed an important issue but, although the flood of official documentation often paid lip-service to it, it was never adequately explored. This view of the curriculum was much more difficult to get to grips with — in fact it was difficult even to find the language with which to do so. It involved a range of concerns — pupil-teacher relationships, teaching and learning methods, policies for the grouping of pupils at different stages and places, the feel of the school community and the ways in which pupil differences are both accepted and built upon. In short, once the content debate started to move on to an examination of the ideas of curriculum *process*, it was never fully pursued. Certainly some interesting ideas, and even projects, developed — for example the ILEA *Hargreaves Report* (1984) on modularity, the best of TVEI, or more recently, the report on *Records of Achievement* (DES, 1988). The feature which all of these initiatives had in common was that of a process view rather than a content view of the curriculum — and of its management. Whilst some parts of the profession pursued these issues with enthusiasm, many are now left wondering to what extent they were considered by those creating the National Curriculum — or about how some elements of them can be salvaged as the latter is introduced and, one by one, the more radical initiatives have their support withdrawn.

Throughout much of the period of the debate, curriculum management work in schools was therefore heavily conditioned by a rather narrow content perspective and, also, by a second strand to the debate — that of curriculum control.

In 1979 the DES required local authorities to:

> . . . improve their capacity to develop and implement more effective approaches . . . to curricular policies and aims of schools.
>
> DES (1979)

Consequently, LEAs set about this task in the early 1980s, and the feeling gained ground that a tide to central control was running. In fact most, if not all LEAs, adopted a very flexible approach to this and left much in the hands of schools and teachers. However, the accountability tradition (see chapter 10), and the moves to enhance it via reformed governing bodies, was also in full swing and the question of who controls the curriculum was gradually but surely being answered — some may feel that the answer was found in the 1986 and 1988 Acts, but they may yet be surprised.

These two strands to the debate — content and control — were to be enshrined in the 1986 Act and the National Curriculum legislation of 1988 but, importantly, they had diverted or weakened attention, at all levels, from other very significant issues in curriculum management — issues which are referred to above in the context of the hidden curriculum. In some situations this can lead to attempts to reduce curriculum management largely to a rather static matter of resource management — with planning, implementation and evaluation seen as adjuncts to an apparently value-free (or value-determined) process. However, it is in the curriculum above all that we cannot abandon a value-driven approach to school management, and the proposal to separate the *what* from the *how* is, in that sense, an attempt to enshrine the division between content and process in the curriculum. This apparently weakens the possibility of establishing approaches to curriculum management which can integrate all the variables involved.

However, if the National Curriculum does represent something of an end to the conceptual limitations imposed by the content/control debate then it may make it possible for us to start to see the other issues — pedagogy, pupil grouping arrangements and a whole series of questions concerning relationships between pupils and teachers — in an integrated curriculum management context rather than in the fragmented and subsidiary manner in which they have been approached to date. The National Curriculum has to be managed, moreover, in relation to other features of the Education Reform Act — the assessment, open enrolment and local management provisions in particular are of interest, although in some local circumstances, the Grant Maintained Schools provision or even the City Technology College elements could be of importance. To what extent do these other parts of the Act affect the prospect for an integrated, school-wide approach to curriculum management? A sanguine view would suggest not only that it is possible but indeed that the possibility is enhanced.

Taken singly, these various elements of the Reform Act are significant, but taken together they have the potential to change major elements of the whole education service in ways which we can only begin to see at this stage.

One simple example of how an apparently non-curriculum-related element of the Act could impact upon curriculum management has already been indicated in chapter 1. If the local management proposal, or more narrowly the financial delegation element of it, is allowed to push us towards the 'chief executive' view of headship, then that alone could result in the withdrawal from curriculum management of the one person in the school who should have the most to offer in this regard. Similarly, open enrolment could have dramatically populist impacts upon the curriculum in some schools as competition for pupils intensifies — marketing the curriculum has already been indicated in chapter 9. However, these are relatively simple cause and effect possibilities. The more powerful ideas emerge when we consider the impact upon our curriculum management thinking of a combination of the various elements of the Act. Take, for example, an issue which could bring together effects in the areas of assessment testing, open enrolment and financial delegation.

The introduction of standard assessment testing — relating levels of achievement to particular age-groups within a broadly criterion-referenced framework — could have major implications for the whole way in which we approach, say, both pupil age and ability grouping and approaches to the management of pupils' curricular time.

What are the implications, for example, of discovering, in a large primary school, that there is a significant minority of seven-year-olds operating well above level 3 in a wide range of the foundation subjects? Should this cause us to rearrange the delivery of the curriculum in some way — perhaps by challenging deeply held beliefs in the value of single-age groupings? Alternatively, will we be designing programmes of study which are flexible enough to deal with this possibility whilst maintaining single-age groupings? In the secondary sector, the rigidities created by external pressures and inflexible timetable structures have long exhibited similar problems (Osborne 1986) for both pupils and teachers. The most eloquent statement of this is provided by Knight (1983) who uses the concept of seat-time:

> Seat-time is a basic feature of our school economy — as characteristic and as obstructive of change as slavery or strip farming in other economies. Seat-time decrees that all students of the same age shall sit in their places for the same amount of time, whether they need it or not, whether they benefit or not, whether they progress or not. And the dose is a fixed ration: students must have no less — but like Oliver Twist, they cannot have more.
>
> Knight (1983) p. 101

At the moment in secondary education the relationship between time and subjects is enshrined, via periods, in the timetable and it is the starting point for much of our curriculum management work — while ignoring the other variables of pupils' different needs, and our different methods of teaching. The result is often that considerable numbers of children tread water for long periods of time in some areas of the curriculum — perhaps even for years at a time. As in the primary example outlined above, are we going to be prepared to live with this once the situation is made clear by the National Curriculum assessment process at ages 11 and 14, or are we going to adopt curriculum management approaches to deal with the situation? Again, as in the primary example, the possibility of a challenge to grouping arrangements — either by age or ability — is rapidly exposed.

In such cases, we may also need to consider the views of parents once the results of the assessment programmes are published. It would certainly seem to be likely that a school which is able to *demonstrate* its ability to manage the curriculum process, in a way which relates it to the needs of particular pupils at various points, would have a marketing advantage over one which could not do so! The link from assessment to curriculum management and on to open enrolment and financial delegation is clear enough.

In these ways, and more, the Education Reform Act is likely to change, quite significantly, our views about the scope and nature of curriculum management and to challenge some deeply held beliefs. The secret garden has been breaking down for some considerable time, and the future will require an approach to managing the curriculum which no longer isolates it from the other management processes going on, or leaves the connections to chance. Paradoxically, the Education Reform Act may well lead to a greater diversity of school experience, rather than the greater commonality that is conjured up by the vision of a National Curriculum. Success will go to those management teams that can keep curriculum management at the centre of their concerns, while relating all of their other management processes to it, and that do so in a way which both draws upon, and keeps under control, the context established by local management of schools, open enrolment and the National Curriculum framework itself. Chapter 1 hinted at the kind of management teams which are likely to succeed in such an undertaking and it remains here to examine the broad approaches which are available to them in bringing about an integrated approach.

## Managing the National Curriculum

It is now necessary to consider the ways in which the various management processes in schools relate to, and indeed emanate from, curriculum management. It is proposed that in practice there are two broadly defined approaches to managing the curriculum. The first perspective gives primacy to a decision-making/resource management process, while the second gives primacy to a change and staff development-led strategy.

### *1. Curriculum management as a decision-making/ resource management process*

The need for management information with which to facilitate the process of planning was indicated earlier. Decision making then occurs at the point where alternative courses of action are measured against certain criteria in order to make a final choice. In the context of the curriculum, we could ask the following questions:

(i) what kind of decisions are made about the curriculum?
(ii) by whom are the decisions made?
(iii) on what basis are the decisions made, i.e. against what criteria and against what information base?

It is possible to suggest some, but by no means all, of the answers to these questions.

*(i) What kind of decisions are made about the curriculum?*
With the introduction of the National Curriculum, teachers felt that their judgement was being undermined and that decisions about curriculum content were no longer to be made by those 'at the chalkface'. There is only limited validity in this since, while the legislation concerns that knowledge and those skills which are to be acquired, it is not prescriptive about other skills and attitudes. Schools have also been left with scope concerning time allocation for core and foundation subjects with the opportunity to 'develop' and 'experiment' (as provided for by Section 16 of the 1988 Act) and the possibility of including non-statutory curricular areas. If we maintain our belief in the 'hidden curriculum' and 'extra curricular' activities, then here is yet further scope for decision making at the school level. Decisions regarding the process of curriculum delivery remain, largely, in the hands of the professionals and the outcome of such discussion can provide a hidden curriculum in itself. It is important to retain some control over both the content and the process aspects, otherwise teachers will feel that they are being deprived of their professionality and are being left to implement someone else's ideas and also, of course, to have their 'success' evaluated by others.

*(ii) Who makes the decisions?*
Having established that many curriculum management decisions will continue to rest within the school, rather than at national level, it should logically follow that decision making is further decentralised within the school. While the head and governors have a strategic role to play, tactical and operational decisions should be made by teams and individuals drawn from the staff as a whole. This has implications for communication, staff development, change management and the whole gamut of management strategies because a whole school approach will be needed, coupled with the availability of skills in making such curriculum management decisions. One of the underlying themes of this book is that different management structures may be needed in the future — structures which

will release and harness professional skills and knowledge rather than control or inhibit them. We are getting close to the value bases of curriculum management at this point.

*(iii) On what basis are the decisions made, i.e. against what criteria and against what information base?*

This is the critical question to consider because the key to curriculum management as a decision-making process is to have a clear view of the criteria, i.e. what they are and on what they are based. The criteria against which curriculum choices will be evaluated are multiple, in that they may be based on a variety of factors (for example educational or resource ones), and dynamic, in that they are always changing. However, these criteria are not all of equal importance and it is in prioritising or weighting the criteria that *values are operationalised.* The criteria used should integrate professional knowledge with management information, resource availability, (including staff and staff development) change management and evaluation strategies. When the various courses of action are measured against these criteria, the chosen one should, therefore, create the most effective learning experience for the pupils.

Are those criteria to be found entirely within the National Curriculum or do we base some of them on the principle (which the government uses to justify LMS) that those closest to the children are best able to decide how to identify and cater for their needs? Those closest to the children are clearly parents and teachers. If we take a populist view and consider the wishes of the parents as clients, to what extent do their values and perceived needs determine the criteria? What is the balance between the strength of market forces and the professional judgement of the staff? Many teachers feel that this balance should lie heavily towards the professionals although schools with falling rolls may compromise their beliefs (consider for example, the issue of uniform). Does the solution lie in chapter 9 — i.e. should teachers improve the way in which they market the *philosophy* of the school and tie it in with the perceived needs of parents, possibly attempting to adjust those perceptions? For example, can an infant curriculum be based on 'learning through play' or will the clients' perception of this as 'time-wasting' begin to determine the teaching approach?

Alternatively, the criteria for choice may be based on micropolitical, rather than rational factors. The preferences of powerful individuals or the influence of tradition may be given more weight than is given to rational argument. Some of the indicators which could be used to assess this rational/micropolitical balance were highlighted in chapter 4 on resource management.

Some of the most obvious curriculum decisions are made about the use of resources within the curriculum and it is therefore possible to see curriculum decisions being made largely on resource grounds. Is that acceptable? Resource decisions may sometimes be very powerful to the extent that they are fairly easy to quantify and, thus, present very precise problems to be considered. The danger is that they emerge as *the* critical decisions so that the less clearly defined, more value-driven, non-quantifiable factors are squeezed out. Also, it is usually 'easier' to compromise on values (and to blame someone else for their non-realisation) than to create the resources which would be needed to realise them.

In the secondary sector, an example of this tendency to rely on quantity rather than quality can be found in the curriculum analysis approach which is put forward as an MIS for managing the secondary curriculum. Such a system defines 'bonus' (teachers allocated to a number of pupils) in terms of *quantity*, but does not take account of the *quality* of those teachers. This technique also shows that *curriculum decisions* are sometimes made by *resource equations* rather than by people and we should question whether or not we accept this. Such a situation arises when a school contracts and curriculum drift occurs so that there is a shift in bonus between year groups, although no decisions have been taken about this. It is simply that numbers drift has determined the richness of provision. Furthermore, because an overt MIS tends to emphasise the quantifiable at the expense of quality issues, it needs to be underlaid by an unofficial MIS which should be taking on board the quality issues. It is also worth reflecting on the rationale behind the increases in the 'core curriculum' at 14 to 16 in the 1980s. Was this educationally desirable or was it a resource-driven policy to reduce the number of uneconomical option groups during contraction?

In primary schools vertical grouping has often been adopted in the past as an efficient means of dealing with an inconveniently sized year group. How far have professional views (and even effective teaching) been compromised by this resource-based decision? As the 1990s progress there may be a reversed situation in which vertical grouping according to National Curriculum levels (i.e. fast-tracking) is perceived as a way of delivering effective education and meeting the parents' demands for education 'according to ability' (to steal a phrase from the 1944 Education Act). Interestingly, this form of rationalisation may also accommodate the teachers' demands for more time in which to carry out their management responsibilities.

Although curriculum management is clearly a decision-making process, seeing the curriculum simply in those terms without exploring the decision-making *process* is too narrow a view. Resources, while they are important, should not dictate the curriculum but should empower it so that objectives are achieved. It is therefore necessary to consider a different and more powerful perspective.

This book has highlighted the need for increased pastoral care of staff based on the premise that *real* change can only be managed by changing the attitudes of those concerned, i.e. by professional development. The section which follows proposes that the most effective approach to curriculum management is one which is based on evaluation followed by change through professional development.

## *2. Curriculum management as a change management and staff development process*

Chapter 1 drew attention to the view, held by some, that one more big push (especially in terms of curriculum change) would allow us to reach the 'Holy Grail'. Despite the evidence of the last 20 years this view is still the one emanating from central government — when the National Curriculum is in place that will be it, subject to 'modifications' of course — and the whims of successive Secretaries of State. This centralist approach is very old fashioned and, as a model for curriculum management or change management, it is seriously flawed. Chapter 1 raised the question of whether schools are obliged to follow this top-down strategy or whether it is possible to break away and adopt a different management model at the level of the individual school. Assuming the latter (and more promising) case, then the view of change put forward by West-Burnham as being essentially a learning process for individuals provides us with the strategy at the school level for thinking about curriculum management. The professional and on-going evaluation of the curriculum is a major element in this broader change management approach to the curriculum.

This learning process requires that we reflect on existing practice, i.e. evaluate with a view to development (rather than an accountability model). At various levels within the school there is a continuous process of curriculum evaluation in order to build on identified strengths and to eliminate weaknesses. It is especially evident at the operational level where the classroom teacher critically appraises each lesson and, perhaps, modifies future learning experiences in the light of this evidence. The starting point for change is, therefore, evaluation, in however informal a way. It should be possible to move on from here and gradually to make the evaluation more formal and more wide-ranging. This can involve groups of pupils as well as groups of teachers and may utilise some particular management techniques such as force field analysis or fishboning but, above all, it is concerned with the development of management skills in all staff, and especially with team building, so that there is a genuine whole-school approach to change.

Looking at curriculum management primarily as a change and staff development process appears to be much more promising than

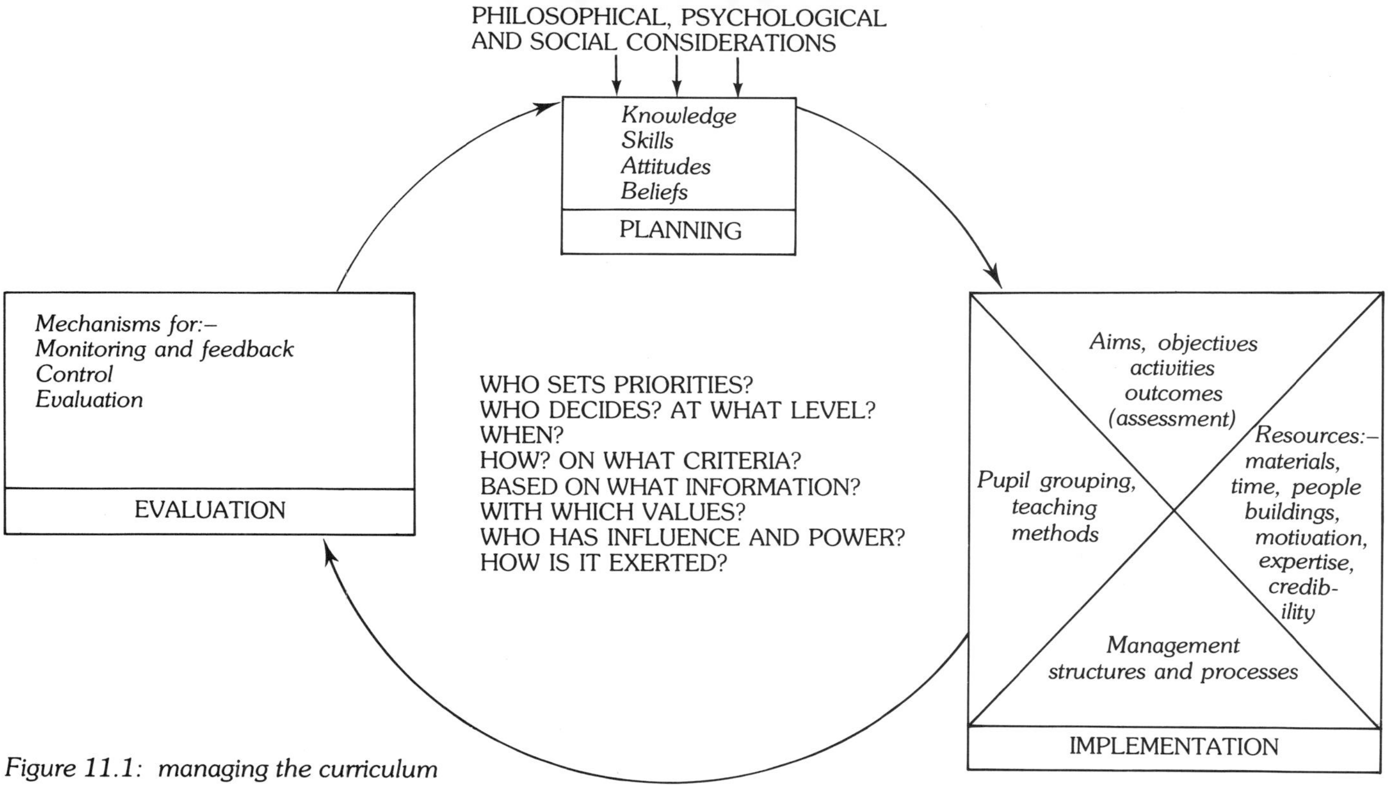
PHILOSOPHICAL, PSYCHOLOGICAL
AND SOCIAL CONSIDERATIONS
Knowledge
Skills
Attitudes
Beliefs
PLANNING
Aims, objectives
activities
outcomes
(assessment)
Resources:–
materials,
time, people
buildings,
motivation,
expertise,
credib-
ility
Pupil grouping,
teaching
methods
Management
structures and processes
IMPLEMENTATION
Mechanisms for:–
Monitoring and feedback
Control
Evaluation
EVALUATION
WHO SETS PRIORITIES?
WHO DECIDES? AT WHAT LEVEL?
WHEN?
HOW? ON WHAT CRITERIA?
BASED ON WHAT INFORMATION?
WITH WHICH VALUES?
WHO HAS INFLUENCE AND POWER?
HOW IS IT EXERTED?

*Figure 11.1: managing the curriculum*

looking at it initially as a decision-making/resource management process. It provides opportunities for development based on identified strengths and weaknesses, taking account of the human and qualitative dimensions.

Taking these two broad approaches into account, what we need is a perspective which accommodates all aspects of them. The model proposed in Figure 11.1 is based on the simplified management cycle (plan-act-review) which has been applied several times earlier in this book. It sets out the central considerations (many of which have been discussed earlier in this chapter) at each of these stages but, more importantly, it puts forward various questions which should be answered before any of the stages take place.

The questions posed in the centre of Figure 11.1 are critical ones since they underpin the curriculum management process. In the introduction, Davies put forward the view that, for curriculum management to be effective, many other management principles and processes must be given a high priority. The focus of this book has been on these principles and processes which, when put into place, decide the answers to these critical questions. If schools are successfully to implement the many changes with which they are faced then the solutions will probably be very different in the 1990s to those put forward in the past.

## References

DES 1979 *Local Authority Arrangements for the School Curriculum*, DES
DES 1984 *Organisation and Content of the 5–16 Curriculum*, DES
DES 1989 *Records of Achievement*, DES
HMI 1985 *The Curriculum from 5 to 16*, HMSO
ILEA 1984 *Hargreaves Report*, ILEA
Knight BAA 1983 *Managing School Finance*, Heinemann
Osborne, A. 1986 'A Comprehensive Approach to the Management of Time' *School Organisation* Vol. 6 No. 2

# Names Index

# Subject Index